M000013778

# THE ACTOR'S GUIDE TO
# PERFORMING SHAKESPEARE

## FOR FILM, TELEVISION AND THEATRE

## MADD HAROLD

 lone eagle

THE ACTOR'S GUIDE TO PERFORMING SHAKESPEARE
For Film, Television and Theatre
Copyright © 2002 Madd Harold

All rights reserved. No part of this book may be reproduced or utilized in any form or by any means, electronic or mechanical, including photocopying, scanning, recording or by any information storage and retrieval system now known or hereafter invented, without permission in writing from the publisher. Inquiries should be addressed to:

LONE EAGLE PUBLISHING COMPANY, LLC™
1024 N. Orange Dr.
Hollywood, CA 90038
Phone 323.308.3400 or 800.815.0503
A division of IFILM® Corporation, www.hcdonline.com

Printed in the United States of America
10 9 8 7 6 5 4 3 2 1

Cover concept by ADVANTAGE, London
Book design by Carla Green
Photo of author by Ben Philippi

Library of Congress Cataloging-in-Publication Data

Harold, Madd
    An actor's guide to performing Shakespeare : in film, television, and theater / by Madd Harold.
        p.  cm.
    ISBN 1-58065-046-5
    1. Shakespeare, William, 1564-1616—Dramatic production.
2. Shakespeare, William, 1564-1616—Film and video adaptations.
3. Acting.  I. Title

    PR3091 .H38 2002
    792'.028—dc21                                2002034213

Books may be purchased in bulk at special discounts for promotional or educational purposes. Special editions can be created to specifications. Inquiries for sales and distribution, textbook adoption, foreign language translation, editorial, and rights and permissions inquiries should be addressed to: Jeff Black, Lone Eagle Publishing, 1024 N. Orange Drive, Hollywood, CA 90038 or send e-mail to info@ifilm.com.

Distributed to the trade by National Book Network, 800-462-6420.
IFILM® and Lone Eagle Publishing Company™ are registered trademarks.

For my Grandmother

Beulah "B" Bridge

January 4th, 1917—December 3rd, 2001

## HOLD THIS THOUGHT

To the actor who poses bravery when approaching The Bard's work, Madd Harold's *The Actor's Guide to Performing Shakespeare* is, indeed, first aid toward their efforts to commune with the muscular language and spirit of Lady Macbeth, Richard III, Julius Caesar, Antony and Cleopatra, Henry IV and the like. Madd Harold has given us an exhilarating and comforting road map to self and self-confidence when approaching Shakespeare's monolithic characters. The *Guide* is unique and accessible, shoring up a belief in ourselves as capable of carrying out the integrity of line and verse "until you fuel through to the end of the thought." And with assured confidence that his work is done, Madd Harold allows the reader: "You decide."

Frederick Ward
Professional Theatre Department
Dawson College
Montréal, Qc. Canada

# CONTENTS

# ACKNOWLEDGEMENTS

Acknowledgements are tricky.

How can a few ink-blots on paper express my deepest thanks and extend my great appreciation to the scores of thousands of people who have informed, shaped, loved and guided me in life?

The best I can do is clack down the major influencers, aiders and abetters.

For the love of Daisy Thomas—*thank you*.

For the strong, practical and sometimes fierce love of my mother, Evelyn Reid; "B" Bridge, Fr. Bill Hunt, Catherine Thomas, Joseph Flynn, Nicola Morry, Jamie and Chris Morry, Kate Duncan, Brett and Meredith Hendricks—*thank you*.

For Niamh Flynn—*thank you*.

For the formative and supporting love of Jim Ryan, the St. Francis House in Brooklyn, Charles Waxberg, Nicholas Kepros, Céline Robbé, Joshua Schwartz, Glenn Cruz, Michael Cumes, Elena Gonzales, Grant Navin, Eureka Joe of New York, Robert Perillo, the Farrell clan, Gabor Zsigovics, Claire Boivin and Gail Lawrence of A.K.A. Artists Management; the extraordinary and peerless artist, Frederick Ward; Richard Zeman—*thank you*.

For the inspiring and positive love of Stephenie Farrell—*thank you*.

For seeking me out and believing in me: Tony Palermo—*thank you*.

For the imagination, unbridled creativity, talent, industry and future greatness of the artists comprising Gravy Bath Productions: Tony Palermo, Anthony Kokx, Nicolas Wright, Mike Hughes, Yann Bernaquez, and Geneviève Genest—*thank you*.

For the theatres, studios, films, and schools in which I have acted, directed, taught or written for: specifically in New York, London, Edinburgh, Toronto, and Montréal—*thank you*.

For the actors, directors, writers, designers, theatre and film crews, and students I have worked with—*thank you.*

For the peculiarities of Montréal artists, theatre professionals, and critics who have supported and inspired me, or disappointed and angered me enough to continue fuelling the creation of important work—*thank you.*

For the people I will work with in the future, for the work we will create and the further discoveries we will make—*thank you.*

For the entire staff at Lone Eagle Publishing: specifically, Lauren Rossini, for her acceptance, intelligence, humor, skill, warmth and ability to un-complicate; Jeff Black for his industry; Stephen Falk for his careful insight and Carla Green for her artistry—*thank you.*

For all of the people in my life, positive or negative, helpful or hindering, for teaching me about living—*thank you.*

And for the amorphous but ubiquitous Spirit that has guided, tickled, badgered, reminded, loved, goaded, pushed and nurtured me into living more deeply, exploring more boldly, and imagining more infinitely—*thank you.*

# WHO IS THIS BOOK FOR?

So there you are. You've picked up this little book I've written, and you're curious—you want to know if this book is right for you. After all, there are lots of other Shakespeare books on the shelves; why should this one be any different?

It *is* different.

I've written this book for you—the actor. It's *not* an academic book. If you want the pencil-scratch snobbery of literary criticism and philosophical dissection, go get another book. You should find dozens, probably hundreds, of professors and intellectuals blathering away, pouring minutiae all over the paper, snoring over things that are inconsequential to this book.

What I want to do is to show you *how to play* Shakespeare— how to really *work* this stuff. How to lift his words off the page, and into active, vigorous life.

Really, it's a lot easier than you think.

If you want to learn about history, costumes, beards, quills, inkpots, clogs, lye, or the recipe for mead—please reshelve this book nice and neat and be on your merry way.

However, if you want to sink your teeth into Shakespeare, and really wrestle with his text—really learn how to *act it*, how to *live it*—and you need a straightforward, practical, easy-to-read book, written *by an actor for other actors*, then keep on reading.

I've struggled with Shakespeare myself, playing a lot of his parts. I've fretted and lost sleep over how to get control of his language, and how to make it real and exciting for the audience. But I've been lucky; I've worked with some of the best people in the world, and have had a lot of techniques poured into me— techniques that have been around for a long time, passed down from generation to generation. And I've finally been able to filter them into a concise, hands-on, fresh new book written for *today's* actor. I'm still young enough to be in touch with the needs of new actors, drama students, and early professional actors, yet experienced enough to guide you straight to the most important ways to play Shakespeare well.

So if you're a student, a young actor, or an older skilled actor who's never really tasted the joy of playing Shakespeare—then this book is for you. If you're an untrained amateur, this book will give you all the skills you need to play this electrifying stuff. If you're a pro with years of experience behind you, and you want to relearn some of the things you've forgotten or gain completely new insights into playing Shakespeare—then this book is for you.

## PART ONE

# BEGINNING THINGS

# WHY SHAKESPEARE?

"Shakespeare" as an idea, an entity, or as some kind of beast needing constant grooming, feeding, and fawning over evokes very strong and mixed feelings in all actors. The need for the actor to *play* Shakespeare—to *taste* it, even once—is stronger than even the most interested non-actor can understand. A beginning actor instinctively feels that there is something in Shakespeare—some quality of depth and power—that he knows he has to wrestle with, maybe without quite knowing why. An experienced actor understands this itch perfectly well, and knows firsthand the fulfillment and power that lies in connecting with an audience through Shakespeare's text. He will often come back to the plays time and again, desperate to scratch that itch, to unearth new concepts, and discover new insights he might have missed when he was younger.

It's fascinating to speak with old stage actors who have now gone into film—they often miss the fire and hot-blooded wholeness of their "Shakespeare Days." There is a nagging polarity visible within them: both a contentment and sense of having had overwhelmingly rich experiences, and a glint-in-the-eye hunger to tackle Shakespeare again. For the experienced actor, grappling with Shakespeare is not a curiosity—it's a necessity. And tickling somewhere in the back of his brain will be the desperate wish to be onstage again, chewing into the work.

But why? What is it about Shakespeare's writing that hovers over an actor's consciousness and hooks its talons in so deeply? Why is playing Shakespeare so essential to the formation of the complete actor? Why do we keep producing his plays, and why do generations of actors still aspire to play his roles? How many times have we heard (in reference to this or that famous actor), "Yes, but can he do Shakespeare?" Why do we hold Shakespeare up as the embodiment of the highest standard of living writing, as guru to hungry actors, and as the ideal of those who seek the most power, invention, and grounded fire in the theatre?

We can't really find the answers in the man himself. We can't find them in the Elizabethan times. We can't find them in the snore-worthy banalities of academic dissection. We can—and do—find them only in Shakespeare's text.

The answers lie in the characters he created, and in their ideas, their words, their depth of living, their insights into life, and in their compelling situations. The answers lie in the stretched gut-girth of living that Shakespeare squeezed into thirty-two plays and one hundred and fifty four sonnets. Each one of his characters is a full-blooded breathing force; alive, and clearly defined. We live with the same characters today, and hear the same dilemmas, ideas, sufferings, and joys found in Shakespeare's work that we experience in our own lives.

He just puts it all together and writes it all down so damn well.

You will come across those actors who try to shrug off the Shakespeare itch. They complain that he is "boring," "too hard," or "out-of-date;" table scraps from another time and place, out of touch with today's world. This comes from a lack of understanding with regards to his work, and an ignorance of living in and experiencing powerfully human situations. Shakespeare, more than any other playwright (indeed, more than most writers and thinkers) explores so many shades of the human condition, so many nuances of relationship and situation, and so many strands of thought which have at one time or another flitted through the minds of people everywhere, that it may take a lifetime to absorb the bulk of his work. It is not only this resonant commonality that we respond to, but also the depth of thought that is most exciting in Shakespeare. Not his own thoughts, but the staggering, jaw dropping, sheer *variety* of thought in every one of his characters, birthed from both ordinary and extraordinary situations. Peeping out of the ideas and mouths of his collection of characters comes a joy, an anger, a reflection, an experience, and a melancholy infused with insight that we can only marvel at, and hope to capture a bit of. He explores and exposes the complexity of his characters fully. Shakespeare, like all great writers, can put aside his own points of view about a character in order to get to the gut of the beast.

It is the quality of his language—his invention, his wit, his raw power, his mercurial turns of phrase—that is so remarkable. You will find yourself engaging the tongue with words and thoughts of such strength and elegance that you will be left hungry for more. He is unique in that his language is so varied dependent on character and situation; it can be visceral and primal or elegant and refined, and everything in between.

The instinctive rhythms he uses reflect both the outward situation and the inner psyche or mood of a character; they bleed off the page and cut right to the gut when played well. At every instant, and every turn of thought, there is a new rhythm underneath the language that grabs an audience emotionally, giving the actor clues for how to play particular moments.

And it is the scale of emotion that is the bone and marrow of Shakespeare's magnetism. Shakespeare's characters have a depth, change, and an expanse of emotion, which allows them to cut a big chunk out of the totality of the human experience. Because they lead big lives, they experience life more fully than most, and this gives you more to play with. Although most of Shakespeare's characters are larger than life, and may experience different situations or use different phrases for the same experiences in life; they may seem to be different from us—they're not; they are extraordinarily real. They're big, yes, and they're not "natural." But they *are* fully and completely real from every angle and every turn of thought. Shakespeare allows us to know these people, and by knowing them, we understand a bit more about ourselves.

The quality of language, the instinctive rhythms, and the scale of emotion are not separate from each other in Shakespeare's work. It's all one beast, and Shakespeare is a full, *alive* experience that no actor can afford to ignore.

Now, let's talk a little bit less romantically.

You, the actor, need Shakespeare because no other playwright gives you more to play with—no one will challenge your strongest experiences in life and make you go 'larger,' no one will require you to engage your full mind, your full body, your full soul, your full voice, and the totality of who you are in order to portray powerful situations and characters. And your reward is that the audience will be engaged with you, and will breathe with you. You need to play Shakespeare in order to understand what *real* breath, *real* emotion, *real* situational truth, *real* language, *real* thought, *real* connection with the audience, *real* exploration, and *real* imagination are all about. I think we're all a bit burnt out on weak, namby-pamby network pablum. In the best of Shakespeare-playing, there is a circle of thought, breath, and energy created through the exchange of thought and experience between actor and audience. The *modern* actor needs to re-experience this excitement and intimacy of life with all its belligerent waves.

You need to play Shakespeare and fail. And play him again and succeed. You need to sink your teeth into the glutton's feast that is Shakespeare's text and learn what it means to really communicate, breathe, live, inspire, raze and plunder an audience's senses and intellect, and to offer that audience chunks of human experience that it will gobble down with recognition and understanding. The actor needs to relearn what the *real*, quality theatre is about. And that tidal wave of insight, inspiration, and human breath is found at its most concentrated—in Shakespeare.

And, on an entirely practical note, by playing Shakespeare, you will acquire skills very quickly. Once you learn to play Shakespeare well, everything else will be easy. When you start jumping between higher and more primal levels of thinking, your more ordinary roles become that much more simple to play. Once you can wrap your tongue around Shakespeare's verse, your film and television dialogue will feel ridiculously effortless. If you can dig deep into yourself to embody complex characters and live through huge situations, your other acting gigs will be a breeze. Everything you encounter in your films, television shows, commercials, and plays will be easy, easy, easy. If you can play Shakespeare well, you can play anything well.

So. Enough about the actor for now. The world needs Shakespeare's theatre as it needs the theatre itself. It needs to relearn how to learn, to listen, to breathe with people, to hear its own truths reflected back at itself, to gain new insights into living, to be entertained, and to imagine. It needs to buzz with ecstasy, and to scrape the granite bedrock of human despair, ugliness, and rot.

I think the modern world needs Shakespeare. Needs him to help us *really hear* the human voice again. We're floundering in a whirlpool of synapse-exploding soundbites, flash images, and quick-wink suggestion and innuendo. As a people, we have become disconnected from our bodies and voices, even as we *seem* to be drawing closer to each other via the Internet and technology. The truth is, we have become used to the *virtual* existence of one another, but have forgotten what it means to be in each other's *real* presence. We need to re-experience the *reality* of each other—our real foibles, our real beauty, our real situations. We need to slide out the filter of the *virtual* world, and we need to be *here* again, as real people doing real people things. We need to gather together in a room, and hear our joys and sorrows relived and re-examined so we can reconnect with who we are. Only when we are firmly grounded in the present can we move forward.

Through sharing Shakespeare with an audience, the actor knows that there is a scope of life in Shakespeare's text that no other writer (so far) has been able to match in invention, volume, and quality. He wants the experience of Shakespeare—and longs to give it to the world. The need for the actor to play Shakespeare is not a narcissistic one; it is a generous one.

Don't worry about what you *think* Shakespeare is or isn't about. You'll learn. Don't be afraid of not knowing anything about Shakespeare. You'll learn. Don't be afraid of not understanding the texts. You will. Don't be afraid of licking the brains and tongues of Shakespeare's characters. You'll stretch yourself, you'll crack open his Pandora's Box, and it will make you a better actor.

And don't be afraid of faltering a bit at first. Ultimately, you will not fail. Playing Shakespeare is easier than you think. You're just missing a few basic skills, and by the time you finish the book—you'll have them.

Remember: if you can learn to play Shakespeare well, you can play *anything* well. And Shakespeare is *easy* to play well. Let me show you how.

# FROM THERE TO HERE—WHERE WE ARE

Before we jump into our practical work, I want to reflect on a few things with you. Let's take a quick sketch look at where we are today as actors. The influence the previous two or three generations have had on artists cannot be underestimated—all art comes out of a strongly informed social background, and is as much a response to immediate political and social concerns as it is an exposition and illumination of human truths. We can't separate ourselves from the influence of society, politics, economics, spiritual traditions, and so forth. Nor can we easily dismiss whatever good and bad changes our parents' and grandparents' generations left in their wake.

You certainly don't have to agree with my take on things, but think about them before we start our work. I make a lot of sweeping generalizations that may irritate the hell out of some of you—so be it. I want us to feel out where we are *right now* and to do that, we have to look back into the past

Let's take a general look at the three major generations of this century. I have to use a few cliché terms and thoughts, because we're quite familiar with the broader spectrum: we have the G.I. Generation, the Baby Boomers, and Generation-X. Three radically different waves of influence, spilling all kinds of styles and personalities onto the theatre and into the media—and therefore, into our collective unconscious.

## G.I. Generation

We'll start with the G.I. Generation, which I rather like. I'm fond of them because, many respects, they are very different from me and my world. Essentially conservative, small-town, hard-working, and self-sacrificing, this generation produced all kinds of interesting actors and styles in theatre and film.

What marked them, of course, was World War II—a huge and life-changing war that galvanized the world into action, and which culminated in a personal and social sense of victory and accomplishment. After the war, the G.I. Generation created all kinds of tremendously positive things for their kids: a good economy, a secure family-life, and—despite the problems of the '50s and early '60s—a relatively stable and positive outlook on life. They were secure, had the foresight to think ahead to the next generation, and set up a strong foundation for those who would come after them.

By today's standards, the G.I. Generation lived simple lives, lacking the complications and confusions of the modern age. But in that relative simplicity, they developed strong *character*; they grew up in hard times, and went through a war that was both traumatic and fulfilling. They had a strong experience of having *achieved an important purpose*, and they tried both to stabilize life (not wanting to return to the desperation of the Depression), and to live in the *here* and *now*—a celebration of existence, marked with consideration and caution for the next generation. They knew who they were.

The actors of the G.I. Generation are distinguished by *confidence, style, romance*, and *character*. They created a deeply stylistic and elegantly precise clipped-tongue delivery; no nonsense dramas and a sweepingly romantic, completely over-the-top musical comedy style that swept away the war years in a wash of fantasy, mood, and fun. Though they may seem hopelessly formulaic and a bit ridiculous to us today, the escape into style and whimsy with bigger-than-life situations and powerfully unique characters resulted in a *strong connection with the audience,* and a desire to live life more deeply. Theatre of the time was generous—they *gave*. They gave fun, they gave life, they gave ambiance and mystery—they gave what audiences *needed*.

And their actors were real characters—full, round, singular people. They were completely themselves. They brought a real sense of life to the stage and screen; you got a sense that these people had lived and actually had some insights to share. They knew how to use language well, how to flip a phrase around, how to engage an audience without self-consciousness, and how to lift us from the mundane into a richer experience of life. They stripped their characters down from the overdone *Nosferatu*-stuff they grew up with and infused them with personalities people could relate to, and look up to.

Of course, they had ample opportunity to practice their craft. They listened to radio, which honed the ear and sparked the imagination. They told stories, engaged in community activities, and interacted with one another. Nightclubs, revues, and dance halls buzzed with life and excitement. Believe it or not, people actually *wanted* to go to the theatre, and made an event out of it. Actors had plenty of opportunities to work—they always had a chance to try out a new joke on an audience, or to present some kind of stage play or vaudeville act, no matter how amateur. People wanted that kind of life, and responded to it.

And importantly, most people did not have television. If they wanted entertainment, cultural contact, or community interaction, they were required to go out for it. They had to leave the house, switch their brains around, and actively pursue their social lives. And they listened and participated—people danced, played cards, planned socials and attended mixers. It was very much a time of "team efforts" and group activities; people did not have the option of staying in and watching one of five hundred channels at the touch of a button.

## Boomers, Inc.

Then we have the Baby Boomers, a generation I have grown to rather dislike. Let me qualify for a moment—I like what they once were, but detest what they have become. The Boomers are a talented, educated, and intelligent group of people who have given a lot to the world. They've molded society very powerfully—some would say strangled it—and their influence can be felt in every part of the globe. There are a lot of reasons why they're so influential, not the least of which is because there are so damn many of them.

Born to the G.I. Generation, this great flood of a humanity was raised with the benefits given to them by their parents (little debt, an open future, the sense of possibility and potential in life), and very few of the hindrances they would later toss at their own kids. This was the first generation raised with television—which was imaginative and entertaining, steeped in fantasy and illusion...and programmed. They were *fed* culture, but didn't have to earn it or participate in it. And this sense of belonging to a wider, more uniform culture, removed from the actual event, instilled in them idealism without the sense of connection their parents had. Television, the overwhelming number of people in their generation, their relatively strong education, and the social unrest of the '50s and '60s, all contributed to giving the Boomers a strong idealistic streak and a desire for radical change.

Both the legitimate need for change, and the war in Vietnam, gave the Boomers a strong focus onto which they could launch their craving for self-expression and self-reflection. Through self-glamorizing and actively calling for needed changes, they raised the voice of protest and freedom. Some of the protest movements were real and admirable. Many of them were fashionable. Most were a mixture of both. I have my own little theory: I think the Boomers were actually *envious* of their parents, not angry with them. In their envy, they craved some of the trauma and fulfillment, some of the depth of living their parents experienced due to the Depression and WWII. And so, envy caused them to generate that trauma and fulfillment through their various social movements—some of which were extremely influential. The protest against the Vietnam War, the birth of Feminism, the call for equality among the races—so many of these things that we now take for granted were born of the Boomer idealism. Early Boomer consciousness also produced fantastic music, new art, good literature, and inspiring films.

However.

When the Vietnam War ended, the Boomers lost that focal point of self-expression and protest. The soldiers came home and were either dismissed or despised. The "reality" of life, of kids, and of aging set in—and the Boomers made a complete about-face. What they once denounced, they became. Self-expression became self-indulgence; self-reflection became self-absorption. The sense of personal opportunity they had as kids became opportunistic. The wider social opportunity for change became selfish opportunism. Their talent for self-glamorizing grew into commercial greed, and the superb armor of rebellion became a prison, locking in the status quo.

Am I being harsh? Maybe. Keep on reading.

The fantastic Boomer protest sentiment twisted into a collective sense that they were owed, and that they would collect—no matter what the cost. The harmonious freedom chants jarred and fragmented into harsh mantras, ringing out over the world as a new song: *Profit from whatever you need to, because you, and only you, matter. Do anything that suits your own interest, and take no responsibility.* And slough off responsibility, they did. Mesmerized by the siren-call of success, many Boomers pursued their careers at the expense of their children and relationships. And whatever economics they once benefited from (affordable education, the prospect of employment, etc.), they now ripped apart—gobbling down the immediacy of profit and leaving only a few scraps behind.

The early Boomer actors are marked by *emotion, invention, naturalness, risk-taking, strength, analytical depth,* and *rebellion.* However, a lot of those actors have now evolved into *peacock coolness, effortless understatement,* and sometimes even a *parody* of what they once were.

I find that it's with the Boomer generation that dramatic changes in theatre and film take place. Language, as a strong theatrical device, begins to fade away, replaced by stronger and more intricate visual images. The connection between artist and audience as a foil to poke at universal truths begins to weaken as artists become more self-involved and removed from the crowd. Character, and the excitement of character clashes, fade away— replaced instead by group searches and more *collective* dynamic. Bold character development becomes a situational encounter, with a more esoteric purpose. It's all quite interesting. You can follow the development of Boomer philosophy and economic situation very clearly in their theatre and film. At the moment, I sense that their art is washed-up, completely engulfed by the commercial, without the zest of invention and passion they once had, and desperately empty (as always, there are generational exceptions that prove the rule, like Julie Taymor or Robert Lepage). But I find that actors I once had faith in no longer hold my attention, and their formerly "naturalistic" style of playing has become laughably unreal. Their animal passion is gone, and they're mostly tame little lap dogs. All in all, I find Baby Boomer theatre and film—for all its remarkable accomplishments—to be ultimately *ungenerous.* It was once self-reflective, and has since spiraled into the absurd.

## X-pe(a)nd-able?

Generation-X. What to say? It is impossible for me to even hint at objectivity with this generation, because I am part of it. I was born at the tail end of Gen-X, and even I can't quite come to terms with it. It is a small, but very complex and complicated generation. As a whole, Generation X is just not that big. Or at least, it seems that way because of the hulking shadow and complete control of the Boomer generation. The biggest contribution we've made to the world so far has been in the field of technology. I suppose it's pop-media cliché to list the general characteristics of my generation, but I'll do it anyway, and hope we can find a little insight into the whys and wherefores.

Yes, we are cynical, often void, inconsistently educated, and without a sense of responsibility; we have trouble firing up *real* passion. We're also deeply anti-social, unlike the previous two generations. But the strongest sense, I think, is a feeling of impotence; a feeling that no matter what our intentions are, we may never be able to *achieve* an objective or dream. And yes, it's true, we have bumbled around for a while, directionless and confused—not without a strong desire for radical change, but without clear thought and expression, and lacking the ability to act or to take initiative. So we're quite plaintive and sometimes even whine. We're often characterless and dull, and wallow in isolation. Yes, yes, yes. But I am a great apologist for my generation, and I would like to point out a few things.

First, we were raised entirely on television. A *lot* of it—hours and hours a day of half-wit sitcoms, empty, horn-blowing game shows, and our parents' situational dramas. This brain-tap programming—mixing completely unreal "reality," high illusion, unattainable dreams, and the banal into a sort of idiot stew— served to drill a quiet desperation into our souls. We furthered our escape in video games, a diet of rotten junk food, and the mournful "grunge" style of the early '90s. We emptied our brains with the hardness of rap, hip-hop, dance, and electronica— rhythm without melody and sound without musicians.

Second, Gen-X is the first generation to be raised substantially in single-parent households, or with career-absorbed parents; this left many of us entirely without confidence of direction— isolated from positive passions and character definition. You would think that this kind of self-raising would result in a liberation or self-definition, but that doesn't seem to be the case. Minor key, doleful inflections of the voice (from our music and TV-talk), droopy body language, and pessimism and sarcasm seem to be the most dominant characteristics of my peers. I suppose the wacky economy we grew up with (seemingly strong, but quietly riddled with debt) helped to instill in us an overall sense of futility and bleakness. A lot of suicides, and a lot of self-abuse through drugs have marked our generation, along with low-key daily living, mixed with clutching, clawing attempts to find some kind of purpose in life, some kind of truthful passion. We live small and curious lives, partly because we had nothing *big* happen in our lifetime—nothing traumatic or fulfilling like our parents and grandparents had. Our trauma-and-fulfillment search is completely *internal*.

I realize that I may sound like a complaining romantic. Of course, the rough sketch I have just drawn is riddled with clichés. Like every generation, there are individuals and groups who champion opposite philosophies—those who go against the grain, or who were raised differently from their peers. There is hope, and I think that Generation-Xers are finally starting to get over themselves and beginning to grow up.

What else do I notice about this generation? Well, we have a lot of naked intelligence, and quirky invention. And though Gen X lives mostly in a supporting role, continuing and holding up institutions and businesses created by Boomers, I see a stiffening of the spine beginning, and the potential for quiet rebellion. The dark events of 2001 leave open two very clear avenues: complete submission and bowing to the gods of the status quo, or the invitation of new ways of thinking and fresh insights in order to solve complex and complicated new problems. Because this generation *is* complex and complicated, there is an untapped resource here—a mine of possibility and passion waiting to offer up its riches.

Our actors are marked by *irony, wispy generalizations,* an *entitled arrogance,* and *wide-eyed dolefulness.* Sometimes, we find *idiosyncratic sardonic humor.* But recently, I notice the beginning of fresh invention and a resurgence of odd passion, as we shake off the malaise of our upbringing and find out who we really are. I hope this book will contribute something to the rekindling of ardor, and ignite a clearer direction in our acting.

## The Decline of *Real* Emotion

You have probably noticed a pattern through these three major generations—a pattern of dwindling emotion. As our lives get quicker and busier, they also get smaller. As we divorce ourselves from the natural rhythms of life, and lose the time to *really* get to know people and to delve into experience (as opposed to the practices of professional success, money-making, and career goal-setting), we begin to erode the connection to our emotions. As we spend more time staring at the tube, living vicariously through the doldrums of television, we begin to lose our depth of living, our life-giving emotions, and replace them with a wash of the general and the common. Real emotion is easy to lose if we shoo it away or tape over it in favor of what we think is a better program.

With our Shakespeare work, you're going to need to peel away your cynicism and start poking around among all those emotions and thoughts you've perhaps let shrivel up. You're going to need to get in touch with your fire, your anger, your joy, your love, your jealousy, your sorrow, and everything else you may have turned a deaf ear to. Shakespeare doesn't tap dance around these things— he dives into them. He makes you, the actor, *eat* them.

And you've got to *fall in love with language*, and really take time rediscovering words and strong thoughts. You will have to start ripping and devouring language; drinking, eating, licking, and tasting it. Shakespeare's work is visceral, and you'll need a vibrant tongue.

It's a good idea to live big and to embrace everything that comes your way; sucking the marrow out of every experience life throws at you. You'll need that resource because you will need to draw on that variety and depth of experience to fully inhabit the souls of Shakespeare's characters. Only when you can wear their skin can you gnaw the bone of life with them.

## So Where Are We Now?

We find ourselves in an interesting spot today—we have the opportunity to open up some completely new concepts by going over some very old ground. If we can relearn some of what we have forgotten, and then take that to the next level, I think we have the opportunity to create a new Art, and a new zest for life.

Our Shakespeare work will teach you the things you should have learned, but never did. It will help you uncover what you need as an actor, and will teach you some completely new things. Once you learn them, use them. Your work will be both old and new: old, because this stuff has been around for a while. New, because I will give you fresh insights; because it's new to you, and because you're living *right now*—you can offer us Shakespeare that is informed by *you*, teach us new things, and bring us in a new direction, informed by your own experience of life.

## From Here to There

The biggest challenge you may face is actually just getting used to Shakespeare's text. What do I mean? Well, compare the two texts below. The first, written by prolific young playwright Anthony Kokx, comes from his play *UnfoundedFearOf* (2001):

| | |
|---|---|
| MS. DEREAFA: | Amen. It's a good thing you did. |
| MRS. RUEPAL: | You think? |
| HANK: | 'Obstacles will come and go, but the exit signs remain visible. Can you see a light?' |
| MS. DEREAFA: | I'm not sure, but only 'cause I haven't thought about it. You know? |
| MRS. RUEPAL: | I've never known, but then again; you never know. |
| HANK: | They ask, 'Can you see it flashing 11:11 on your digital clock? Or turn and see it turn 11:11 on your digital clock? How's making a wish at 11:11, closing your eyes, only to re-open them and find it's still 11:11? Could you have made twins?' |
| MS. DEREAFA: | No, I know. I'm pregnant. |
| HANK: | 'Or towering up at night and it's 1:11, so you close your eyes in custom, but sleepy conditions only permits the re-opening at the digital sound of your flashing alarm the next morning. And so superstitions state you must re-open to confirm and finalize the wish. Does that mean whatever you dreamt might come true?' |
| MRS. RUEPAL: | Wha—? |
| MS. DEREAFA: | I said I'm pregnant. |
| MRS. RUEPAL: | You? That bastard. |

| | |
|---|---|
| HANK: | I'm completely stumped, and they want me to ask, 'What if 11:11 is four ones switching on in your head? Does it make you smarter?' |
| MS. DEREAFA: | No. |
| HANK: | 'How many times have you seen 11:11?' |
| MS. DEREAFA: | Never—not your dirty German. |
| HANK: | 'How smart are you now, Hank?' |
| MS. DEREAFA: | I've been infected by something way beyond Europe. |
| HANK: | And I say, 'I was born on November eleventh'. |
| MRS. RUEPAL: | Does he speak English? |
| MS. DEREAFA: | Not exactly. |
| HANK: | And they say, 'Good'. They smile, and now I remember them being there. |
| MRS. RUEPAL: | Good luck. |

## And the second, from *Henry V*:

| | |
|---|---|
| BARDOLPH: | Here comes Ancient Pistol and his wife. Good corporal, be patient here. How now, mine host Pistol! |
| PISTOL: | Base tike, call'st thou me host? Now, by this hand I swear, I scorn the term; Nor shall my Nell keep lodgers. |
| HOSTESS: | No, by my troth, not long; for we cannot lodge and board a dozen or fourteen gentlewomen that live honestly by the prick of their needles, but it will be thought we keep a bawdy house straight. |
| | *Nym and Pistol draw* |
| | O well-a-day, Lady! if he be not drawn now; we shall see wilful adultery and murder committed. |
| BARDOLPH: | Good lieutenant! good corporal! offer nothing here. |
| NYM: | Pish! |
| PISTOL: | Pish for thee, Iceland dog! thou prick-ear'd cur of Iceland! |
| HOSTESS: | Good Corporal Nym, show thy valor, and put up your sword. |

NYM:          Will you shog off? I would have you solus.

PISTOL:       'Solus,' egregious dog? O viper vile!
              The 'solus' in thy most mervailous face;
              The 'solus' in thy teeth, and in thy throat,
              And in thy hateful lungs, yea, in thy maw, perdy;
              And, which is worse, within thy nasty mouth!
              I do retort the 'solus' in thy bowels;
              For I can take, and Pistol's cock is up,
              And flashing fire will follow.

NYM:          I am not Barbason; you cannot conjure me. I
              have an humor to knock you indifferently well.
              If you grow foul with me, Pistol, I will scour you
              with my rapier, as I may, in fair terms: if you
              would walk off, I would prick your guts a little,
              in good terms, as I may; and that's the humor of
              it.

PISTOL:       O braggart vile and damned furious wight!
              The grave doth gape, and doting death is near;
              Therefore exhale!

BARDOLPH:     Hear me, hear me what I say: he that strikes the
              first stroke, I'll run him up to the hilts, as I am a
              soldier.

              *Draws*

PISTOL:       An oath of mickle might; and fury shall abate.
              Give me thy fist, thy fore-foot to me give.
              Thy spirits are most tall.

NYM:          I will cut thy throat, one time or other, in fair
              terms: that is the humor of it.

PISTOL:       'Coupe le gorge!'
              That is the word. I thee defy again.
              O hound of Crete, think'st thou my spouse to get?
              No; to the spital go,
              And from the powdering-tub of infamy
              Fetch forth the lazar kite of Cressid's kind,
              Doll Tearsheet she by name, and her espouse:
              I have, and I will hold, the quondam Quickly
              For the only she; and—pauca, there's enough.
              Go to!

The differences are obvious, but don't let them frighten you.
You get used to Shakespeare's text very quickly the more you
read, and the more you play with it. So let's begin our work.

# SHAKESPEARE'S WORLD

Let's stretch our brains a bit here. Let's just crack open our time-closet, and take a little peek into Shakespeare's world. Before we start exploring the techniques of playing Shakespeare well, we should sniff out the world he lived in, and the way people of his time understood man, the world, and the universe.

Don't worry, I'm not going to switch into dry and crusty "Academic Mode." This is a book for actors, not for scholars, so I'll just peel back the tiniest layer of the "worldview," and reveal only as much information as you need in order to understand the Elizabethan world, and to start gnawing on Shakespeare's work. If you want to dig more deeply into the day-to-day workings of the Elizabethan mind, its politics, philosophy, and so on, I strongly suggest E.M.W. Tillyard's book, *The Elizabethan World Picture*. You should also read Virginia Woolf's novel, *Orlando: A Biography*, which will let you inside the skin of characters of the time, and which will give you insight into the textures, thinking, passions, smells, tastes, and relationships. Renting the film *Shakespeare in Love* isn't a bad idea either.

You might think it's hard for us in the present day to click into the Elizabethans, and to get a full, round picture of their worldview, but it's not. Although a lot of their notions are quite foreign to us, it might give you some relief to know that we can find solace in the camaraderie of our ancestors. The Elizabethans, for all their minor differences, are much like us. The basic truths of our lives don't change all that much from century to century. Despite our technological achievements and our progress in science, medicine, and so on, our basic qualities are all the same. We've always had geniuses, idiots, and a mighty host of mediocres shuffling through life. We've always had the same questions about existence, about our place in the world and about the meaning of life. And I suppose we will *always* have the same dilemmas; problems in marriage and relationships, unrequited love, sexual hunger, soul-bashing betrayals, neuroses surrounding achievement, financial anguish, and on and on.

But what brings us joy today also brought us joy four hundred years ago: discoveries, soul-fulfillment, transcendence and love, laughing, love-making, satisfaction of accomplishment, and whatever else picks our souls out of the sticky monotony of living.

When Queen Elizabeth came to the throne, she began to sweep away the Dark Ages and to transform England into an extraordinary place. It was a time of discovery, of renewal, of flourishing art, bold exploration and tricky colonization. England began to become a strong force at sea and in trade. Confidence was flowing back into many lives.

The English language was really coming into its own, and was exploding with invention. New words were created all the time, popping into popular consciousness with novelty and ease. The harsh Saxon, meaty-mouthed speech was changing, just as society was changing.

In some respects, we're living in a similarly transformational time. Our language is changing, too—think of all the new words and expressions in our vocabulary; or words that have taken on new meanings with the boom of technology: data, input, downsize, laptop, DVD and so on. And our worldview is being challenged, as we're sucked forward into an ever-widening whirlpool of events and momentous changes. We, too, are living in juggernaut time, and, except for a few important factors, we can find a lot of connection with the Elizabethans.

The Elizabethans were *complex*—but probably not as complicated as our lives have become. Today's world is both complex and complicated. For example, Freud came along early this century and left an army of psychoanalysts in his wake—we can't underestimate the changes he brought to our experience in life. Instead of looking to God and the natural forces as controlling influences in our lives, we now understand that we are more likely to be ruled by our subconscious needs and urgings. Our concept of free will has shifted from the unfathomable Outer into the thickly-layered Inner. And thanks to Einstein and our moon-leaps in science, we realize now that we know very little about the nature of the universe, time, and space. We can't rely on our old concepts any more as our scientific theories come and go—we open one Russian doll only to find another one underneath it. We question Divine Reality more than ever before, and we are in a collective limbo of acute despair and existential pain that this lack of knowing brings. We have no solid worldview that makes sense when shone in the spotlight of modernity. We scramble faster and faster both to look at ourselves and to get away from ourselves. The more strides we make, the more we know we've only scratched the surface.

It's an exhilarating and liberating reality; it invites a freedom to make real advances, unchained from the dusty, archaic traditions of the past. At the same time, it's a quietly desperate situation; what's the point in living if there is no purpose, no *order*? ("Order" will be an important part of the concepts to come; remember it.)

But guess what: even as our scientists and philosophers search for their "Grand Unified Field Theory," we have to recognize the fact that the Elizabethans had their own. They called it the *Chain of Being*.

## Elizabethan Cosmology, the Earth, and the Divine Order

Even though Copernicus published his heliocentric view (that the sun was the center of the universe, and not the Earth) in 1546, it wasn't really in the popular consciousness until a bit later. Elizabethans accepted *both* this view *and* the geocentric one (that the Earth is the center of the universe). This side-by-side living of two opposing thought-strands is an important theme in the Elizabethan mind, which you'll discover as you continue to read. Let's take a look now at this geocentric view of the universe; it's the one that informs Shakespeare and his audience most powerfully. Let's try to get inside the heads of the Elizabethans:

> *The Earth is the center of the universe. The Sun, stars, and cosmic bodies revolve around it as the focal point of creation. The Earth is the center of God's mind, and God's attention. Most of us know by now that the Earth is round, not flat—but we don't really care. The focus of glory and cosmic beauty is the Earth itself, and Man is the apple of the Universal Eye.*

*We are either Catholic or Protestant. Though we have our troubles, both religions remain in practice side by side. This is the smooth paradox of our age—both the helio- and geocentric views of the universe exist side by side. Catholic and Protestant live side by side. We are comfortable with our churches' teachings and images, but we are equally at ease with Greco-Roman mythology and symbolism. We know as much about Neptune, Vulcan, and the heroes of the Ancient World, as we know about the Father, Son and Holy Ghost. We are fun-spirited, drinking, cavalier good-time people. We are also dour-faced, humorless Puritans. Most of us are poor— some of us are not. Life is very hard, and it takes a lot of energy to exist day to day, but there is a pulsing of exciting circumstance and events around our lives. We see extraordinary people from exotic places coming off the boats, and we are curious. We have a powerful Queen, but we sense drastic political changes when she dies.*

*We have been created by God, and he has set the universe according to a Divine Order, or 'Chain of Being.' There is a natural hierarchy that we understand and obey:*

- *God*
- *the Seraphim*
- *the Cherubim*
- *the other angels and the spirit world*
- *Emperors, Kings and Queens (close to the angelic realm)*
- *the Aristocracy, with its own strong hierarchy*
- *the wealthy*
- *the common people*
- *the poor and outcast*
- *animals*
- *plants*
- *minerals*

*This is the Chain of Being set forth by God Himself. Every man, woman, and child has a superior or inferior, according to the Divine Order—and we abide by it. There are, of course, more hierarchies even within these larger groups.*

Listen to Sir Walter Raleigh describe this Divine Order:

> *"For that infinite wisdom of God, which hath distinguished his angels by degrees, which hath given greater and less light and beauty to heavenly bodies, which hath made differences between beasts and birds, created the eagle and the fly, the cedar and the shrub, and among stones given the fairest tincture to the ruby and the quickest light to the diamond, hath also ordained kings, dukes or leaders of the people, magistrates, judges, and other degrees among men."*

This worldview was deeply imbedded inside people's consciousness. For Elizabethans, it's just the way it was. They understood their place in the world and stuck to it. They were comfortable with who and what they were. If they weren't, they sucked it in and dealt with it. Everyone knew his place, and lived it. The only way one could advance socially was to marry into a higher class (which was rare), or to have some strange accident of Fate throw you up the ladder. Of course, there were opportunists, schemers, and those who tried to advance socially by other means—but this usually resulted in disaster. People could fall on the scale of degree by committing serious sins.

When this order was broken, when some link in the chain of being was misplaced, usurped, rebelled against, or had fallen, the universe itself went out of whack. Any upset in the Divine Order resulted in cataclysmic difficulties: the weather raged, spiritual omens were seen or heard, souls were in turmoil—bad luck, evil, sickness, wars, and even death followed—until Order was restored.

This is the basis of a lot of the action in Shakespeare's plays:

- order is upset
- disaster and trauma follow
- order is restored

When you come across references in Shakespeare's work to storms raging, animals shrieking, ghosts being seen and heard, you know that "Time is out of joint." Nature reflects the disorder of man, and the internal struggles to restore order are mirrored by natural phenomena.

Listen to Shakespeare describe this Elizabethan worldview, in the voice of Ulysses on the battlefield (from *Troilus and Cressida*, Act I, Scene 3):

> Troy, yet upon his basis, had been down,
> And the great Hector's sword had lack'd a master,
> But for these instances.
> The specialty of rule hath been neglected;
> And look, how many Grecian tents do stand
> Hollow upon this plain, so many hollow factions.
> When that the general is not like the hive
> To whom the foragers shall all repair,
> What honey is expected? Degree being vizarded,
> The unworthiest shows as fairly in the mask.
> The heavens themselves, the planets, and this center
> Observe degree, priority, and place,
> Insisture, course, proportion, season, form,
> Office, and custom, in all line of order.
> And therefore is the glorious planet Sol
> In noble eminence enthron'd and spher'd
> Amidst the other; whose med'cinable eye
> Corrects the ill aspects of planets evil,
> And posts, like the commandment of a king,
> Sans check to good and bad. But when the planets
> In evil mixture to disorder wander,
> What plagues, and what portents, what mutiny,
> What raging of the sea, shaking of earth,
> Commotion in the winds, frights, changes, horrors,
> Divert and crack, rend and deracinate
> The unity and married calm of states
> Quite from their fixture? O! when degree is shak'd,
> Which is the ladder to all high designs,
> The enterprise is sick. How could communities,
> Degrees in schools, and brotherhoods in cities,
> Peaceful commerce from dividable shores,

The primogenity and due of birth,
Prerogative of age, crowns, scepters, laurels,
But by degree, stand in authentic place?
Take but degree away, untune that string,
And hark what discord follows; each thing meets
In mere oppugnancy. The bounded waters
Should lift their bosoms higher than the shores
And make a sop of all this solid globe;
Strength should be lord of imbecility,
And the rude son should strike his father dead;
Force should be right, or rather right and wrong,
Between whose endless jar justice resides,
Should lose their names, and so should justice too.
Then everything includes itself in power,
Power into will, will into appetite.
And appetite, an universal wolf,
So doubly seconded with will and power,
Must make perforce an universal prey
And last eat up himself. Great Agamemnon,
This chaos, when degree is suffocate,
Follows the choking.
And this neglection of degree it is
That by a pace goes backward with a purpose
It hath to climb. The general's disdained
By him one step below, he by the next,
That next by him beneath; so every step,
Exampled by the first pace that is sick
Of his superior, grows to an envious fever
Of pale and bloodless emulation:
And 'tis this fever that keeps Troy on foot,
Not her own sinews. To end a tale of length,
Troy in our weakness stands, not in her strength.

The Elizabethans had a real horror of chaos, and tried to maintain their stability by honoring this chain of being. It was, for them, the natural state of the universe. As such, this sense of order, the chain of being, was reflected in the design of the Globe Theatre.

## The Globe Theatre

A lot of Shakespeare's plays were performed in the Globe Theatre—one of the more popular theatres, but certainly not the only one. It wasn't really unique in design, but it reflected the beliefs and thinking of the Elizabethans.

The theatre was constructed as a fully enclosed circle—a "wooden O." It was as popular an arena for bear baiting and cockfighting as it was for plays. I imagine the actors played many performances slipping over puddles of blood and bits of gut from the morning's action. Really try to imagine this theatre before you begin playing Shakespeare, not only because of its design and function, but because of the throngs of people who gave the theatre its life. Imagine:

You're standing downstage center. Immediately up and to your left, there are people; across from you, more people; to your right, more people; and at your feet, rippling like a little lake a few hundred feet to the opposite wall—hordes of stinking, living, bristling, jostling, peering, yelling (probably drunk), whistling, smart-mouthed, excited, toothless, filthy Elizabethans, all hanging on your every word and expecting their money's worth.

There is no roof above your head. The theatre is open to the sky, and to its elements. It doesn't matter if the sun is beating down, or if rain, cold, or chill is slashing down upon the crowd, you keep playing. Your acting is as open to your audience as your audience is open to the sky. You are a part of them; your playing is for them, and your breath is for them. You respond to anything they throw at you: catcalls, cheering, or booing. You're an actor, and you celebrate, examine, and gnaw the bone of life with your audience.

Keep imagining:

> Directly above your head is an overhanging plat-
> form, onto which is painted the Sun, the Moon,
> the stars, and the signs of the Zodiac in blue,
> gold and other strong colors. This represents the
> Higher Order.
>
> The "wooden O"—the Globe Theatre—represents
> the globe of the Earth. The theatre is the world.
> You're standing on a strong, solid wooden stage.
> This represents the Earth we all stand upon. This
> stage juts out almost into the middle of the the-
> atre. When you, the actor, stand downstage
> center, you are standing in the "middle of the
> world."
>
> Underneath you is a trapdoor, leading to a pit.
> This represents the Underworld, from which an
> assortment of ghosts or evil spirits will emerge.

Even the layout and design of the theatre reflects the thinking of your time.

## The Ultimate Elizabethan Statement

I think the people of Shakespeare's day lived in more clarity than we do. Night was night—black, dangerous, secretive. Day was day—bright, open, warm. They didn't have the neon haze of per-petual day that bright city lights give us. They knew their place in society, understood right from wrong (even if they ignored it), and knew their superiors and inferiors. They existed in a world of order, no matter how glorious or horrible it was for them.

I also think they had heightened senses. Their sense of smell was sharper because of the horrendous stink in the streets; their ears sharper because of the eruption of language; their eyes more penetrating because of the clear difference between night and day.

And I think it's the combination of their sense of order, the distinction of environment, the pulsing sense of change, and their acute senses that brought on a *real* melancholy. Not the weepy, sentimental, fashionable, and overblown romantic melancholy of the 19th Century, and not the hard, cynical blackness of the 20th Century, but a real "defect of the spleen;" a truthful melancholy. They knew joy and sorrow intimately, and suffered through it all with a clear-cut sense of the Divine nature of humanity, as well as man's frailty and life's futility. The clearest insight into Elizabethan thinking comes from Hamlet, when he makes the "Ultimate Elizabethan Statement":

> I have of late—but wherefore I know not—lost all my mirth, forgone all custom of exercises; and indeed, it goes so heavily with my disposition that this goodly frame the earth seems to me a sterile promontory; this most excellent canopy, the air, look you, this brave o'erhanging firmament, this majestical roof fretted with golden fire—why, it appeareth nothing to me but a foul and pestilent congregation of vapors. What a piece of work is a man, how noble in reason, how infinite in faculties; in form and moving how express and admirable, in action how like an angel, in apprehension how like a god: the beauty of the world, the paragon of animals! And yet to me what is this quintessence of dust? Man delights not me....

This is most telling and typical of Elizabethan thinking. In a way, it sums up the whole of Shakespeare's writing: "Man is glorious—almost Divine. And yet man and life mean nothing to me. He is a 'quintessence of dust,' and I take no joy in him, even as I recognize that he is a miracle." Even so, Shakespeare's work is a burning celebration of man.

Read this "Ultimate Elizabethan Statement" again, and this time picture your Globe Theatre. Hamlet makes this statement standing downstage center (remember: in the center of the "world"). He subtly refers to the "wooden O" when he says, "this goodly frame the earth seems to me" and the bare, protruding stage when he says, "a sterile promontory." He also uses the painted ceiling as "this brave o'erhanging firmament, this majestical roof fretted with golden fire." Yes, I know he had the open sky to use ("this most excellent canopy, the air"), but it's interesting that Hamlet is standing on his platform, underneath the "majestical roof" and on top of the Underworld pit. In that carefully chosen position, he extols the virtues of man, and then dismisses humanity as meaningless. He does all this as he stands with great authority in the center of the Earth, between Heaven and Hell.

## How Good Were the Elizabethan Actors?

I can only guess. But knowing Shakespeare's work, understanding the Elizabethan mind, tasting the quality of the time, and by piecing other fragments together, I think that the actors were undoubtedly excellent. By our standards, they had almost no rehearsal time. Each actor received his—and only his—part (not the whole play) in little bits and fragments, and probably had only the cue lines of the other actors. Some playhouses produced forty or fifty plays a year, so I suppose they had less than a week to cobble a production together. Judging from the popularity of the Globe, I imagine the actors kept the audience on edge, and were very exciting.

And I think they played very, very *swiftly*. The crowds had to cross the Thames River in order to get to the playhouse—a bit out of the way. So the actors had to get them in and out and back over the Thames before the cutthroats came out at night to rob the audience as they left the theatre. And don't forget, the Puritans were hanging around, skulking in the corners of the theatre...watching, just waiting for the chance to close the place down. And they succeeded, at times. Not long after Queen Elizabeth's day, Oliver Cromwell and his Puritans took control of England, so we can't underestimate the pressure of Puritanical presence. The Chorus, in *Romeo and Juliet* refers to the production as "the two hours' traffic of our stage." These days, Shakespeare productions take 2½ to 3½ hours to play, with cuts! So how did they do it? Swiftly. They came on, did their business, and got the hell off the stage.

## Audio

In Spain, crowds are called "spectatorio;" to see, to observe a spectacle. It's a visual word. In France, they have "le publique;"

the public—a gathering of people for an event. In the English-speaking world, we have an "audience;" audio—to hear, to listen. This is an important thing to keep in mind. Shakespeare's work is to be actively listened to. We're a lot more visual than aural now—we're used to "watching" television and "seeing" a movie. We used to "hear" a play, but now we "see" a show.

Of course, there were no moving images in Shakespeare's day, so he pours language into the ear to set a scene. He creates scenes, moods, and strong visual images by weaving a fabric of audio imagery. In your practice, you'll really have to work at these images slowly, setting up a situation for the audience with detail. By speaking a visual image to the crowd, you allow them to use their imaginations to "see" it, and to fill in the gaps. They will take your picture, and reshape it in their minds. You get an intimacy and connection with an audience when you do this well; you offer an image, let them sort it out, and they follow you. In a way, it's more imaginative than the visual "show;" when you present a visual image, we all see the same *external* thing—we're *given* an imagination. Through the ear, we can *suggest*, plant a seed, and let it flower.

As we get into our Shakespeare work, remember this acute sense of the audio. Remember, too, the notion of order, the depth of living Elizabethans experienced, and the swiftness in playing. It will inform all your work, as you reach to dig deeper into yourself for a stronger, meatier you.

# OBJECTIVES, ACTIONS, INTENTIONS? THROW THEM AWAY!

Ah, good old Stanislavsky.

In the nineteenth century, there was a very popular acting style: maudlin. After the introduction of opulent costumes, amazing mechanical contraptions, opera, and richly embroidered sets and theatres in the late-seventeenth to late-eighteenth centuries, actors became at home in this other-worldly, over-rich environment. Their playing changed from the intimate, dynamic, and alive, to the sing-song, removed-from-reality, and self-absorbed precious. I know I'm making a sweeping generality— there were always actors and styles that people of the time considered "natural"—but I just want to give you a small overview of shifting styles.

It's hard for us to judge styles objectively. Every generation produces actors important to their immediate time and culture. To people in a particular time, actors reflect the reality of that time. To later generations, they appear ridiculous. John Gielgud, for example, was unique and popular in his day. He was considered very "real" and "natural," at the time (in comparision to his contemporaries), but today his style seems overblown and romantically affected. Likewise, Laurence Olivier was the most galvanizing, "natural" actor in his day. Now his style seems less so; clipped, overdone, and overly theatrical. Every generation changes perspective, and has new ideas of what is real and what is not. To us, a lazy, throwaway, never-changing attitude is considered "natural;" later generations will look back on us and laugh, just as we laugh at the maudlin actors of the late nineteenth century.

In response to this high-falutin' stuff in the theatre, Stanislavsky embarked on a series of important discoveries. He changed the theatre, and his influence continues to be felt. He discovered the idea of an *objective* in a play or scene. What you want; what you need from another character. He thought of the idea of *actions*: when you want something, what do you *do*, actively, to attain it? For his day, he and his actors were remarkably realistic and natural. They delved into the emotional truth of a character, and broke plays down analytically. Not that actors weren't emotionally truthful before him, or didn't break down their plays properly—of course they did—but his discoveries continued into the Group Theatre in New York, and on and on down the line; they're still trickling through to us today, though our styles have changed considerably. Interestingly, the Moscow Art Theatre and Group Theatre both followed very strict acting styles, which seem considerably less natural to us than to audiences of their day.

But this kind of analysis is important when you have plays written with a lot of subtext. Good twentieth century plays have overtures, subtext and hidden meanings; you have to incorporate strong analysis into your acting work in order to uncover your objectives, and make the scenes playable. Today's plays have a barrier between the actor and the audience—a "fourth wall." We carry on our stage-lives in front of the audience, as if they were peeking through an invisible wall; voyeurs into other people's lives.

It's not like that with Shakespeare. There is no fourth wall. Everything is open, and everything is for the audience. Even when you have an intimate scene between two people, or a larger scene in a specific setting, you will still refer to the audience and bring them into your world. Nothing is private. Everything is shared. So you have to get rid of the idea of a fourth wall right away.

And because you're not living a secret, private life with thousands of voyeur eyeballs blinking at you, you have:

## No Subtext

With the Shakespeare work (and all classical work) you have absolutely *no subtext*. You tell the audience what's going on with your little asides, and they follow you. When you have something to reveal to the audience, you reveal it through a monologue or soliloquy. The audience never needs to guess what is going on in your head, and you don't have to break down your scene and analyze it. You don't need to bust your brain figuring out what you need in a scene, and what actions will support and fulfill your need. Shakespeare gives you everything you need, right there on the page. Every line guides you to the next, and every line is active. You just need to live each line, and share it with the audience.

There is a way to incorporate our theatre traditions (text analysis, objective breakdowns, etc.) with the classical work. But I'll show you that in the very last section of the book, because it's not important to the bulk of our work. Right now, I want you to throw away your notion of the fourth wall, and scrap your ideas of objectives, intentions, actions, emotional recall, sense memory, and all those acting notions. Go on, purge your brain of it right now, and put it away.

## "Real" vs. "Natural"

Shakespeare's work is *not "natural."* It's *real*—about as real as you can get. You have *real* complex characters, and *real* situations and relationships. You have *real* problems and dilemmas, and so on. He is deeply real, even if that reality is heightened. But that doesn't mean Shakespeare is natural—he isn't at all.

What do I mean? Well, for me, "natural" is just that. You come into a room, mumble, collapse, scratch your ass, pick your nose. I walk around in my pajamas all day talking to myself, spilling coffee, and sit hunched-over. I shuffle around "naturally." My "natural" existence, however, doesn't reflect my "real" existence. The reality of my life is bigger and more dynamic than the "naturalisms" that affect it. There's not much time for "naturalism" in Shakespeare's theatre. Yes, you inhabit your characters fully, but you must get away from the idea of "natural." Play instead the core reality of your character-in-situation. It's more exciting.

Naturalistic playing works mostly for films, where the visual environment supports the mood and thoughts of a character. You can play a very subtle inner-life because the camera picks up every nuance, and the microphone picks up your tiniest breaths. It can work, too, for plays with a strong visual background and intimate audience. But it doesn't work all that well with Shakespeare. It *can* (as we'll see much later on), but for now just get rid of the idea. I want to guide you from the *core* outwards.

Now, even as I tell you this, Shakespeare both supports and contradicts me by giving you instructions through Hamlet:

Speak the speech, I pray you, as I pronounced it to you—trippingly on the tongue. But if you mouth it, as many of our players do, I had as lief the town crier spoke my lines. Nor do not saw the air too much with your hand, thus, but use all gently; for in the torrent, tempest, and (as I may say) the whirlwind of your passion, you must acquire and beget a temperance that may give it smoothness. O, it offends me to the soul to hear a robustious, periwig-pated fellow tear a passion to tatters, to very rags, to split the ears of the groundlings, who for the most part of capable of nothing but inexplicable dumb shows and noise. I would have such a fellow whipped for o'erdoing Termagant. It out-herods Herod. Pray you, avoid it.

Be not too tame neither, but let your own discretion be your tutor. Suit the action to the word, the word to the action—with this special observance: that you o'erstep not the modesty of nature. For anything so overdone is from the purpose of playing, whose end, both at the first and now, was and is, to hold, as 'twere, the mirror up to nature, to show virtue her own feature, scorn her own image, and the very age and body of the time his form and pressure. Now this overdone, or come tardy off, though it make the unskillful laugh, cannot but make the judicious grieve; the censure of the which one must in your allowance o'erweigh a whole theatre of others. O, there be players that I have seen play, and heard others praise—and that highly (not to speak it profanely)—that neither having the th' accent of Christians, nor the gait of Christian, pagan, nor man, have so strutted and bellowed that I have thought some of Nature's journeymen had made men, and not made them well, they imitated humanity so abominably.

What we want to find, eventually, is a harmony between more naturalistic playing and its deeper reality. And it's easy to find when we first get to the essence of playing Shakespeare.

# PART TWO

# YOUR SHAKESPEARE TOOLBOX

## CAN YOU ASK A QUESTION?

Well, can you? I know it seems like a silly thing to ask any actor taking his first steps into playing Shakespeare, but it is one of the most important. The question would have been unnecessary thirty or forty years ago, but is endemic to the modern age—and specifically to my X-Generation—the fact that we have a very hard time asking *real* questions.

There are many reasons why, but let me just point out some of the most important. First, for the most part we are an urbanized people. And urbanization brings a hardness, a cynicism, a psychologically protecting veil, and an unwillingness to show any weakness. It's hard to be open, because we reveal that we have a need that must be met. And when we ask someone a genuine question, what we're really saying is: "I need to know something from you that I don't know. Do you have the answer?" Or, more succinctly: "You have something I don't. Are you willing to share?"

We leave ourselves open and vulnerable to the possibility that the other person may respond negatively, snidely, or mockingly. Perhaps they'll ignore us completely. Asking a question means revealing a need, and opening up to potentially negative possibilities. So what we do instead is: *ask a question without really asking a question.* We ask the question, yes, but through use of inflection, we actually *make a statement.*

What do I mean?

Pretend there's someone else in the room with you. Ask them this question:

"You got any sugar?"

Now, say it flat, monotone, from beginning to end. Follow the arrows:

"You got a - ny su - gar..."

Now, say it so that "sugar" ends on a lower tone. Follow the arrows:

"You got a - ny su - *gar*..."

This is how we commonly ask questions today.

Now, open up and ask the question truthfully. Let the "gar" in "sugar" lift up, on a higher tone. Follow the arrows.

"You got a - ny su - *gar*..."

That little lift on the final syllable is the vulnerable one. That's the inflection that leaves us open. But you must get used to asking questions this way.

## Baby-Talk

We do it naturally, from our very first words. "Ma-*ma?* Da-*da?*" As soon as we can speak, we began to phrase our need through inflection. We have to keep that inflection in our psyche. When you ask a question, hit a higher tone on the last syllable in the sentence. Try it again:

"Ma-*ma?*"

"Da-*da?*"

"You got any su-*gar?*"

## Always?

No. Sometimes we ask rhetorical questions, questions we know the answer to. And sometimes, we *conclude* with a question. But for now, just practice asking real, open questions.

## What Does This Have to Do with Shakespeare?

Everything.

A big bulk of Shakespeare's text has to do with argument. And in order to argue well, you have to lift off the end of the line in order for the other character (or *your* next thought) to come in fresh underneath it. Lift up in pitch, then enter your new thought on a lower tone. When you move up on the last syllable, you keep your listener (and the audience) engaged. They hold with you, and they ask with you. They follow your pitch, and leave themselves open for the reply. You'll soon see how important asking a question is in Shakespeare's text.

Practice asking questions, and then use them in life. It will feel strange at first, but it forces you to crack yourself open and to be exposed.

# WHAT IS A CLASSICAL MONOLOGUE?

"Prepare one modern, and one classical monologue."

I'm sure you've heard that one a hundred times already in your career. It's pretty easy to find a modern monologue—flip through any Shepard, Miller, or Mamet, and you can probably find a decent monologue to suit. There are dozens of books in print with monologues for actors taken from movies and modern drama. It's just as easy to find a meaty monologue from the classical repertoire, but you may feel overwhelmed by the bulk of the text and not know exactly what you're looking for.

What is a classical monologue, *really*?

Is it just a fancy piece of text from an old-fashioned play? Convoluted poetry written in strict meter or form? Or is it simply anything written by Shakespeare, Molière, or Marlowe—*any* series of words using flowery language and a maudlin acting style?

Of course not.

In order to understand what a classical monologue really is, what its form and purpose are, we first have to define "classical." A lot of plays are touted as "classics," or "modern classics." All this means is that they tower above others as artistic monuments—that they are somehow "more important" than other plays, that they hone in on eternal truths more sharply than their contemporaries, and that they strike both an immediate and long-lasting chord with the audience. That's a good start.

A dictionary will tell you that "classical" refers to a system or form of thought of early significance, before modern times. But this is too vague; you could argue that humanity has *always* lived in its modern time. Each new year lived is as fresh and groundbreaking as the fallen year is old. Each new generation born lives in its immediate, modern world, and it is only through technology and hindsight that we see previous decades as being primitive.

So let's forget about the dictionary.

For our purposes, let's define "classical" as "the time before the Industrial Revolution." I think this is a good definition because it puts us in a mind-time before machines of mass-production, before a regulated nine-to-five work day broke us from the natural rhythms of life, before we left our search for meaning in gods, philosophy, astronomy, and the natural forces; and before we replaced that search with mechanization, urbanization, and faith in exponential technological advancement as the solution to our problems.

Next, we have to define "monologue" as "a series of thoughts spoken by a single person to a group of listeners." The listeners are either onstage partners in the scene, or the audience. Technically, a "soliloquy" is a series of thoughts spoken by a single actor *to the audience*, and a "monologue" is spoken *to onstage partners*. But for our purposes, let's lump them both together.

So now we can figure that a classical monologue is a spoken series of thoughts dealing with a personal, social, moral, physical or intellectual situation in which a person has some important problem to work out. And when we have a problem to work out—we argue. So then what is a classical monologue?

## A Classical Monologue Is an Argument

It's possible to hear classical argument occasionally if you really listen for it. You might find it in our law courts, Congress, debating forums, and politicians' rhetoric. You might—if you really stretch the ear—even hear it in university lectures. But even as real "open" intellectual examination is creeping away from us, so too is classical argument fast becoming an archaic discipline.

An argument? Sounds easy enough. And it is. But a lot of actors overlook the argument in soliloquies, monologues, and scenes, looking instead for the "emotional truth" of a character. It's easy to equate classical argument with some dusty old vintage tradition—with periwigs, powdered faces, and Greek togas. But it's actually a fundamental way of thinking, and of expression. Classical argument, when properly and passionately played, is full of emotional truth. How? When you honestly argue a situation, you find the truth of who, where, and what you are.

The only problem is this: many of us received a mediocre education at best, and we've never learned how to argue well. You must learn this simple structure as an actor. Real argument will not interfere intellectually in your playing. Rather, it will unlock the passions behind your thoughts and your real objectives in a scene.

## So Why Do We Argue?

We argue because we have a point of view that conflicts with someone else's point of view. We're right and they're wrong! Or maybe they're right and we're wrong, but we're stubborn and we defend our thoughts! Or perhaps we're openly trying to work out an idea or a plan, and we come up with reasons to back up our objective, or reasons to give up.

## So What Is an Argument?

An argument is a list of reasons for or against something. *It is a discussion that persuades*:

- a change in mind
- a change in course of action

I know this seems a bit academic, but it's vitally important that you understand it as we get into our classical monologues. It has *everything* to do with Shakespeare.

A classical monologue is an argument shared with the audience. It is formed in a particular way:

Ask the Question
(or Share Your Problem)


Give the Arguments
(Pros and Cons)


State the Conclusion

Shakespeare gives his characters monologues in order to fill the audience in on what's happening in the characters' heads. Your character will speak a monologue in order to:
- figure out a plan, or decide on a course of action
- react to a series of events, and reason through them
- assess his critical situation
- share a plan or an insight with the audience
- give us reasons for what he is doing/not doing
- share what he thinks life or his situation is all about

This is how Shakespeare fuels the action of the play. He has no establishing shots or stage effects to switch a character's point of view or mood. So the actor *shares* with the audience his problem (asks the question), *weighs* the pros and cons (gives the arguments), and *states* his conclusion (what he *will* do, what he *will not* do, or what is *inevitable*).

So, once more for clarity's sake: You will
- share your problem with the audience (ask your question).
- weigh the pros and cons.
- state your conclusion (what you *will* do, what you will *not* do, what is *inevitable*, what you *hope* for, what you *fear*, etc.).

## Are *All* of Shakespeare's Monologues Arguments?

Mostly.

When a monologue isn't a clear argument, it is a series of disclosures, discoveries, and decisions. We'll take a look at these "Three Dynamic D's" a little later on. You will find that the arguments often include the Three D's, and the Three D's often include arguments.

But first, let's take a look at some of Shakespeare's monologues as arguments.

I'm sure you're at least somewhat familiar with Hamlet's "To be or not to be" speech from Act III, Scene 1. It's a good piece of writing. It's also one of the clearest, best examples of a classical monologue. Actors often have little trouble understanding it, but struggle with the playing of it. It's actually quite simple to play well, if you just:
- Ask the question (or Share Your Problem).
- Give your arguments (Pros and Cons).
- State the conclusion.

If you can do these three things clearly, you won't have to gnaw out vague emotions, force a whimper, gnash your teeth, grunt, and so on. You won't have to ask, "How do I play this? What do I do?" It's easy if you remember that *the emotion is* in *the thought.* It's not on top of the thought, after the thought, or between the thoughts, but it actually *is* the thought itself.

Hamlet presents us with his dilemma. He says:

To be, or not to be—that is the question:
Whether 'tis nobler in the mind to suffer
The slings and arrows of outrageous fortune
Or to take arms against a sea of troubles
And by opposing end them. To die, to sleep—
No more; and by a sleep to say we end
The heartache and the thousand natural shocks
That flesh is heir to, 'tis a consummation
Devoutly to be wish'd. To die, to sleep;
To sleep: perchance to dream: ay, there's the rub;
For in that sleep of death what dreams may come
When we have shuffled off this mortal coil,
Must give us pause: there's the respect
That makes calamity of so long life;
For who would bear the whips and scorns of time,
The oppressor's wrong, the proud man's contumely,
The pangs of despised love, the law's delay,
The insolence of office and the spurns
That patient merit of the unworthy takes,
When he himself might his quietus make
With a bare bodkin? Who would fardels bear,
To grunt and sweat under a weary life,
But that the dread of something after death,
The undiscover'd country from whose bourn
No traveler returns, puzzles the will
And makes us rather bear those ills we have
Than fly to others that we know not of?
Thus conscience does make cowards of us all;
And thus the native hue of resolution

Is sicklied o'er with the pale cast of thought,
And enterprises of great pith and moment
With this regard their currents turn awry,
And lose the name of action.

The first thing Hamlet does is *ask his question* (or share his problem).

To be or not to be—that is the question.

He says, "To live or not to live. That is the question. Should I live or should I die? That's my problem." He even *tells* us that he's asking a question.

The second thing he does is *give his arguments* (weigh the pros and cons).

Whether 'tis nobler in the mind to suffer
The slings and arrows of outrageous fortune,

*—or—*

...to take arms against a sea of troubles,
And by opposing end them?

"I ask myself," he says, "what's the nobler thing to do? Suffer the rot and difficulties of this ridiculous life...*or*...stand up to the problems, and by standing up to them, end them. Which is better?"

Then he says: "Here, folks—let me *argue out the* good *things about dying.*"

To die, to sleep—
No more; and by a sleep to say we end
The heartache and the thousand natural shocks
That flesh is heir to, 'tis a consummation
Devoutly to be wish'd.

"To die. To sleep. And nothing more. And by 'sleep,' I mean we put and end to all the heartache, and the thousand natural shocks that comes from being alive...that's an end and a completion to be wished for."

Then he says: "Here, folks—let me *argue out the* bad *things about dying.*"

> To die, to sleep;
> To sleep: perchance to dream: ay, there's the rub;
> For in that sleep of death what dreams may come
> When we have shuffled off this mortal coil,
> Must give us pause: there's the respect
> That makes calamity of so long life;

"If we die, we sleep. If we sleep, we might dream—and that's the problem. In that sleep of death, what dreams will come...when we have shaken off our bodies? What happens afterwards? That has to make us pause and think. That's the problem, and that's the thing that makes our lives so difficult: *what happens afterwards?*"

Then he says: "Here, folks—let me give you *arguments* for, *and* against, *living.*"

> For who would bear the whips and scorns of time,
> The oppressor's wrong, the proud man's contumely,
> The pangs of despised love, the law's delay,
> The insolence of office and the spurns
> That patient merit of the unworthy takes,
> When he himself might his quietus make
> With a bare bodkin?

"Who (in their right mind) would put up with life's garbage? All these things suck: people in power are always wrong, proud people are contemptuous of others, the pain that comes from being rejected in love, the slow and unjust nature of the law, the insolence of people in office, and the injustice that people who are deserving receive. These things are intolerable—so why should we put up with all this when we can make our own sleep with a knife? Why deal with all this when you can just kill yourself?"

Then he says: "Here's another *argument* against *life."*

> ...Who would fardels bear,
> to grunt and sweat under a weary life...

"Who would put up with these burdens, to grunt and sweat under a tiring life?"
And here, Hamlet explains *why* we all do it:

> But that the dread of something after death,
> The undiscover'd country from whose bourn
> No traveller returns, puzzles the will
> And makes us rather bear those ills we have
> Than fly to others that we know not of?

"We put up with it because of the fear of what comes after life; that *something,* that *undiscovered country,* from whose borders no traveler ever returns. We don't know what's in the next life (if there is one) and that confuses us; it *puzzles the will.* And so we put up with the problems we have, instead of flying to problems that we don't know about."
The third thing Hamlet does is: *state his conclusion.*

> Thus conscience does make cowards of us all;
> And thus the native hue of resolution
> Is sicklied o'er with the pale cast of thought,
> And enterprises of great pith and moment
> With this regard their currents turn awry,
> And lose the name of action.

"And so, conscience (thinking about these things, life/death/life after death/what happens afterwards) makes us all cowards. We don't dare kill ourselves for fear of what comes after. And thus, the true color of our resolve is diluted by the cold, pale light of reason. And movements of importance (like mine), with these things in mind, turn away and stop. They lose the name of action. Just like *I'm* doing; I'm losing my resolve."
Easy.

It takes away a lot of the frustration and worry when you realize that this monologue is only just a well-written argument about living and dying.

## Does That Mean There Is No Emotion in the Speech?

Absolutely not.

Though playing the argument might seem cold, or without emotional truth—it isn't. The more pointedly and clearly you can lift arguments for an audience, the more you can pick apart mini-arguments within arguments, and the more you can *debate* your convictions, ideas, and problems, the more an audience will be engaged by your thought and situation.

## Where Is the Emotion, Then?

The emotion is the thought. The emotion is *that particular thought* at *that particular moment*. Yes, you will have an underlying emotional state in a monologue—rage, joy, despair, etc.—but it's very dangerous for an actor to play this general wash of emotion. Never play a general mood. In life, we're rarely in a static, general mood. Although we might *feel* a vague emotional state, the truth is that our moods change instant by instant, thought by thought, encounter by encounter. It's the same in Shakespeare. You can look at a monologue and figure out what the general state of the character is, but never *act* this generality. Play each thought specifically, moment by moment. Each new thought *is the new emotion*.

For example, take the first line in *The Merchant of Venice*:

In sooth I know not why I am so sad.

The weakest choice would be to play this line sadly. Antonio tells Salerio and Solanio that he's sad and that he doesn't know why. But if you wash this line over with a vague, sad sentimentality—it's boring; it's unspecific and it gets you nowhere. However, if you play this as the beginning of an argument, trying to figure out the reasons for your sadness, scrabbling to find the cause, sharing your problem openly with Salerio and

Solanio, you begin to play this line truthfully and dynamically. How much more interesting would this line play if you try to find the reasons for your sadness in your mind, find nothing, and decide to share your problem through a short temper, or humor, or just by giving us the line as a plain fact? If you *live* this argument, the audience will follow you. But if you whine it out as flabby and sad, you will lose the audience even on the first line.

I often get very frustrated with actors who hem and haw, pause, and cough out indistinct "feelings" before, between, or after the lines. I know why they do this—*they don't trust the thoughts*. This is a very important note as you journey into Shakespeare—trust his thoughts. Trust the power of his thoughts alone. You don't need to sprinkle a shower of nebulous emotion onto them.

It is the impact of these living thoughts that move an audience to a greater experience of life. All of Shakespeare's thoughts are fuelled by *real* love, *real* hatred, *real* whimsy, *real* jealousy, *real* lust, *real* desperation, etc. The only trick for you as an actor is to be in tune with your passions, and to be ready to resonate within these thoughts. Just as your mind, your tongue, and your body must be poised for the moment you step onstage, you must be able to resonate with emotionally powerful thoughts without washing everything in a scrub of vagueness.

Are you up to it? Well, if you are a living, breathing human being who has had some experience in life—you are. But always keep your mind, body, tongue and passions tuned. Now, if you can remember that your emotion is *in* your argument, half your worries are gone. Play your arguments to the audience and to your scene partners—they're for them, not for you. All you need do is:

*Ask your question* (or share your problem): To be or not to be—that is the question.

*Give your arguments* (the pros and cons): Life? Or death? Good and bad qualities of each.

*State your conclusion*: Thinking about these things makes us cowards; we lose our resolve, upon open contemplation, and lose the name of action.

Now go back and try the monologue again. Fuel your first line with *real questioning*. Fuel your arguments with *real doubts about life,* and *real fears of death.* Fuel your conclusion with *the sickening realization that true reflection on life and death makes us all cowards.*

Once you play these arguments fully, you will receive a very clear character clue. You will notice that Hamlet explores one side of his argument fully—and then swings over and matches that argument with a counter-argument, weighing both sides with equal measure. He is like a scale, trying desperately to balance itself, but getting nowhere in the process. His conclusion solves nothing for him. Instead, it comes right back to the beginning. He has solved nothing, he has decided nothing, and he has only succeeded in arguing with himself. So your character clue is this: Hamlet is a scale, having no fundamental strength of his own. He lives his life instead by balancing internal and external arguments. He teeters from one side to another, without any weight of his own to support him. Use the image of a delicate balance scale, trying both to maintain equilibrium and to measure, under the stress of an insupportable burden.

Now let's take a look at another monologue, perhaps not as obvious as Hamlet's, but an example of a slightly different kind of argument. In Act III, Scene 1, Macbeth debates with us:

> To be thus is nothing;
> But to be safely thus. Our fears in Banquo
> Stick deep; and in his royalty of nature
> Reigns that which would be fear'd: 'tis much he dares;
> And, to that dauntless temper of his mind,
> He hath a wisdom that doth guide his valor
> To act in safety. There is none but he
> Whose being I do fear: and, under him,
> My Genius is rebuk'd; as, it is said,
> Mark Antony's was by Caesar. He chid the sisters
> When first they put the name of king upon me,
> And bade them speak to him: then, prophet-like,
> They hail'd him father to a line of kings:
> Upon my head they placed a fruitless crown,
> And put a barren scepter in my gripe,
> Thence to be wrench'd with an unlineal hand,
> No son of mine succeeding. If 't be so,

For Banquo's issue have I filed my mind;
For them the gracious Duncan have I murder'd;
Put rancors in the vessel of my peace
Only for them; and mine eternal jewel
Given to the common enemy of man,
To make them kings, the seed of Banquo kings!
Rather than so, come fate into the list,
And champion me to the utterance!

The first thing Macbeth does is *make his case* (i.e. share the problem/ask the question).

To be thus is nothing;
But to be safely thus....

*—and—*

Our fears in Banquo
Stick deep; and in his royalty of nature
Reigns that which would be fear'd.

"To have this power," he says, "is nothing unless I am *safely* in power. My fear of Banquo runs deep. In his noble nature reigns that which would be feared (like honor, valor, truth). I fear it now, and his subjects would fear it (in the good sense of the word), were he in power."

Next, Macbeth *gives his arguments.*

- These are the reasons I fear and hate Banquo:

(1) tis much he dares;
(2) And, to that dauntless temper of his mind,
He hath a wisdom that doth guide his valor
To act in safety. (3) There is none but he
Whose being I do fear: and, (4) under him,
My Genius is rebuk'd; as, it is said,
Mark Antony's was by Caesar. (5) He chid the sisters
When first they put the name of king upon me,

And bade them speak to him: (6) then, prophet-like,
They hail'd him father to a line of kings:
(7) Upon my head they placed a fruitless crown,
And put a barren scepter in my gripe,
Thence to be wrench'd with an unlineal hand,
No son of mine succeeding.

1. Banquo is daring, ambitious, and he is on the move.
2. Along with his fearless mind, he has a wisdom that makes his bravery act in safety.
3. I fear no one but him.
4. Next to him, my genius is thwarted (as they say Mark Antony's was by Caesar).
5. He chastised the witches when they first called me king, and asked them to speak to him.
6. Then, like prophets, they proclaimed him father to a whole line of kings.
7. They put an impotent crown on my head and an empty scepter in my grip (which will be wrenched away from me by an un-ancestral hand—no son of mine will succeed me as king).

• These are the reasons I fear my fate:

If 't be so,
(1) For Banquo's issue have I filed my mind;
(2) For them the gracious Duncan have I murder'd;
(3) Put rancors in the vessel of my peace
(4) Only for them; (5) and mine eternal jewel
Given to the common enemy of man,
To make them kings, the seed of Banquo kings!

1. For *Banquo's ancestors* have I ruined my mind.
2. For *Banquo's ancestors* have I murdered the gracious King.
3. I have put bitterness in my peace.
4. Only for them!
5. I have sold my soul to Satan in order to make *them* kings; the sons of *Banquo*—kings!

And last, Macbeth *states his conclusions.*

> Rather than so, come fate into the list,
> And champion me to the utterance!

"Rather than all this," he says, "come on, Fate, fight me to the death! I'll fight my fate until I can fight no more."

What do you notice about this monologue? With Hamlet, you had clear arguments—one side and then the other, with pros and cons. With Macbeth, you have instead a *list*, without the weighing of opposites. This is very common in Shakespeare. He gives you lots of lists to work through for the audience. Don't worry—they're just grocery lists.

## A Shakespearean Grocery List

Shakespeare scribbles out lots of lists for you to play with. Common among them is a *list of arguments* for or against a particular course of action, without the actual weighing of pros and cons. You will also encounter *lists of reasons, lists of facts, lists of actions,* and *lists of complaints.* These lists are still arguments—they're just detailing a situation through a crafted series of objective or subjective facts.

Put a very simple grocery list into your mind for a moment. Apples, bananas, bread, milk, cheese, and so on. Now, change each individual item to one of the numbered arguments from Macbeth's speech. Instead of apples, use "'tis much he dares," instead of bread, use "there is none but he whose being I do fear," and so on.

You find that Macbeth's speech is really a very simple grocery list of facts, fears and complaints. When you come across monologues like these, it will help you to look at each individual item on the list on its own terms, and then to join these individual thoughts together into a larger string or ladder of thoughts, building to the conclusion in the last line or two. Build slowly, allowing each individual item to be more anger-making than the last, more saddening than the last, more frustrating than the last, funnier than the last, etc., swelling you up for the climax of the conclusion. Play around with the individual items on the list—

let the first one frustrate you, the second one make you laugh, the third one enrage you, the fourth one worry you, and so on. Change, change, change between each thought, as long as you're climbing up the ladder item by item.

For example:

1. 'Tis much he dares. *Find this ominous.*
2. And, to that dauntless temper of his mind, he hath a wisdom that doth guide his valor to act in safety. *Find this admirable.*
3. There is none but he whose being I do fear. *Give us this plain fact.*
4. Under him, my genius is rebuked. *Find this infuriating.*

And so on. Build your list of items up to the point where you can explode onto Fate, and challenge her to the death. It's always a good idea with these lists to find a few items funny or ironic in order to break up the monotony of heavier notes.

So, as you scan these kinds of monologues for the first time, remember that they are simply grocery lists of arguments, reasons, facts, actions, and complaints. It will keep your playing more focused, and the audience will follow your train and change of thought.

## Argument as 5th Grade Math

There's one more kind of monologue-as-argument we need to take a look at before we get on with things. It's the kind of argument we learn early on in math classes.

$$x + y = z$$

If x represents 2, and y represents 3, then z represents 5. Remember those long-ago math classes? Believe it or not, this simple formula comes in handy right now. It's a basic chain of logic that you'll play with in certain kinds of monologues. Often your character will try to work through a situation by trying to set up a thread of logic—and then something in that thread breaks, or doesn't follow, or needs to be resolved. Troilus's monologue, from *Troilus and Cressida* (Act V, Scene 2) is an excellent example. I won't interrupt you too much in this speech; I want you to follow the logic and argument for yourself now. But before you read it, remember: though Troilus tries to figure out his situation by using logic (he is Greek, after all), it is the *inability to piece things together* that is the core of his *emotional situation*. Each strand of logic comes through anger, worry, confusion, frustration, the realization of betrayal, jealousy, and desperation. Notice the following: he attempts reason, he is unable to hold onto that reason, he is enraged that he cannot find a logical way out of his situation, he desperately tries to find another example of his situation to analyze, and, because he cannot find one, he fractures and disintegrates into apoplectic jealously, repeating "mine, mine." Because he cannot *reason the situation*, he gives into his *primal nature*.

Remember the "if": *If* x = 2, and *if* y = 3, *then* x + y = 5.

This she? Troilus Asks his Question No, this is Diomed's Cressida: *and* Makes his Case
If beauty have a soul, this is not she; Troilus Gives his Arguments
If souls guide vows, if vows be sanctimonies,
If sanctimony be the gods' delight,
If there be rule in unity itself,
This is not she. O madness of discourse,
That cause sets up with and against itself!
Bi-fold authority! Where reason can revolt
Without perdition, and loss assume all reason
Without revolt: this is, and is not, Cressid.
Within my soul there doth conduce a fight
Of this strange nature that a thing inseparate
Divides more wider than the sky and earth,
And yet the spacious breadth of this division
Admits no orifex for a point as subtle
As Ariachne's broken woof to enter.
Instance, O instance! Strong as Pluto's gates;
Cressid is mine, tied with the bonds of heaven:
Instance, O instance! Strong as heaven itself;
The bonds of heaven are slipp'd, dissolv'd, and loos'd; Troilus Gives his Conclusion
And with another knot, five-finger-tied,
The fractions of her faith, orts of her love,
The fragments, scraps, the bits and greasy relics
Of her o'er-eaten faith, are bound to Diomed.

Work through the logic, grapple for reason, and live through each strand of argument. You will find—as you build through the "ifs" and try to find previous examples of this kind of betrayal—that your sense of logic will begin to break. As you break, your jealously takes over, and you will find the emotional truth of Troilus in this situation.

Remember: a classical monologue is just an argument. You will always have to set it up, live through each specific detail, and give your emotional conclusion. That argument is just a *form*—not meant to turn you into a cold, blank automaton, but a form you must work with in order to make your objective clearer. It is an old form, belonging to the "classical world," infused with as much emotion as rational thought. If you look at argument as the *starting point* in your monologue work, you will have the clarity of thought and detailed ladder-building necessary to push forward in your Shakespeare playing.

# ANTITHESIS

And here we come to another vital part of playing Shakespeare, which most drama teachers have forgotten about. It is as basic an ingredient to good classical acting as any you will find. Without antithesis, you can't have good argument—and Shakespeare's writing is riddled with it. I think the whole Elizabethan age was, in a sense, antithetical, and that the people were drunk with antithetical thinking.

## What Is Antithesis?

Just take a look at the word itself. That's part of the answer.

*anti-thesis = anti-argument*

It's the examination and balancing of one argument with its opposite. More specifically, it's making an argument and then looking at its opposite argument. This is really the heart of all argument, and of open, detailed thinking.

## Why Do We Look at an Argument and Its Opposite Argument?

In order to find an answer, a course of action, the way out of a situation, or a fresh perspective, we propose one side of an argument, and then we examine its complete opposite argument. The interplay of these two extremes very often reveals what is in the middle, the truth—the essential dilemma, or a solution to an essential dilemma. In drama, as in life, human truths very often *are* our essential dilemmas.

Since we've just worked with Troilus's speech, let's look there for good examples of antitheses:

O madness of discourse,
That cause set up *with* and *against* itself;

- the simple antithesis is: with / against
- the broader antithesis is: my cause (my reason) sets up *with itself* / my cause (my reason) sets up *against itself*

Where *reason can revolt*
*Without perdition*, and *loss assume all*
*Reason without revolt.*

- the antithesis is: my reason can revolt against itself without destroying itself / and that destruction can take control of my reason without my reason revolting

Remember, Troilus begins by saying, "O madness of discourse," or "What a crazy way of thinking this is!" The struggle through these antitheses is his essential problem.

This *is*, and *is not* Cressid.

- obvious antithesis

Within my soul there doth conduce a fight
Of this strange nature that *a thing inseparate*
*Divides more wider than the sky and earth;*

- the antithesis is: a thing *indivisible* (Cressida) / *divides* herself wider than the sky and earth (through her sexual betrayal of Troilus). (In addition to the antithesis, you have the sexual image of "divides herself.")

And yet *the spacious breadth of this division*
*Admits no orifice for a point as subtle*
*As Ariachne's broken woof to enter.*

- the antithesis is: the giant breadth of this division / cannot even admit a tiny strand of spider-web into itself (Cressida, although she is widely divided—and therefore open—lets nothing in.)

Cressid is mine, tied with the bonds of heaven:
Instance, O instance! Strong as heaven itself;

The bonds of heaven are slipp'd, dissolv'd, and loos'd;
And with another knot, five-finger-tied,
The fractions of her faith, orts of her love,
The fragments, scraps, the bits and greasy relics
Of her o'er-eaten faith, are bound to Diomed.

The last antithesis is the interplay of the first and last three words of this passage.

- *Cressid is mine...but the rotten scraps of her love—are bound to Diomed.*

## Why Is Any of This Important?

Well, you can always jump onstage and start hacking away at a monologue blindly. But you won't get very far if you don't understand the finer components in an argument. You'll save yourself a lot of work when you clarify your antitheses—and if you highlight them for yourself and for the audience, your monologue will be that much easier to play.

It is the contrasting of argument and counter-argument that fuels the action and drama. In *this*, we find the conflict of objectives, and clash of situations; this *play of opposites* makes for good comedy and tragedy. In your acting work, you can't forget that in tragedy there is always something funny, and in comedy there is always something deeply tragic.

It is trying to *make sense of these extremes* that fires Troilus's turmoil, his frustration, his rage. He is trying to figure it all out, and can't. That's why he tells us that his revelation that Cressida has bound herself to another is "bi-fold authority"—it's a double-truth that makes no sense. He tries frantically to discover some parallel, some reference point to anchor himself to, and calls out for it twice: "Instance, O instance." "I need a previous example of this kind of treachery, double-dealing, dual nature." He *needs to make sense out of these extreme polarities*.

## Do I Need to *Play* Antithesis?

Yes.

*Discover* one argument, and then its opposite, onstage, *in the moment*. Share these with the audience, and then together with the audience try to figure it all out. In playing this, you will find the bulk of your action.

Richard, in *Richard II*, Act V, Scene 4 has some good antitheses to work with:

> I have been studying how I may compare
> This prison where I live unto the world:
> And for because the world is populous,
> And here is not a creature but myself,
> I cannot do it; yet I'll hammer it out.
> My brain I'll prove the female to my soul,
> My soul the father; and these two beget
> A generation of still-breeding thoughts,
> And these same thoughts people this little world,
> In humors like the people of this world,
> For no thought is contented. The better sort,
> As thoughts of things divine, are intermix'd
> With scruples and do set the word itself
> Against the word:
> As thus, 'Come, little ones,' and then again,
> 'It is as hard to come as for a camel
> To thread the postern of a needle's eye.'
> Thoughts tending to ambition, they do plot
> Unlikely wonders; how these vain weak nails
> May tear a passage through the flinty ribs
> Of this hard world, my ragged prison walls,
> And, for they cannot, die in their own pride.
> Thoughts tending to content flatter themselves
> That they are not the first of fortune's slaves,
> Nor shall not be the last; like silly beggars
> Who sitting in the stocks refuge their shame,
> That many have and others must sit there;
> And in this thought they find a kind of ease,
> Bearing their own misfortunes on the back
> Of such as have before endured the like.
> Thus play I in one person many people,
> And none contented: sometimes am I king;

Then treasons make me wish myself a beggar,
And so I am: then crushing penury
Persuades me I was better when a king;
Then am I king'd again: and by and by
Think that I am unking'd by Bolingbroke,
And straight am nothing: but whate'er I be,
Nor I nor any man that but man is
With nothing shall be pleased, till he be eased
With being nothing. Music do I hear?
 *Music*
Ha, ha! keep time: how sour sweet music is,
When time is broke and no proportion kept!
So is it in the music of men's lives.
And here have I the daintiness of ear
To check time broke in a disorder'd string;
But for the concord of my state and time
Had not an ear to hear my true time broke.
I wasted time, and now doth time waste me;
For now hath time made me his numbering clock:
My thoughts are minutes; and with sighs they jar
Their watches on unto mine eyes, the outward watch,
Whereto my finger, like a dial's point,
Is pointing still, in cleansing them from tears.
Now sir, the sound that tells what hour it is
Are clamorous groans, which strike upon my heart,
Which is the bell: so sighs and tears and groans
Show minutes, times, and hours: but my time
Runs posting on in Bolingbroke's proud joy,
While I stand fooling here, his Jack o' the clock.
This music mads me; let it sound no more;
For though it have holp madmen to their wits,
In me it seems it will make wise men mad.
Yet blessing on his heart that gives it me!
For 'tis a sign of love; and love to Richard
Is a strange brooch in this all-hating world.

These are great examples of antitheses and the interplay of opposite ideas, because Richard tells us that this is exactly what he's doing to do. "I want to compare *this* with *that*, but because of *this* and *that*:

> I cannot do it; *yet I'll hammer it out*."

He basically tells us, "Here we go; here comes the list of antitheses." (It may look a little confusing, but I will italicize for you the arguments and counter-arguments.)

> I have been studying how I may compare
>
> *This prison* where I live *unto the world*:
>
> And for *because the world is populous*,
> And *here is not a creature but myself*,
>
> *I cannot do it*; yet *I'll hammer it out*.
>
> My *brain* I'll prove the *female to my soul*,
> My *soul* (I'll prove) the *father*;

- Brain and soul; female and father.

>                         and *these two* beget
> A *generation* of still-breeding thoughts,
> And these same thoughts *people this little world*,
> In humors like the *people of this world*,
>
> For no thought is contented. The better sort,
> As thoughts of *things divine*, are intermix'd
> With *scruples*
>
> and do *set the word itself*
> *Against the word*:
>
> As thus, 'Come, little ones,' and then again,

*'It is as hard to come as for a camel*
*To thread the postern of a needle's eye.'*

- This whole Biblical saying is an antithesis.

Thoughts tending to ambition, they do plot
*Unlikely wonders;*

               how these vain *weak nails*
May tear a passage through the flinty ribs
Of this *hard world*, my ragged prison walls,

And, for they cannot, die in their own pride.
Thoughts *tending to content flatter themselves*

That they are not the *first* of fortune's slaves,
Nor shall not be the *last*; like silly beggars
Who sitting in the stocks refuge their shame,

That many have and others must sit there;
And in *this thought* they find a *kind of ease*,

Bearing *their own* misfortunes on the back
Of *such as have before* endured the like.

Thus play I in *one person many people*,

And none contented: sometimes am I *king*;
Then treasons make me wish myself a *beggar*,

And *so I am*: then crushing penury
Persuades me I was better when a *king*;

Then am I *king'd* again: and by and by
Think that I am *unking'd* by Bolingbroke,

And straight am nothing: but whate'er I be,
*Nor I nor any man* that but man is

*With nothing shall be pleased*, till he be eased
*With being nothing.*

Music do I hear?
    *Music*
Ha, ha! keep time: how *sour sweet* music is,

When *time is broke* and *no proportion kept*!

So is it in the music of men's lives.

And here have *I* the *daintiness of ear*
To check *time* broke in a *disorder'd string*;

- *I* with *time...daintiness of ear* with *disorder'd string*.

But for the concord of my state and time
*Had not an ear to hear my true time broke.*

*I wasted time*, and now doth *time waste me*;

For now hath time made me his numbering clock:
My thoughts are minutes; and with sighs they jar
Their watches on unto mine eyes, the outward watch,
Whereto my finger, like a dial's point,
Is pointing still, in cleansing them from tears.
Now sir, the sound that tells what hour it is
Are clamorous groans, which strike upon my heart,
Which is the bell: so sighs and tears and groans
Show minutes, times, and hours:

- This whole section, while not a clean antithesis, is still is argument and counter-argument. We make time *our numbering clock*—now time makes Richard *his numbering clock*.

                                       *but my time*
Runs posting on in *Bolingbroke's proud joy*,

- Not clean again, but still argue *my time* with *Bolingbroke's proud joy*.

While I stand fooling here, his Jack o' the clock.

*This music* mads me; let it *sound no more*;

For though it have holp *madmen to their wits*,
In me it seems it will make *wise men mad*.

Yet blessing on *his* heart that gives it *me*!

- Though you have *his* and *me,* try not to play personal pronouns—it rarely sounds good—
  instead, play the whole thought.

For 'tis a sign of love; and *love to Richard*
Is a strange brooch in this *all-hating world*.

You see that the whole damn speech is nothing but antitheses. No, some of the italicized passages aren't *exactly* opposing arguments, but they are still comparisons of *this versus that*. So, for our purposes, let's include any idea that compares one thing with another (in order to hash out an argument) in our definition of antithesis. If we get any more technical and separate our ideas into minutiae, we will just dilute our playing.

Then let's qualify antithesis in the playing of Shakespeare.

## When You Play Shakespeare, Antithesis Is:
- *arguing two opposite points of view*
- *balancing (or trying to balance) those opposite points of view*

and

- *comparing or contrasting two images*

## Why?
- *to gain a fresh perspective on life*
- *for a change in course of action*
- *to make a disclosure, a discovery, or a decision*

Here is another example, this one taken from from *Julius Caesar*. See if you can pick out the antitheses on your own, and I'll list them at the end.

The Greeks and Romans were masters of oratory and argument. They understood this art, and fuelled it with great irony, tongue-in-cheek, and barbed sarcasm. Try to sniff out the irony in Marc Antony's speech. We'll look more at irony later on, but I'll give you a hint: he repeats the same line over and over again...to make a point. In ironic monologues, antithesis is used to pick away at a person or situation, trying to lift an ironic scab.

Friends, Romans, countrymen, lend me your ears;
I come to bury Caesar, not to praise him.
The evil that men do lives after them;
The good is oft interred with their bones;
So let it be with Caesar. The noble Brutus
Hath told you Caesar was ambitious:
If it were so, it was a grievous fault,
And grievously hath Caesar answer'd it.
Here, under leave of Brutus and the rest—
For Brutus is an honorable man;
So are they all, all honorable men—
Come I to speak in Caesar's funeral.
He was my friend, faithful and just to me:
But Brutus says he was ambitious;
And Brutus is an honorable man.
He hath brought many captives home to Rome
Whose ransoms did the general coffers fill:
Did this in Caesar seem ambitious?
When that the poor have cried, Caesar hath wept:
Ambition should be made of sterner stuff:
Yet Brutus says he was ambitious;
And Brutus is an honorable man.
You all did see that on the Lupercal
I thrice presented him a kingly crown,
Which he did thrice refuse: was this ambition?
Yet Brutus says he was ambitious;
And, sure, he is an honorable man.
I speak not to disprove what Brutus spoke,

But here I am to speak what I do know.
You all did love him once, not without cause:
What cause withholds you then, to mourn for him?
O judgment! Thou art fled to brutish beasts,
And men have lost their reason. Bear with me;
My heart is in the coffin there with Caesar,
And I must pause till it come back to me.

Did you find the antitheses? Let's list them:
- bury/praise
- evil lives after them/good is interred with their bones
- noble/ambitious
- grievous fault/grievously answer'd it
- many captives home to Rome/whose ransoms did the general coffers fill
- poor cried/Caesar wept
- I thrice presented the crown/He thrice refused
- I speak not to disprove what Brutus spoke/I speak what I do know
- You all did love him once, not without cause/What cause withholds you then, to mourn for him?
- judgment/brutish beasts
- My heart is in the coffin with Caesar/I must pause till it come back to me

Mark Antony is using his antitheses here—well-crafted, well-thought out, and perfectly rehearsed—to penetrate a few points into the Roman psyche. He tries to get them to understand their potential hypocrisy, and to sway them to another way of thinking, by using a logic they understand. His antitheses are not discovered in the moment—rather he *pretends* to find them in the moment, using irony.

How many times does he use the word "honorable"? And how many times does he say "Brutus is an honorable man"? In this, he uses another rhetorical device:

## Repetition
You'll find a lot of repetition in Shakespeare. That is deliberate, and there is an important reason for it. You must use repetition cleverly.

Why do great speakers use repetition? In order to hammer home a point? Yes. Think of how many times Dr. Martin Luther King repeated the phrase, "I have a dream." And think of *when* the phrase is lifted out of his speech, and *how many different intonations* he used for the same four words.

But often, characters use the same phrase over and over again, gently changing the intonation each time, leading us somewhere *else* with the repeated thought. Do they mean the *opposite* of what they repeat so that you can draw your own conclusions without them having to spell it out for you? Do they trick you into thinking that you're coming up with your own revelation? This is what Mark Antony is after. Speak the first "Brutus is an honorable man" as a statement of fact. Mean it. And for its repetition, try and lead us into doubt about that phrase. Use it as a little joke. Next use it as a question. Then barb the phrase with anger. Finally, use irony—get us to believe that Brutus is the opposite of "an honorable man."

This incongruity between what Antony *says*, and what he *means*, is interesting to keep in mind for later, when we look more closely at irony.

# VERSE, PROSE, HIDDEN DIRECTIONS AND OVERRUNS — WHAT YOU PROBABLY *DON'T* KNOW!

Like most actors, you probably know a little about verse and prose. You might *sense* a difference between them, but you aren't exactly sure *what* that difference is. And if you're like most actors, you probably play verse and prose as the same beast, ordinary, conversational text.

Of course, you don't want to be like "most actors." If you pay very close attention to this chapter, you will learn to use a few tools that will lift you above the common ranks and help you become a more finely tuned, living actor.

If you want to play Shakespeare well, you must learn the difference between verse and prose, and then you must *use* them differently. They are not the same thing. Shakespeare writes some parts of his plays in verse, other parts in prose, and there is a happy difference between them that will both *inform* and *help* your acting. Shakespeare also loads his text with important *hidden directions* that will help you unlock your thought-speaking, your action, your objective, and your character.

Many directors and teachers—even excellent ones—have either forgotten or dismissed the difference between verse and prose. Or else they don't help the actor to use these thought-shapes differently or to find out what the obvious and subtle hints and pointers are in those differences. Actors are mostly encouraged to play all of Shakespeare's text as a natural, modern conversation—rushing to script analysis, using objectives, motivations, actions, and needs, without fully understanding that part of the *ease* in playing Shakespeare well lies in his *form*.

Your skills will improve by:

- Learning what these forms *are*
- Learning how to *use* them
- Learning how to use the directions Shakespeare gives you *through* his form
- Learning how to use the directions Shakespeare gives you *directly from his language*
- Understanding that your primary motivations come directly from his spoken text, and not from an overlaid "interpretation"

This last point often gets me into trouble. Yes, yes, I know—you make an "interpretation" the moment you filter Shakespeare's thoughts through your own experiences and out your mouth and body. That's true. But before we get there, I think we first have to empty out and take a look at how all of this stuff *works*, and how it works on its own terms. Then, the thoughts and form will resonate within you, and you'll be able to make more informed personal choices.

## What Else Did I Miss in My Shakespeare Classes?

Overruns.

A few old-timers remember how to use an Overrun, but it's an almost-forgotten technique—much to the weakening of contemporary Shakespeare productions. Power, action, sublime emotion, and the ability to move an audience very quickly can all be found in a simple, little, Overrun.

Overruns can be a touchy subject. There might be a few teachers or directors who have sniffed out a vague notion of the Overrun, but they're usually loath to suggest it to an actor. Why?

Well, when I first teach the use of this tool, most actors react with either slack-jawed disbelief, or deep skepticism. I get a lot of refusal to attempt, and some open hostility—that is, until some brave soul in class or production tests the waters and plays the first few Overruns of his or her career. The usual choir of "Ohhh" sings out, and my actors then realize that Shakespeare can't be played in a diffuse and undefined way. They understand the brawn, discovery and insight that a little Overrun can give to them, and to the audience. I hear their playing changed, and improved, dramatically.

I want to pass all of this on to you.

But before we get into all that, let's begin at the beginning and ground ourselves in the basics. Shakespeare writes his plays in two forms:

**Verse**          **Prose**

They are not to be played in the same way.

## What Is Prose?

Prose is not really a form at all. It is the *lack of form*. It is a piece of text written in a straightforward, conversational style. There is *no defined rhythm or meter* (though there's usually an inherent internal rhythm), and no real structure other than "beginning, middle, and end." In other words: "blah blah blah." This is how novels and contemporary plays are written—in ordinary, informal thoughts.

If you are very unfamiliar with Shakespeare's plays, you will know if the scene or speech is in *prose* if:
- the sentences continue all the way to the end of the page without a line break, and
- if each new line doesn't begin with a capital letter.

In other words—a big, black, messy chunk of text.

Shakespeare is writing in *verse* if:
- you see a more-or-less tight column of words, and
- each new line begins with a capital letter, regardless of punctuation.

Shakespeare is unusual in that he is one of the first writers to use prose in the theatre. Before he came along, most playwrights used a tight, strictly defined meter (verse) to heighten their text. But Shakespeare throws bits of prose in with his verse, peppers it freely here and there to add a measure of everydayness to his theatre. And there is a lot of it—something like 1/4 to 1/3 of his text is written in prose—so it's pretty important to learn how to play.

While *many of his prose conversations are still arguments,* there is a down-to-earth and engaging quality to them, afforded by this lack of form. Here is Benedick with an example of this easy conversation from *Much Ado About Nothing,* Act II, Scene 3:

"I do much wonder that one man, seeing how much another man is a fool when he dedicates his behaviors to love, will, after he hath laughed at such shallow follies in others, become the argument of his own scorn by falling in love; and such a man is Claudio. I have known when there was no music with him but the drum and the fife; and now had he rather hear the tabor and the pipe. I have known when he would have walked ten mile afoot to see a good armor; and now will he lie ten nights awake carving the fashion of a new doublet. He was wont to speak plain and to the purpose, like an honest man and a soldier; and now is he turned orthography; his words are a very fantastical banquet—just so many strange dishes. May I be so converted and see with these eyes? I cannot tell; I think not. I will not be sworn but love may transform me to an oyster; but I'll take my oath on it, till he have made an oyster of me he shall never make me such a fool. One woman is fair, yet I am well; another is wise, yet I am well; another virtuous, yet I am well; but till all graces be in  one woman, one woman shall not come in my grace. Rich she shall be, that's certain; wise, or I'll none; virtuous, or I'll never cheapen her; fair, or I'll never look on her; mild, or come not near me; noble, or not I for an angel; of good discourse, an excellent musician, and her hair shall be of what color it please God. Ha, the Prince and Monsieur Love! *(retiring)* I will hide me in the arbor."

Notice how little "heightened" language Shakespeare uses in this text? There are very few metaphors, no long and complex images to chew on, no "grand statements" about life and death, no "poetic" insights. It is a simple, fun, ordinary (but clever) conversation. Yet, you still have the components of argument. Benedick compares Claudio's present state of mind with his former one, mocks his change in character, contrasts Claudio's soldierly attributes with his "shallow follies," and so on. Benedick also explores and argues the possibility that he himself might be "converted," and gives us his grocery list of criteria. But it is a straightforward and down-to-earth conversation Benedick has with the audience.

When you find a piece of text written in prose, Shakespeare is telling his actor:

"Relax and chat openly with the audience—be direct. Drop the conventions of heightened language and level with us. It's time to speak plainly and to bounce your ideas off the audience. Come down to earth, engage us with your discoveries, and be easy. It's time to drop the form and to have an open conversation."

Shakespeare rarely gives you long and intricate images to offer the audience in prose, and very little "poetic" language. His thoughts are usually direct and immediate. (This isn't always true, of course, so we'll take a look at exceptions later on.)

## Prose Tools

Now comes the technical stuff. Notice how many colons, semi-colons, and commas punctuate Benedick's speech. *Shakespeare is telling you something* with these seemingly innocuous marks[1]. Benedick makes his discoveries by speaking his thoughts in snippets, working through his problem in quick half-thoughts, leaping one idea over the other, pausing to think, catching new insights on new breaths, and jolting forward again. It's not that his thoughts are disjointed—they are quick and spontaneous. He catches his ideas *directly from the men and women in the theatre*, and *uses the audience as a catalyst for his arguments*.

What do I mean? Well, you can't come onstage with your lines carved into your skull and deliver them mechanically. Benedick will *use the people* listening to forward his speech. He will get his ideas *from* the women peeping up at him, in the moment.

For example: Benedick, scanning the audience as he chats with them, spots a good-looking woman and gets his idea, "One woman is fair." Then, very pleased that he's still in control of his libido, he boasts to the guys in the theatre, "yet I am well." Or,

---

[1] The First Folio punctuation is a bit different from modern-edited texts. And you will notice subtle disparities in your Complete Works, depending on the publishing house, edition, culture, etc. Over time, and through hosts of different editors, some changes were made to Shakespeare's original flow of thought in order to modernize spelling, fiddle with punctuation, and sometimes change a word or two. Don't worry too much about these changes—most editors are careful in their work and pay attention to punctuation, working thought by thought. The more Shakespeare work you do, the more you will be particular about which edition suits you.

he will let his gaze linger on her for a moment and try to convince himself, "yet I am well." Then he scans again, notices a smart woman, and says, "Another is wise, yet I am well." He sees a virtuous woman, and so on, building his argument. He is engaging, reflexive, and down to earth.

## Pay Attention to Punctuation!

When Shakespeare gives you this kind of punctuation, *use it.* Generally speaking:

- A *period* is a full stop, or a *full breath.* Use it to separate one full idea from a new one.
- A *comma* is a half-stop, or *half-breath.* Use it to add on to an existing idea, detaching momentarily from a full thought in order to build on that thought, or to offer a new insight onto that thought.
- A *colon* is a full stop, or *full breath* (slightly shorter than a period). Use it to change direction entirely within the structure of one full thought, or to make a dramatic conclusion to that thought.
- A *semi-colon* is a half-stop, or half-breath (longer than a comma). Use it to make a mini-conclusion, or to give a mini-insight before the full stop of a period.

## Redefining Punctuation

For our purposes, let's define punctuation as:

*A note of pause or change in thought or breath.*

Remember this well as we push ahead. It's an important tool.

- a note of pause in thought
- a note of change in breath

Of course, your use of punctuation will vary, depending on the speech or scene, the rhythm of the text, your director's notes, and so on. But it is a good thing to keep in mind when you begin working through Shakespeare's text with your new eyes and ears. Be sensitive, not only to the text, but to its punctuation. Notice where these full and half-stops are and what they mean. Try to *change the direction of your thought by observing the punctuation.*

## Breath Workout

Try this as an exercise:

1. Go back and speak Benedick's speech out loud, just as you would normally read it—in your own normal breathing pattern.
2. Read it again. This time, notice *where you take breaths*, and how these breaths *help or interfere with the flow of thought.* Notice when you're chopping up your thoughts needlessly, just to take a breath.
3. Now speak his speech again, breathing only where (and how) I have noted. Notice how this will fuel your thoughts:

"I do much wonder that one man, *(quick breath)* seeing how much another man is a fool when he dedicates his behaviors to love, *(quick breath)* will, *(quick breath)* after he hath laughed at such shallow follies in others, *(quick breath)* become the argument of his own scorn by falling in love; *(medium breath)* and such a man is Claudio. *(Stop. Fill up your lungs.)* I have known when there was no music with him but the drum and the fife; *(medium breath)* and now had he rather hear the tabor and the pipe. *(Stop. Fill up your lungs.)* I have known when he would have walked ten mile afoot to see a good armor; *(medium breath)* and now will he lie ten nights awake carving the fashion of a new doublet. *(Stop. Fill up your lungs.)* He was wont to speak plain and to the purpose, *(quick breath)* like an honest man and a soldier; *(medium breath)* and now is he turned orthography; *(medium breath)* his words are a very fantastical banquet— *(mini-conclusion)* just so many strange dishes. *(Stop. Fill up your lungs.)* May I be so converted and see with these eyes? *(Stop. Fill up your lungs.)* I cannot tell; *(medium breath)* I think not. *(Stop. Exhale. Now fill up your lungs.)* I will not be sworn but love may transform me to an oyster; *(medium breath)* but I'll take my oath on it, *(quick breath)* till he have made an oyster of me he shall never make me such a fool. *(Stop. Fill up your lungs.)* One woman is fair, *(quick breath)* yet I am well; *(medium breath)* another is wise, *(quick breath)* yet I am well; *(medium breath)* another virtuous, *(quick breath)* yet I am well; *(medium breath)* but till all graces be in one woman, *(quick breath)* one woman shall not come in my grace. *(Stop. Exhale. Now fill up your lungs.)* Rich she shall be, *(quick breath)* that's certain; *(medium breath)* wise, *(quick breath)* or I'll none; *(medium breath)* virtuous, *(quick breath)* or I'll never cheapen her; *(medium breath)* fair, *(quick breath)* or I'll never look on her; *(medium breath)* mild, *(quick breath)* or come not near me; *(medium breath)* noble, *(quick breath)* or not I for an angel; *(medium breath)* of good discourse, *(quick breath)* an excellent musician, *(quick breath)* and her hair shall be of what color it please God. *(Stop. Fill up your lungs.)* Ha, *(quick breath)* the Prince and Monsieur Love! *(Stop. Fill up your lungs.) (retiring)* I will hide me in the arbor."

4. Now try it again, this time using the breaths I have indicated to *change direction* in your thought. After each breath, use a new intonation, a renewed vigor, and a completely new thought; allow each new breath to *fuel* your next thought

## Do I Need All Those Breaths?

Probably not. We all have different lung capacities: some people can speak great chunks of text on a single intake of breath, while others can barely squeeze out a few words. Punctuation merely gives you your *opportunities* to breathe. Whether or not you take them will depend on the strength of your lungs.

For the sake of the exercises in this book, however, breathe where and when I tell you; don't breathe in the middle of a thought, or when you don't have a note of punctuation. This is not only a good prose tool, but also the beginning of good phrasing. We'll do more detailed breath exercises later on, when you will learn "Good Phrasing and Bad Phrasing = Good Breath and Bad Breath."

## What About Prose in Dialogue?

Prose in dialogue is the same as prose in a monologue. It is unfettered by "shape," and is a free-flow of realistic and lifelike conversation between two or more people. See if you can hear how easy and naturalistic this conversation is between the Duke and Claudio in *Measure for Measure*, Act III, Scene 1:

Duke: Son, I have overheard what hath passed between you and your sister. Angelo had never the purpose to corrupt her; only he hath made an assay of her virtue to practice his judgment with the disposition of natures. She, having the truth of honor in her, hath made him that gracious denial which he is most glad to receive. I am confessor to Angelo, and I know this to be true; therefore prepare yourself to death. Do not satisfy your resolution with hopes that are fallible: tomorrow you must die; go to your knees and make ready.

| Claudio: | Let me ask my sister pardon. I am so out of love with life that I will sue to be rid of it. |
|----------|----------------------------------------------------------------------------------------------|
| Duke: | Hold you there: farewell. |

Keep in mind Shakespeare's acting note. He asks you to have a plain, open, truthful talk with a free-flow of wit and ideas, without a "formal" structure.

## I Lied to You

And now I have to qualify everything I've just told you about prose by saying: *most of it isn't true*. I told you to play prose as an easy, lifelike conversation—because that's what I want to *hear* in your playing.

However, prose is often just as complex as verse—sometimes even more so. It has twists and turns of phrase, swiftness of thought, complicated images and complex thought-patterns that can be very difficult to play. It's not always as straightforward as our Benedick or our *Measure for Measure*. Listen to Falstaff for a moment from *Henry the Fourth, Part One*, Act II, Scene 4:

"Peace, good pintpot. Peace, good tickle-brain—Harry, I do not only marvel where thou spendest thy time, but also how thou art accompanied. For though the camomile, the more it is trodden on, the faster it grows, yet youth, the more it is wasted, the sooner it wears. That thou art my son I have partly thy mother's word, partly my own opinion, but chiefly a villainous trick of thine eye and a foolish hanging of thy nether lip that doth warrant me. If then thou be son to me, here lies the point: why, being son to me, art thou so pointed at? Shall the blessed sun of heaven prove a micher and eat blackberries? A question not to be asked. Shall the son of England prove a thief and take purses? A question to be asked. There is a thing, Harry, which thou hast often heard of, and it is known to many in our land by the name of pitch. This pitch, as ancient writers do report, doth defile; so doth the company thou keepest. For, Harry, now I do not speak to thee in drink, but in tears; not in pleasure, but in passion; not in words only, but in woes also: and yet there is a virtuous man whom I have often noted in thy company, but I know not his name."

Or the Fool from *King Lear*, Act I, Scene 4:

Fool:  No, faith; lords and great men will not let me. If I had a monopoly out, they would have part on't. And ladies too, they will not let me have all the fool to myself; they'll be snatching. Nuncle, give me an egg, and I'll give thee two crowns.

Lear:  What two crowns shall they be?

Fool:  Why, after I have cut the egg i' th' middle and eat up the meat, the two crowns of the egg. When thou clovest thy crown i' th' middle and gav'st away both parts, thou bor'st thine ass on thy back o'er the dirt. Thou hadst little wit in thy bald crown when thou gav'st thy golden one away. If I speak like myself in this, let him be whipped that first finds it so.

You can hear in these two examples, that there still exists a kind of formal shape—a logic sequence, components of argument, and ladder-building imagery that we find in verse. Even though these thoughts are hard to play, and they're more complex than the simple prose of Benedick, you must still play it in a naturalistic, down-to-earth way. Though the shape of prose itself is endlessly variable, Shakespeare wants you to play it as conversationally as possible. Prose is very often the most difficult, wittiest of dialogue you'll have to play in Shakespeare, but you still throw it away in a straightforward manner.

## Why Does Shakespeare Switch from Verse to Prose?

If I could give you an easy, all-encompassing answer, I would. But there isn't one. There is no real, consistent reason for Shakespeare's switches from verse to prose (documented or otherwise); it is impossible to give you any absolutes. This is why prose is more difficult to dissect than verse. Usually, your character will speak in prose if:

- he or she is from a lower class
- he or she is *trying* to appeal to a lower class (trying to be "one of the gang")
- Shakespeare wants a fun, easy conversation
- he or she is engaging in wit-play for its own sake
- he or she is caught up in a "common" situation

- he or she is trying to level one-on-one with the audience
- if the play is more social or conjugal in setting than formal

However, these are not hard-and-fast rules. For example, take this conversation between Celia and Rosalind from *As You Like It*, Act I, Scene 3. These two young women are both daughters of dukes, so there's no reason why they should be speaking in prose. Yet their conversation is so quick, witty, and flippant, I can't see how this would work in verse:

| | |
|---|---|
| Celia: | Why, cousin! why, Rosalind! Cupid have mercy! Not a word? |
| Rosalind: | Not one to throw at a dog. |
| Celia: | No, thy words are too precious to be cast away upon curs; throw some of them at me; come, lame me with reasons. |
| Rosalind: | Then there were two cousins laid up; when the one should be lamed with reasons and the other mad without any. |
| Celia: | But is all this for your father? |
| Rosalind: | No, some of it is for my father's child. O, how full of briers is this working-day world! |
| Celia: | They are but burrs, cousin, thrown upon thee in holiday foolery: if we walk not in the trodden paths our very petticoats will catch them. |
| Rosalind: | I could shake them off my coat: these burrs are in my heart. |
| Celia: | Hem them away. |
| Rosalind: | I would try, if I could cry 'hem' and have him. |
| Celia: | Come, come, wrestle with thy affections. |
| Rosalind: | O, they take the part of a better wrestler than myself! |
| Celia: | O, a good wish upon you! you will try in time, in despite of a fall. But, turning these jests out of service, let us talk in good earnest: is it possible, on such a sudden, you should fall into so strong a liking with old Sir Rowland's youngest son? |
| Rosalind: | The duke my father loved his father dearly. |
| Celia: | Doth it therefore ensue that you should love his son dearly? By this kind of chase, I should hate him, for my father hated his father dearly; yet I hate not Orlando. |

| | |
|---|---|
| Rosalind: | No, faith, hate him not, for my sake. |
| Celia: | Why should I not? doth he not deserve well? |
| Rosalind: | Let me love him for that, and do you love him because I do. Look, here comes the duke. |
| Celia: | With his eyes full of anger. |

So, even though there isn't any consistent reason for switching from verse to prose, you can be sure that there is always an *important theatrical reason*.

Though you may not be able to figure out why exactly your character is speaking in prose at a particular moment—chances are—if you are sensitive to the larger shape of the scene or the play as a whole, you will always discover a theatrical reason for Shakespeare's switch from verse to prose. You can't always say what it is, but the switch resonates with the audience at the right time, and resonates with you at the right time, *in the playing* of it.

For example, Celia and Rosalind have just engaged in the above prose-dialogue. After Celia's last line, Duke Frederick enters with his Lords. He addresses the girls in verse, and they respond in verse, suddenly formal. The theatrical reason is obvious.

| | |
|---|---|
| Duke: | Mistress, dispatch you with your safest haste And get you from our court. |
| Rosalind: | Me, uncle? |
| Duke: | You, cousin. Within these ten days if that thou beest found So near our public court as twenty miles, Thou diest for it. |
| Rosalind: | I do beseech your Grace Let me the knowledge of my fault bear with me. If with myself I hold intelligence Or have acquaintance with mine own desires, If that I do not dream or be not frantic, As I do trust I am not; then, dear uncle, Never so much as in a thought unborn Did I offend your Highness. |

The situation has suddenly changed, and the stakes are higher. Celia and Rosalind and thrust into a "heightened" state and need to respond accordingly.

Here is another example, from *King Lear*, Act II, Scene 4. Kent speaks in verse in Lear's presence; but the moment Lear leaves, Kent's verse switches to prose, in order to respond to the Fool:

| | |
|---|---|
| Gentleman: | Made you no more offense but what you speak of? |
| Kent: | None. |
| | How chance the King comes with so small a number? |
| Fool: | An thou hadst been set i' th' stocks for that question, thou'dst well deserved it. |
| Kent: | Why, fool? |
| Fool: | We'll set thee to school to an ant, to teach thee there's no laboring i' th' winter. All that follow their noses are led by their eyes but blind men, and there's not a nose among twenty but can smell him that's stinking. Let go thy hold when a great wheel runs down a hill, lest in break thy neck with following. But the great one that goes upward, let him draw thee after. When a wise man gives thee better counsel, give me mine again. I would have none but knaves follow it since a fool gives it. *(sings)* |
| Kent: | Where learned you this, fool? |
| Fool: | Not i' th' stocks, fool. |

Lear and Gloucester enter the scene again, and the conversation stays in verse. Again, the theatrical reason is obvious.

You will find, too, some highly romantic verse-passages that are undercut by a character speaking in prose. Shakespeare keeps us on our toes by sounding out changes in tune, in situation and in emotion by switching at the right time. He keeps the audience's emotions changing, and gives the actors clues about their characters. In this scene from *Troilus and Cressida*, Pandarus cuts the highly charged romance with his earthy, bawdy prose:

| | |
|---|---|
| Troilus: | How were I then uplifted! But, alas, |
| | I am as true as truth's simplicity, |
| | And simpler than the infancy of truth. |
| Cressida: | In that I'll war with you. |

| | |
|---|---|
| Troilus: | O virtuous fight, |
| | When right with right wars who shall be most right! |
| | True swains in love shall in the world to come |
| | Approve their truth by Troilus. When their rhymes, |
| | Full of protest, of oath, and big compare, |
| | Wants similes, truth tired with iteration, |
| | 'As true as steel, as plantage to the moon, |
| | As sun to day, as turtle to her mate, |
| | As iron to adamant, as earth to th' center,' |
| | Yet, after all comparisons of truth, |
| | As truth's authentic author to be cited, |
| | 'As true as Troilus' shall crown up the verse |
| | And sanctify the numbers. |
| Cressida: | Prophet may you be! |
| | If I be false or swerve a hair from truth, |
| | When time is old and hath forgot itself, |
| | When waterdrops have worn the stones of Troy, |
| | And blind oblivion swallowed cities up, |
| | And mighty states characterless are grated |
| | To dusty nothing, yet let memory, |
| | From false to false among false maids in love, |
| | Upbraid my falsehood! When th' have said, 'as false |
| | As air, as water, wind or sandy earth, |
| | As fox to lamb, as wolf to heifer's calf, |
| | Pard to the hind, or stepdame to her son,' |
| | Yea, let them say, to stick the heart of falsehood, |
| | 'As false as Cressid.' |
| Pandarus: | Go to, a bargain made; seal it, seal it; I'll be the witness. Here I hold your hand, here my cousin's. If ever you prove false to one another, since I have taken such pains to bring you together, let all pitiful goers-between be called to the world's end after my name; call them all Pandars; let all constant men be Troiluses, all false women Cressids, and all brokers-between Pandars! Say, 'Amen.' |
| Troilus: | Amen. |
| Cressida: | Amen. |
| Pandarus: | Amen. Whereupon, I will show you a chamber which bed, because it shall not speak of your pretty encounters, press it to death. Away! |

Falstaff, in *Henry the Fourth, Part Two*, speaks in his witty, down-to-earth prose during the whole play. I can't find a single line of verse that comes out of his mouth...except at the end. When his buddy Hal becomes King at the end of the play, Falstaff addresses him in verse, because he is in a very different situation:

Falstaff:     God save thy grace, King Hal, my royal Hal!

and

My king! My Jove! I speak to thee, my heart!

Two lines of very regular verse.

Very often, you will find that prose works as a *counterpoint* to really heightened states of emotion, like this one from *King Lear*, Act III, Scene 2:

Lear:     Blow, winds, and crack your cheeks. Rage, blow.
You cataracts and hurricanoes, spout
Till you have drench'd our steeples, drowned the cocks.
You sulph'rous and thought-executing fires,
Vaunt-couriers of oak-cleaving thunderbolts,
Singe my white head. And thou, all-shaking thunder,
Strike flat the thick rotundity o' th' world,
Crack Nature's moulds, all germains spill at once,
That makes ingrateful man.

Fool:     O nuncle, court holy-water in a dry house is better than this rain-water out o' door. Good nuncle, in; ask thy daughters blessing. Here's a night pities neither wise men nor fools.

Sure, the Fool uses prose most of the play, except when he speaks or sings his little ditties. But this time the prose acts as a measure of levity or grounding in the situation—something to try to bring Lear back down to earth from his heightened state.

## Inconsistent...But Not Really

You'll find characters who you would think should speak in prose, speaking in verse. Like Phoebe, from *As You Like It*. She's a common shepherdess, but Shakespeare writes her in verse the whole play. It's as though he wants her to have a poet's heart, and so offers her as a romantic character despite her station; he wants her gentle simplicity to be heightened in verse, and not bound in prose.

> Think not I love him, though I ask for him:
> 'Tis but a peevish boy; yet he talks well;
> But what care I for words? Yet words do well
> When he that speaks them pleases those that hear.
> It is a pretty youth: not very pretty:
> But, sure, he's proud, and yet his pride becomes him:
> He'll make a proper man: the best thing in him
> Is his complexion; and faster than his tongue
> Did make offence his eye did heal it up.
> He is not very tall; yet for his years he's tall:
> His leg is but so so; and yet 'tis well:
> There was a pretty redness in his lip,
> A little riper and more lusty red
> Than that mix'd in his cheek; 'twas just the difference
> Between the constant red and mingled damask.
> There be some women, Silvius, had they mark'd him
> In parcels as I did, would have gone near
> To fall in love with him; but, for my part,
> I love him not nor hate him not; and yet
> I have more cause to hate him than to love him:
> For what had he to do to chide at me?
> He said mine eyes were black and my hair black:
> And, now I am remember'd, scorned at me:
> I marvel why I answer'd not again:
> But that's all one; omittance is no quittance.
> I'll write to him a very taunting letter,
> And thou shalt bear it: wilt thou, Silvius?

## Prose Peppering

Take a look at this scene from *Julius Caesar*. Brutus and Cassius are the more formal men: they speak in verse. Casca uses prose here, peppering the dialogue with a more urgent, earthy tone, breaking up their formality with the immediacy of prose.

| | |
|---|---|
| Casca: | You pulled me by the cloak; would you speak with me? |
| Brutus: | Ay, Casca; tell us what hath chanced today, |
| | That Caesar looks so sad. |
| Casca: | Why, you were with him, were you not? |
| Brutus: | I should not then ask Casca what had chanced. |
| Casca: | Why, there was a crown offered him: and being offered him, he put it by with the back of his hand, thus; and then the people fell a-shouting. |
| Brutus: | What was the second noise for? |
| Casca: | Why, for that too. |
| Cassius: | They shouted thrice: what was the last cry for? |
| Casca: | Why, for that too. |
| Brutus: | Was the crown offered him thrice? |
| Casca: | Ay, marry, was't, and he put it by thrice, every time gentler than other, and at every putting-by mine honest neighbors shouted. |
| Cassius: | Who offered him the crown? |
| Casca: | Why, Antony. |
| Brutus: | Tell us the manner of it, gentle Casca. |
| Casca: | I can as well be hanged as tell the manner of it: it was mere foolery; I did not mark it. I saw Mark Antony offer him a crown; yet 'twas not a crown neither, 'twas one of these coronets; and, as I told you, he put it by once: but, for all that, to my thinking, he would fain have had it. Then he offered it to him again; then he put it by again: but, to my thinking, he was very loath to lay his fingers off it. And then he offered it the third time; he put it the third time by: and still as he refused it, the rabblement hooted and clapped their chapped hands and threw up their sweaty night-caps and uttered such a deal of stinking breath because Caesar refused the crown that it had almost choked Caesar; for he swounded and fell down at it: and for mine own part, I durst not laugh, for fear of opening my lips and receiving the bad air. |

| | |
|---|---|
| Cassius: | But, soft, I pray you: what, did Caesar swound? |
| Casca: | He fell down in the marketplace, and foamed at mouth, and was speechless. |
| Brutus: | 'Tis very like: he hath the failing sickness. |
| Cassius: | No, Caesar hath it not; but you and I, And honest Casca, we have the falling sickness. |
| Casca: | I know not what you mean by that; but, I am sure, Caesar fell down. If the tag-rag people did not clap him and hiss him, according as he pleased and displeased them, as they use to do the players in the theatre, I am no true man. |

## Summing Up with Contradictions

This may seem contradictory, but it's not.

What I want you to play in your prose-work is an *earthy, immediate*, and *naturalistic* conversation. But not too "natural;" prose still has very strong rhythms (stronger sometimes than verse), clear argument, antitheses, and complex language. So don't toss it away—you risk making it flat, monotone, or dull. Keep it alive, light, quick, and strong. *Use its natural rhythms*, and keep it as sharp as your verse, even as you play the *ease*. Keep it conversational, but with body and substance. The balance between naturalism and the observation of form-within-lack-of-form is the key.

Don't worry too much about *why* your character speaks in prose in a particular moment. Shakespeare always has a theatrical reason for it. You will start to discover the reasons as you get more familiar with the text, and you'll start to discover clues about character, relationship, and situation. Let the shape of the play, and the specific reasons for switching from verse to prose resonate within the audience *in the playing of the text*. Let the overall rhythm of the play take care of itself—you just play your prose well.

## What Is Verse?

Verse is metered, orderly form.

Beginning from the very first plays in history, thoughts have been spoken aloud in a fairly strict, metered, rhythmic, and often rhymed pattern. It is an organized structure which lifts language from the day-to-day mundane into the rich, imaginative, poetic, highly tuned, and specific. By heightening language from prose to verse, writers and speakers can grab an audience's ear, galvanize attention, weave complex images, make important comparisons, offer novel, structured insights and arguments about life, and inspire the listener to greater depths of imaginative and intelligent living.

## Where Might You Have Heard Verse Before?

Well, you were probably very familiar with it when you were small. If you did a lot of reading (or were read to) as a small child, you probably still have a bunch of passages rattling around in your head. The best, most memorable phrases were probably in verse. Take an extreme example—an imaginative and rhythmic writer of children's books loved throughout the world: Dr Seuss. I'll bet you can still remember some of his writing, his rhythm, his turns of phrase and lyrical thought. Remember how he roused your ear with his verse?

> *I do not like*
> *green eggs and ham.*
> *I do not like them,*
> *Sam-I-am.*

Part of the power of his writing was the rhythm and structure of his text. Put into your mind now some of the passages from *How the Grinch Stole Christmas*, and listen to how strong the rhythm is, how it pushes you forward, and how it sticks in the brain.

Now I don't want you to get the wrong impression: Shakespeare doesn't use the sing-song, beat-perfect, hoe-down cadence we remember from *The Cat in the Hat*! Neither does he use as many rhyming couplets in his plays, which give Dr. Seuss his universally appealing childlike sound. I only want to make one point: that Dr. Seuss's verse yanked our attention, lifted us from the doldrums of everyday-speak into the specific, and sharpened our ears and our minds from common noise—in a highly concentrated and compact form, rich with limitless possibility.

*That* is what verse does.

Shakespeare's verse isn't country-bumpkin rigid, but is a richly alive, dynamic, highly complex, and ever-changing beast.

So let's begin:

## Classical French Verse

The great French playwrights like Molière and Marivaux used a specific rhythm: twelve beats per line, with rhyming couplets at the end of each (the last syllable of one line rhymes with the last syllable of the next line).

French is an intelligent language, so its verse possesses an intelligent rhythm; it drives straight through to the end of the line, where the point is made (on its rhyming couplet):

> "Zon-zon-zon, zon-zon-zon, zon-zon-zon, zon-zon-*zee*
> Za-za-za, za-za-za, za-za-za, za-za-*zee*."

Take this example, from Molière's *Le Misanthrope*, Act I, Scene 1:

> Non, je ne puis souffrir cette lâche méthode
> Qu'affectent la plupart de vos gens à la mode;
> Et je ne hais rien tant que les contorsions
> De tous ces grands faiseurs de protestations,
> Ces affables donneurs d'embrassades frivoles,
> Ces obligeants diseurs d'inutiles paroles,
> Qui de civilités avec tous font combat,
> Et traitent du même air l'honnête homme et le fat.

> *No, I cannot suffer so base a method*
> *Which your fashionable people commonly affect;*
> *There is nothing I hate so much as the contortions*
> *Of these great makers of protestation,*
> *These affable dispensers of meaningless embraces,*
> *These obliging speakers of empty words,*
> *Who view every one with civility,*
> *And treat the honest man and the fop alike[2].*

[2]Please note that the above is merely a straight translation, and thus is neither the twelve beats of French verse, nor ten beat iambic pentameter. -Ed

It's a fairly uniform rhythm, which keeps the attention of the listener all the way to the end of the line.

Classical English verse follows ten beats per line. It is called:

## Iambic Pentameter

The word "iambic" means simply:
- an *un*accented syllable followed by an *accented* syllable.

The word "pentameter" means:
- a unit *measurable by five.*

So, *un*accented + *accented* = 2 beats.
2 beats x five (pentameter) = *10 beats per line.*

Now that we have that stodgy definition out of the way, I have to tell you that we're dealing with a rhythm that is tremendously exciting. The English "iambic pentameter" is full of life and drive. Why? Because it follows the natural rhythm of the human heartbeat.

Feel your heartbeat for a minute:

"Da-*dum*, da-*dum*, da-*dum*, da-*dum*, da-*dum*
Da-*dum*, da-*dum*, da-*dum*, da-*dum*, da-*dum*."

*That* is iambic pentameter. For example:

Now all the youth of England are on fire,
And silken dalliance in the wardrobe lies.

Beat it out for yourself. Listen to the rhythm:

Now *all* the *youth* of *England* *are* on *fire*,
And *silken* *dalliance* *in* the *wardrobe* *lies*.

Here is another:

Have I a tongue to doom my brother's death,
And shall that tongue give pardon to a slave?
My brother killed no man—his fault was thought—
And yet his punishment was bitter death.

Hear the rhythm?

Have *I* a *tongue* to *doom* my *brother's death*,
And *shall* that *tongue* give *pardon to* a *slave?*
My *brother killed* no *man*—his *fault* was *thought*—
And *yet* his *punishment* was *bitter death*.

*English falls into this meter naturally*. It underscores much of our day-to-day discourse without our being aware of it. For example:

"Give me a Coke, a Snickers, and some gum."

—or—

"Why don't I come and meet you after work?"

Of course, we don't emphasize this rhythm when we speak:

"Give *me* a *Coke*, a *Snickers and* some *gum*."

—or—

"Why *don't* I *come* and *meet* you *after work?*"

Rather, it is a subtle, heartbeat rhythm that is the natural music of the English tongue. And it's very important to note that this rhythm is not a heavy, dead thing. It doesn't fall or collapse with each accented syllable. It's not: "Ba-*boom*. Ba-*boom*. Ba-*boom*. Ba-*boom*. Ba-*boom*," like a 700-pound wrestler. Rather: "Dee-*dum* dee-*dum* dee-*dum* dee-*dum* dee-*dum*," lightly galloping off the tip of the tongue...*understated* and unaffectedly *real*. The iambic rhythm keeps driving forward with momentum, drive, and vigor.

And now that you know what iambic pentameter is, I'm going to try to avoid using the phrase as much as possible. I don't like the term—it sounds too technical, too rigid—and I want you to approach Shakespeare's verse with openness. He writes a living, breathing series of thoughts with a changeable and flexible wrist, and not with the iron fist of a demented overlord. Iambic pentameter is Shakespeare's blueprint, but he often breaks it and plays around with it. It is important to note that *when* and *how* he breaks from the norm will inform your acting enormously. So let's use the term "blank verse" as much as possible. "Blank verse" leaves room for flexibility and change of rhythm as a blanket form, where iambic pentameter forces us to remain locked into a ten-beat rigidity.

I also want to avoid using the technical terms bandied about by Shakespeare teachers. Phrases like "trochaic variations," "dactylic," "anapestic," and so on, *can* serve a purpose: they are more detailed examinations of the intricacies of verse and ways of sorting through the various rhythms Shakespeare employed. But these terms are more useful to academics than to actors, and are not very practical for the performer taking the first steps playing Shakespeare. Technical terms may serve only to confuse you by getting you bogged down in tiny details. When you get extremely good at playing Shakespeare (ironically, to the point where you don't need these technical words, except for interest's sake), then by all means look into them; these phrases might help your acting much later on as you fine tune yourself. But for now, I want you to become a breathing life force of an actor, not a breathing textbook.

Here's a good example of "clean" blank verse from *Henry the Fourth, Part One* (Act IV, Scene 3). Every line has ten beats, and is a good example of a compact, perfect rhythm. Enjoy it, because you will find comparatively few such "perfect" texts in Shakespeare.

> The king is kind, and well we know the king
> Knows at what time to promise, when to pay.
> My father and my uncle and myself
> Did give him that same royalty he wears;
> And when he was not six-and-twenty strong,
> Sick in the world's regard, wretched and low,
> A poor unminded outlaw sneaking home,
> My father gave him welcome to the shore;
> And when he heard him swear and vow to God
> He came but to be Duke of Lancaster,
> To sue his livery and beg his peace,
> With tears of innocence and terms of zeal,
> My father, in kind heart and pity moved,
> Swore him assistance, and performed it too.

Notice how the most of the important words in each line fall on the *accented* syllable.

## Exaggerate

Now read the above passage again. As an exercise, *really exaggerate* the rhythm and listen to its imitation of a beating heart. Keep the momentum forward, driving almost without end. *Listen to it picking up the important syllables, highlighting particular words, and sharpening your ear.* Listen to "Da-dum, da-*dum*," and hear the moment when that blueprint changes.

## So What Does All of This Mean?

Now you know what prose and verse are. You know that prose is a clear, normal conversation, and that verse is an ordered form. But how do you *speak* the verse? What do you *do* with it? Why and how should you *use the verse differently*?

Don't worry, we'll get there. First, I want you to notice a few things:

1. You will know immediately if your scene or speech is in verse or prose.
   - *If it beats out, it's verse.* Sometimes you will notice fewer or more than ten beats per line, which we will get to later. But for now, think of the regular form.
   - *If it doesn't beat out at all* (if it's just a stream of dialogue with no "formal" structure) *it's prose.*
2. You will know that verse demands a sharper focus and a stronger concentration. You will need to use more complex images, longer metaphors, and a more "heightened" use of the language.
3. You will find hidden directions and acting notes within the verse.
4. The verse form will help you discover what the important words are.

This last point is particularly useful to inexperienced actors. Quite often, actors get stuck in a convoluted thought or image and ask, "What's the important word in this phrase? I don't know what to emphasize." To which I reply, of course, "The whole thought is important!" But I understand what's being asked. Sometimes, we need to hone in on a specific word in order help shape our thought. And Shakespeare's pen will usually give you the answer—in his blank verse.

Suppose, for example, that you had to play Titus Andronicus's revenge monologue. Suppose you were stuck and couldn't decide which words were important to emphasize. Where would you find the answer?

> Come, come, Lavinia; look thy foes are bound.
> Sirs, stop their mouths, let them not speak to me,
> But let them hear what fearful words I utter.
> O villains, Chiron and Demetrius!
> Here stands the spring whom you have stain'd with mud,
> This goodly summer with your winter mix'd.

Beat it out. Find *where* the accents fall and on *which words* (note: "Lavinia" is three syllables—La-vi-nia):

> Come, *come*, Lavinia; *look* thy *foes* are *bound*.
> Sirs, *stop* their *mouths*, let *them* not *speak* to *me*,
> But *let* them *hear* what *fearful words* I *utter*.

(Note: this line has 11 beats. Don't worry about this just now—we'll come to it later on.)

> O *villains*, *Chiron and* Demetrius!
> Here *stands* the *spring* whom *you* have *stain'd* with *mud*,
> This *goodly summer with* your *winter mix'd*.

Now list the words or sounds that fall on the *stressed beat*:

*come vi look foes bound*
*stop mouths them speak me*
*let hear fear words ut*
*vi Chi me us*
*stands spring you stained mud*
*good sum with win mixed*

Now imagine you have an audience, and speak these words and sounds out loud. You can almost get the meaning across with these monosyllables, can't you? You can almost speak with Titus's gentleness:

> "Come, Vi. Look—foes bound."
> And with Titus's contempt:
> "Stop mouths...them speak me."
> "Let hear fear words."
> "Stands spring you stain'd mud."
> "Good sum with win mix'd."

You can almost hear the basic thought.

As for the snippets of words that don't make sense, notice that the accented syllables (or *stressed* beats) are the muscular syllables within the word. Take "fearful," for example. The sound in this word that falls on the stressed beat is "fear." This is how the word is pronounced: *"fear*-ful," not "fear-*ful.*" Titus drips this word out with cold threat:

> "But let them hear what *fear*-ful words I utter."

This is part of the muscle of the English language. Our words are often powerful, meaty ones—*their sounds alone mean something,* and sound like what they represent (which you will remember from your high school English classes as onomatopoeia). English words are generally not flowery or poetic like words rooted in the Latin tongue (i.e. French, Italian). Our Saxon noises are harsh, often monosyllabic, and earthy. The softer English words are usually the ones we stole from Latin.

## Got It? Now Let It Go!

Now you understand *what* the rhythm is. You know how it works, and how you can use it to find the important words within the thoughts. Now let it go. You must *never play the rhythm itself; always play the thoughts!* I don't want you to step onstage and dutifully drone out:

> Come, COME, LaVInia; LOOK, thy FOES are BOUND.

As absurd as this may sound, I've heard it more than once.

The rhythm is there—inherent and embedded in the text— whether you emphasize it or not. Play only the thoughts, and the *rhythm will underscore your thoughts*—sometimes vigorously, often subtly, subconsciously driving you forward, exciting the ear of the audience—*as long as you don't add pauses, beats, and breaths where Shakespeare gives you none* (unless you have carefully earned and chosen those pauses).

## But the "Iambic" Doesn't Always Fall on the Right Word! What About Exceptions?

Good. Now we start to get into the real meat of blank verse! And we will learn a little about Shakespeare's hidden directions and acting notes. As with any general rule, you will find as many exceptions to the rule as examples of the rule itself. And you will always find exceptions in Shakespeare's verse, which aren't really exceptions at all.

The rhythm of blank verse can't always be a uniform, rigid, tick-tocking metronome. If an audience were subjected to a continuous monotony of:

> "Da-*dum*, da-*dum*, da-*dum*, da-*dum*, da-*dum*,
> da-*dum*, da-*dum*, da-*dum*, da-*dum*, da-*dum*"

they would be lulled to sleep. This is part of the problem with English translations of classical French or Italian texts: translators are forever sticking to an unyielding rhythm that actors have a horrible time breaking, or making interesting. Remember, I refer to Shakespeare's text as living, breathing, and ever-changing. I told you how important it is never to emphasize the rhythm, because Shakespeare keeps the rhythm of his text interesting and dynamic by *changing the beat*.

You'll find many times that the *unaccented* word is the important word within the phrase. And sometimes an *unimportant* word falls on a stressed beat, which would sound terrible if you were to stick to a strict rhythm. For example, take the fifth and sixth lines of our *Henry the Fourth* speech:

And when he was not six-and-twenty strong,
Sick in the world's regard, wretched and low,

The stressed beats in the first line pick out the important words nicely:

*when was six twen(ty) strong*

But the second line picks up some strange sounds:

*in world's gard tched low*

If you played the rhythm only, and not the thought, the audience would hear:

sick IN the WORLD'S reGARD wretCHED and LOW,

which is, of course, ridiculous.

Very often, you'll notice that "odd-metered" lines like this one play a *counter-rhythm* to the verse. The ordinary, forward-moving "Da-*dum*, da-*dum*, da-*dum*," needs to be reigned in once in a while, the meter changed, played around with, and broken entirely. Shakespeare keeps his text exciting by changing his rhythms as much as possible—as much as any composer sweeps in new melodies and punches holes in a predictable rhythm.

Listen now as I emphasize the rhythm and counter-rhythm in this text. Listen closely once, and then speak it aloud, stressing the words I italicize. This is what the rhythm underscoring your text sounds like:

And *when* he *was* not *six* and *twenty strong*,
*Sick* in the *world's* re*gard*, *wret*ched and *low*,

You hear how the second line is almost an *opposite rhythm* to the first? These are called contrapuntal stresses; they play against the norm, counter-punching. Speak it again, and listen how the stressed word "strong" slides quickly into the stressed word "sick." Also, listen to how quickly the second line runs off the tongue after playing the slower, more regular rhythm of the first line. It flies off the page, completely countering the first rhythm, keeping the dialogue interesting.

Pay very close attention to the rhythms in your text—score them, as you would a piece of music, and highlight the regular and contrapuntal stresses. Exaggerate them in your practice—go way over the top with them musically—and then slowly bring them back down to natural speech, until you can make them work *subtly*. But in performance, never play the rhythm itself. Let academics and linguists fawn over the details and particulars of rhythm and counter-rhythm. As an actor, you want to *play only the thoughts; let the rhythm take care of itself!*

When you practice a lot, get very good, and play many of Shakespeare's parts, then you may try to break this rule. When you are as comfortable with Shakespeare as you are with more ordinary text, you might then begin to occasionally play rhythms deliberately from time to time to underscore a dramatic effect. A really skilled actor can sometimes fuel his character or scene by throwing up contrapuntal stresses and bending the rhythm for particular reasons—but it is a rare actor, and a rare occasion.

In the meantime, if you get stuck, and if you can't shape your thought or don't know which words to highlight, listen closely to the verse (stressed/unstressed beats) to find your clues. If you notice strange sounds falling on stressed beats, and seemingly unimportant words falling on stressed beats, notice this too. It means Shakespeare is changing the rhythm for a reason. Listen carefully to that "irregular" rhythm—note this to yourself, and let these counter-sounds inform your acting.

Sounds easy enough...but how exactly do we do that? Most of your answers are found in Shakespeare's hidden directions:

## Hidden Directions

Shakespeare was an actor, so naturally his text is full of hidden acting notes. You just have to know where to find them. Sometimes he sneaks them to you in rhythm and counter-rhythm. Sometimes he holds his notes out to you plainly. But most of the time, you will need to search out the little hints and signals he gives you in the text.

Let's look at Henry V's speech again:

Once more unto the breach, dear friends, once more
Or close the wall up with our English dead!
In peace there's nothing so becomes a man
As modest stillness and humility,
But when the blast of war blows in our ears,
Then imitate the action of the tiger:
Stiffen the sinews, summon up the blood,
Disguise fair nature with hard-favored rage;

How would you play this? Certainly, there are many different ways, depending on the actor. But the more you listen to the text, the more you realize that it takes a fairly definite shape. Instead of scanning it with our stressed/unstressed rule, let's scan it as a realistic, full thought—the way someone in the middle of a battle would speak:

*Once more* unto the *breach, dear friends, once more,*

So much for the "iambic pentameter," huh? Out of the ten beats in this line, seven are definitely stressed. We have two stressed right at the beginning, then three little unstressed sounds, followed by five strongly stressed beats. If Shakespeare had stuck to the regular "Da-*dum*, da-*dum*," we would never hear this kind of "irregularity," and it would be impossible for Henry to stir his troops. This is Shakespeare giving you a hidden direction. The whole line is squeezed, pushed, off-balance.

Henry starts with two powerfully stressed words; here is your first acting clue. Is Shakespeare telling you:
- Henry is *out of breath,* and *off-balance*?
- Henry is *desperately trying* to squeeze out any strong noise he can?
- Henry is *exhausted,* at the end of his strength?
- Henry is *revitalized* and on fire?
- Henry is trying to *galvanize* his troops, and light a firecracker under them?
- Henry is trying to *scare* the hell out of his men?
- Henry is hopelessly trying to *grab their attention*?

- Henry is *infuriated* with their cowardice?
- Henry is biting into these words to *steel his own courage?*

You decide. But those two stressed beats are there, and you must make use of them.

And why does Shakespeare stress "dear friends"? Is he telling you:

- Henry is *begging?*
- Henry is letting them know he is *one of them?*
- Henry is trying to *regain loyalty?*
- Henry is *desperate?*
- Henry is *ordering* their attention?
- Henry is trying to *inspire confidence?*

You choose. But you *must* use these beats with some kind of real intention behind them. And Shakespeare stresses those two final words, "once more"—a repetition of the first two words. You decide if this is:

- An *order?*
- A *plea?*
- A *roar* meant to shake them from complacency?

Regardless of how you chose to play the line, make a *specific* choice and commit to it. Nothing is more useless than an actor shouting out this full line in a general wash of battle-crazed noise. Use the first "once more" *differently* from the second. Use your commas to make a *specific* point with "dear friends." Use threat, order, begging, or whatever else you come up with, as long as you use each little stressed thought with detail.

Notice too, that—except for the word "unto"—this first line is composed entirely of monosyllabic words. Shakespeare uses these direct, blunt, primitive Saxon sounds to express Henry's urgency. Let this inform your acting.

Let's continue:

> Or *close* the *wall* up with our *English dead!*

More monosyllabic sounds, but fewer stressed beats, beginning to fall more regularly. Shakespeare is giving you another note. Is Henry:

- *Refocused?*
- Regaining his *balance?*
- Being very *specific* and *direct?*
- *Choosing* only the *most important words?*
- *More confident* now that he has grabbed attention?

You decide. But be informed by the *threat* in this line. Henry is telling his troops: *"If you don't get back to work, we'll plug up the wall with the bodies of our brothers!"* Is it a *real* threat, or just a ploy to catch their attention again? Notice the three stressed beats at the end of the line, with that note of exclamation, "English dead!" Is this final *"Dum-dum-dum"*:

- An *order?*
- A *conclusion?*
- An *honest reality?*
- A *blunt threat?*

Hit these last three beats with everything you've got, and then you can take a few beats afterwards to collect yourself, catch your breath, survey your troops, etc., before moving on. Shakespeare gives you the opportunity to stabilize by making the next section fall more regularly:

In *peace* there's *nothing so* be*comes* a *man*
As *mo*dest *still*ness and hu*mili*ty,

Listen to how *even* these two lines are, as Henry tries to level and reason with his men. He tries to collect his emotions and to rationalize; he's more down-to-earth and "regular"—another acting hint from Shakespeare. Now, listen to the rhythm suddenly picking up again, as Henry finds new energy and tries to *inspire* his troops:

But *when* the *blast* of *war blows* in *our ears,*
Then *imitate* the *action* of the *tiger:*

Henry picks up the pace again, stirring his men, his blood beginning to boil away. Now notice the contrapuntal stresses—listen to Shakespeare flip the rhythm around in the next line:

*Stiffen* the *sinews, summon up the blood,*

The first word is now the stressed beat, as Henry orders his men *immediately* to "stiffen" and to steel themselves to courage. He bounces right from "tiger" to "stiffen," both words stressed and vitally important to his speech. Notice all the "s" sounds Shakespeare gives you to spit at your troops—like the lashings of a whip.

Try this:

Tighten your jaw and clench your teeth together as you read this line out loud again. Notice how the rhythm and the "s" sounds force your jaw and body to change into a more steely shape. Another clear acting hint from Shakespeare.

Continue now:

> Disguise fair nature with hard-favored rage;

Clear antithesis. And six out of seven words in this line are emphasized. What does that tell you? How important is this thought? Is it another commandment? Another threat? Or is Henry choosing *exactly the right words at the right time*, which he knows will stir his soldiers' blood? Let this exacting, cold-but-hot-blooded calculation of Henry's inform your acting. He knows exactly *what* to say, *when* to say it, and *how* to say it.

Shakespeare's rhythm is filled with hidden acting notes. Pay attention:

- When is Shakespeare's rhythm "regular"?
- When does he break it?
- Why does he break it?
- How does he sweep in counter-rhythms, contrapuntal stresses, or chop up his text with breaths?

What hints does that give to you, the actor?

- Is your character in his right mind, or off-balance?
- Is your character struggling with something, or confused?
- Is your character broken, ragged, at his wit's end?
- Is your character whole and complete, fueling his thoughts with unyielding momentum?
- Does your character use each word fully and completely, tasting, chewing out each thought ruminatively?
- Does your character spit out quick, monosyllabic words?
- Are there only one or two important words in a single line?
- Are most of the words in a single line important?

## No Dead Beats

Quite often, Shakespeare puts the *most important word* in a phrase on the *final beat*—the whole line drives you straight through to that last word, where the character *makes his point*. You must let this inform your playing, too. In this case, Shakespeare tells you, "Let this whole line trip off the tip of your tongue quickly, and really highlight that last word. Get to that word as fast as you can, and then *taste that final beat!*"

This is a very important point—particularly for North American actors. We have a terrible vocal habit that needs to be completely broken: our tendency is to *emphasize the first few words in a sentence, and then to drop off at the end.* Like this:

"I **never** thought she'd say that."

or

"Can you **believe** Jimmy would do that?"

As a classical actor, you have to break that habit. For classical texts, the whole thought is important, and the most important point is often made on the last few words.

Not:

Have I a tongue to doom my brother's death?

And shall that tongue give pardon to a slave?

When you die at the end of a phrase, you lose energy in a thought, lose energy onstage, and frustrate the audience. Get all the way to the last few words with your energy:

Have I a tongue to doom my **brother's** *death?*

And shall that tongue give **pardon** to a *slave?*

Got it?

Now let's get back to our Hidden Directions. Let's use the same *King Lear* from our earlier discussion of prose, and this time listen to Shakespeare ripping up the stressed/unstressed blueprint:

> Blow, winds, and crack your cheeks. Rage, blow.
> You cataracts and hurricanoes, spout
> Till you have drenched our steeples, drowned the cocks.
> You sulph'rous and thought-executing fires,
> Vaunt-couriers of oak-cleaving thunderbolts,
> Singe my white head. And thou, all-shaking thunder,
> Strike flat the thick rotundity o' th' world,
> Crack Nature's moulds, all germains spill at once,
> That makes ingrateful man.

He continues:

> Rumble thy bellyful. Spit, fire. Spout, rain.
> Nor rain, wind, thunder, fire are my daughters.
> I tax you not, you elements, with unkindness.
> I never gave you kingdom, called you children;
> You owe me no subscription. Then let fall
> Your horrible pleasure. Here I stand your slave,
> A poor, infirm, weak, and despised old man.
> But yet I call you servile ministers,
> That will with two pernicious daughters join
> Your high-engendered battles 'gainst a head
> So old and white as this. O, ho! 'tis foul.

Notice how Shakespeare sometimes comes back to the stressed/unstressed rhythm for occasional balance, but then turns it all upside-down again. Here are the stressed words, as an actor would play them:

> *Blow, winds,* and *crack* your *cheeks. Rage, blow.*
> You *cataracts* and *hurricanoes, spout*
> Till you have *drenched* our *steeples, drowned* the *cocks.*
> You *sulph'rous* and *thought-executing fires,*
> *Vaunt-couriers* of *oak-cleaving thunderbolts,*

*Singe my white head*. And *thou, all-shaking thunder,*
*Strike flat* the *thick rotundity* o' th' *world,*
*Crack Nature's moulds, all germains spill* at *once,*
That *makes ingrateful man.*

*Rumble* thy *bellyful. Spit, fire. Spout, rain.*
Nor *rain, wind, thunder, fire* are my *daugh*ters.
I *tax* you *not,* you *elements,* with *unkind*ness.
I *never gave* you *king*dom, *called* you *child*ren;
You *owe* me *no* sub*scription. Then let fall*
Your *horrible pleasure. Here I stand your slave,*
A *poor,* in*firm, weak,* and des*pised old man.*
But *yet* I *call* you *servile ministers,*
That *will* with *two* per*nicious daugh*ters *join*
Your *high-engen*dered *battles 'gainst* a *head*
So *old* and *white* as *this.* O, *ho!* 'tis *foul.*

So why does he stomp on the iambic blueprint so often? Why does he bust it all up like that?

Well, Lear is slightly round the bend—he's old, he's in grief, he's been used and betrayed cruelly. And here he is, his saggy old balls dangling in a whipping thunderstorm, cursing and raging. Like Lear, Nature itself is rabid and in chaos—Lear rages *with* that Nature, and represents a *part of it*. He's not in sync with the rest of the world—he's out of favor (think, *out of rhythm*). He is now the *world's opposite,* and his internal rhythm is as violent, jangled, and unpredictable as the thunderstorm. His verse-rhythms reflect that.

So why does Lear speak in verse at all? If Lear's verse is so unpredictable and thunderous, why doesn't he just speak in prose?

Shakespeare is once again giving you your acting clues—*in* that blank verse.

Now, I'm not going to give you all the answers—I want you to start thinking about these things for yourself—but here are a few hints:

- Is Lear in a "heightened" frame of mind?
- Are his emotions "highly tuned"?

- Is he having a natural, down-to-earth conversation, or is he dealing with something extraordinary?
- How does Nature reflect his inner turmoil? How does his chaotic verse reflect this struggle? Don't analyze too much, just *play* the chaotic, powerful verse.

## Saxon vs. Latin

Look at the text again, and notice the difference between those often-monosyllabic Saxon sounds and the more refined Latin sounds. Think:

> *blow winds crack cheeks rage spout*
> *drenched steep drowned cocks*
> *thought fires vaunt oak cleaving*
> *thunderbolts singe white head thou*
> *shaking thunder strike flat thick world*
> *crack moulds spill once makes man*
> *rumble thy bellyfull spit fire spout rain*
> *wind daughters tax not you kingdom*
> *called children owe me no let fall*
> *stand slave poor weak join battles*
> *'gainst head old white ho foul*

Really crack and spit these words out of your mouth. Exaggerate the open vowels—hammer out and chew on the consonants. Notice how muscular and meaty these words are, compared with:

> *germains ingrateful elements subscription horrible*
> *pleasure servile ministers pernicious engendered*

These are still good words, but slightly softer and less immediate. These are more delicate, polysyllabic sounds. *This, too, is an acting note.* Why does Lear suddenly begin to use these more intellectual words after blowing his face out with the strong Saxon noises? Answer this for yourself, but notice that he doesn't begin to use them until he says:

> I tax you not, you elements, with unkindness.

Is he:

• Coming to his *senses*?
• *Giving up* on his *"baser" self*?
• Trying to *rationalize* with Nature?
• Using his *brain*, if only for a moment?

Notice when Shakespeare switches to these more rational, polysyllabic sounds, and ask yourself why. What's going on with your character? What is the motivation for his/her switch to "higher" words? Let these changes inform your acting.

If you get stuck and can't figure out which words are important to stress, or what the general shape of the speech should be, remember to play only the full thoughts themselves, and never the rhythm. But do listen to the text very closely, and let the rhythm *inform* your acting. Keep in mind the "iambic pentameter" blueprint, and be sensitive to that basic rhythm. Notice, too, all the counter-rhythms. Direction will reveal itself to you if you scan Shakespeare's text with delicate ears.

## What About Characters Interrupting Each Other? What Happens to the Verse?

As we get into more of Shakespeare's hidden directions, we'll need to get back to the basics a bit. I'll have to use the formal term "iambic pentameter" more in these next sections because we'll investigate maintaining the strictures of the iambic rule in dialogue, and how this will uncover acting clues.

When Shakespeare starts a scene in verse, he usually continues the whole scene in verse. Once in a while, you will see a mixture of prose and verse in one scene (as we saw in our earlier example from *As You Like It*), but generally he will not switch from one to the other unless there is a *significant change on stage* (i.e. someone is left alone, a different group of people enter, or a whole new scene begins).

You'll find a lot of cut-offs, overlaps, interruptions, question and answering, and quick-banter in Shakespeare's verse—just as we speak and interact with each other in contemporary life. But notice how Shakespeare keeps his dialogue within the iambic pentameter form:

| | |
|---|---|
| Benvolio: | Good morrow, cousin. |
| Romeo: | Is the day so long? |
| Benvolio: | But new struck nine. |
| Romeo: | Ay me! Sad hours seem long. |

Benvolio's first line, "Good morrow cousin," has five beats. Romeo's answer, "Is the day so long?" has the next five beats. Add them together and you get the full ten beats of iambic pentameter. This is commonly referred to as a "shared line."

Shakespeare is telling you that Romeo's thought comes in *immediately* after Benvolio's. Romeo's response is quick and ready, almost as though they share a single thought together. Although each thought belongs to, and is unique to, each character, *together* they made up the meter of one full line. Shakespeare is telling his actor:

"Come in right away with your line! Pick up your cue! Don't take a pause, or fill in empty air with action. Respond immediately!"

Listen to the thought continuing, being picked up instantaneously in the next example:

| | |
|---|---|
| Dumaine: | As upright as the cedar. |
| Berowne: | Stoop, I say— |
| | Her shoulder is with child. |
| Dumaine: | As fair as day. |
| Berowne: | Ay, as some days, but then no sun must shine. |
| Dumaine: | O that I had my wish! |
| Longaville: | And I had mine! |

A bit sing-songy with the rhyming couplets there, but never mind them. You have a happy banter taking place here when you pick up your cues immediately, and pay attention to the verse form. There is no room between Dumaine and Berowne's lines for hemming and hawing, posturing, thinking, mulling, emoting, or anything else the beginning actor does. Berowne and Dumaine's thoughts are fresh and spontaneous—they almost trip over each other with excitement and quickness of thought.

Certainly, Shakespeare's quick exchange of thought is not always wit-play. It is just as often a scene of violent confrontation, desperate confusion, terror, chastisement, anger, begging— any natural exchange of swift thought. Listen to the Macbeths share their lines, as their hearts race in a moment of panic:

| | |
|---|---|
| Macbeth: | I have done the deed. Didst thou not hear a noise? |
| Lady: | I heard the owl scream and the crickets cry. |
| | Did not you speak? |
| Macbeth: |                   When? |
| Lady: |                     Now. |
| Macbeth: |                        As I descended? |
| Lady: | Ay. |
| Macbeth: | Hark! |
| | Who lies i' th' second chamber? |
| Lady: |                        Donalbain. |

You can hear the quick desperation in this text—the one tense breath both characters share. Shakespeare's acting note is very clear when he gives you these shared lines:

"Don't stop! Ping-Pong these words between yourselves, and *build the tension* by keeping these worried thoughts bouncing off each other. Keep fueling!"

*This is not to say the actor cannot take a pause if he creates an important need for one.* If you are a skilled actor, or if your director wants to change the stage-tension, and you decide to put a pause into your text, by all means use a pause. Just be careful. Choose your beat conscientiously and deliberately. The scene could work very well like this:

| | |
|---|---|
| Lady: | I heard the owl scream and the crickets cry. |
| | Did not you speak? |
| | (Pause.) |
| | (Macbeth stiffens with sudden realization. Then,) |
| Macbeth: |                   When? |
| Lady: |                     Now. |

| Macbeth: | | As I descended? |
| Lady: | Ay. | |
| Macbeth: | Hark! | |

Just keep Shakespeare's acting notes in mind. If you want to change them by inserting a beat or a pause, make sure there is a very specific reason for it.

All in all, when you notice a scene in Shakespeare's text in which the question and answering, exchange of thought, quick bantering of ideas, etc., *maintains its verse form*, there you have your stage direction. Keep driving your scene forward by picking up your cues, adding in your new thought freshly and immediately, and maintaining the integrity of the ten beat rhythm.

If Shakespeare had wanted you to take your time with responses, or dilly-dally with action, pauses, and "thinking," he would have written your scene in prose. Or he would have slipped extra or fewer beats into the blank verse, which he does all the time. And this is another important hidden direction.


## What About Lines that Have Fewer or More than Ten Beats?

If you have paid close attention to some of the examples in this book, you will have noticed that some lines are eleven, even twelve beats long. And some lines fall short of ten beats.

Yes, this means something, too.

Off the top of your head, can you think of an irregularly long piece of text? I'll give you a hint: we've already looked at it, and it's the most famous of Shakespeare's thoughts:

> To be or not to be; that is the question.

Beat it out.

> To *be* or *not* to *be*; that *is* the *ques...tion*. — eleven beats.

Hmm. So much for "iambic pentameter," right?

Contrary to what you might already have been taught, adding in extra beats is not really a "liberty" Shakespeare takes when writing in verse—nor is it a mistake or accidental. Shakespeare is telling you, the actor, something. He *intentionally* gives you a line that is eleven or twelve beats long. Why? Because this line is of *extra importance* and he wants to make sure you know it. He is saying, "This whole thought is of particular importance in this scene. I'm highlighting it for you. Lift it out to the audience. Give it special consideration. Pay particular attention to this thought."

It doesn't matter what word you emphasize:

> To be or not to be; *that* is the question!
> To be or not to be...that *is* the question!
> To be or not to be; that is...the *question!*

The whole thing is irregular. The audience instinctively feels something odd about this line because they are attuned to the ten-beat rhythm. They will subconsciously prick up their ears at this oddity, and pay a little more attention. That is what Shakespeare wants, and that's why he adds on to the line, lengthening it, shattering the usual rhythm by gently lifting it out to the audience. He grabs the ear with these irregularly long lines, saying, "Listen up, folks! I'm telling you something important!"

In fact, the whole next section of the speech is irregular. You must notice this, because it is Shakespeare's way of using a yellow highlighter. By making the lines irregular, he says:

> "This is Hamlet's problem, folks! This is Hamlet. Listen closely."

> Whe*ther* 'tis *nobler in* the *mind* to *su*-ffer (eleven beats)
> The *slings* and *arrows of* outrageous *for*-tune (eleven beats)
> Or to take *arms* a*gainst* a *sea* of *trou*-bles (eleven beats)
> And *by* opposing *end* them. To *die, to* sleep— (eleven beats)

Strange rhythm. You certainly can't pick out the important words in this text by using the iambic as a clue. Shakespeare is telling you, "Forget the form—highlight these thoughts! This is the crux of my play, so give this whole section a little extra weight!" That whole first chunk of text is irregular, before it settles into a more stable rhythm. Once Shakespeare catches the audience's mind with these important reflections on life and death, he then lets the actor settle a bit into the "normal" rhythm. Notice:

No more—and by a sleep to say we end (ten beats)
The heartache, and the thousand natural shocks (ten beats)
That flesh is heir to. 'Tis a consummation (eleven beats—extra importance)
Devoutly to be wished. To die, to sleep— (ten beats)

And so on. Allow these "irregularities" to inform your playing.

Shakespeare also tells you a little about your character with these irregularly long lines. He says:

"Hamlet is unbalanced...he is trying frantically to balance himself, to pull together his contrary forces. He is really struggling. These thoughts haunt and eat away at him. He is finally sharing them with an audience; he is exorcising his doubts, and he finally examines his dilemma with the crowd. Give these thoughts their due, and let my irregular lines highlight his problem."

These kinds of extra-beat lines are sometimes referred to as *feminine*. A *masculine* ending refers to a line ending on a stressed beat. For example:

Now entertain conjecture of a *time*

ends on a stressed beat, or emphasized word. If the final beat is a monosyllabic word (like "time"), the whole word is stressed. If it is a polysyllabic word, the ending is masculine if the stress falls on the last syllable of the full word. For example:

Others would say, "Where? Which is Boling*broke*?"

A feminine ending (in a ten beat line) refers to a line ending on an unstressed beat. Sometimes it can be:

Note if your lady strain's enter*tain*ment

But it is most often a line ending in eleven (or more) beats, like:

To be or not to be; that is the ques—tion.

You can see where that final, extra syllable seems to fall off the end of the line.

It's important to note that you should never stress the last beat on a feminine ending, even if you're trying to keep the line driving forward. It sounds unnatural and contrived:

My people are with sickness much enfee*bled*

Some old-time actors used to hit that feminine ending, which you can hear today on scratchy library recordings. It may have worked back then, as they tried to project out to a huge house, but it's pretty comical to us today.

Notice when an ending is feminine because of an extra beat or two, but speak the line as you would in life. Use your common sense. You shouldn't have to force out a concocted, jagged emphasis—rather, lift the line out subtly, gently, and let the abnormal length of the line work upon the audience's subconscious ear. Note the irregularity, and use it delicately. Never force it. Keep in mind Shakespeare's clever hidden direction.

## Elisions

Having said all that, I want you to notice when a line is eleven beats because Shakespeare has marked it with his version of your yellow highlighter, and not *because it is an elision*.

Because of different editors, or the changes in language over the past four hundred years, you will often have a line that is eleven beats due to the need for a *different pronunciation*, or the *collapsing of syllables together*. An elision is just that: *the compression of minor words or syllables together in order to subtract a beat*. For example:

Yet I am richer than my base accusers. — is eleven beats
Yet *I'm* richer than my base accusers. — is ten beats

However, if you notice that this line needs to be lifted out for particular attention, then *use* those eleven beats. If not, then the line should be compressed. The choice is yours, but make a specific choice for a specific reason and commit to it.

Another example:

Then, gracious auditory, be it known to you — is twelve beats

It should be:

Then, gracious audit'ry, *be't* known to you.
With treacherous crowns; and three corrupted men — is eleven beats

Not, "treach-er-ous" (three beats), but:

With treach'*rous* (two beats) crowns; and three corrupted men — is ten beats

The same thing goes for names. For example, sometimes the name "Juliet" is pronounced "Joo-lee-ette," and other times, it's pronounced "*Joo*-liet."

*And the opposite can be true, as well.* Sometimes when you have lines *missing* a single beat, you may have to take a second look at the words. For example:

Down, down I come, like glist'ring Phaethon — may seem to be nine beats.

But "Phaethon" is pronounced "Phay-u-thun," and not "Phay-thun." With this, the line beats out perfectly.

How do you know? Well, just use your common sense, and look into those words you're not sure how to pronounce. Look twice at your text before deciding whether it is a collapsible elision at work lengthening the line, or if it is Shakespeare himself poking you with his highlighter. If you notice great chunks of text together that end in extra beats, you have your acting note.

## What About Eleven Beats or More in a Dialogue?

Just as the Romeo/Benvolio and Berowne/Dumaine dialogues fall nicely into ten beats per line, you will find other dialogues that count eleven or more beats. Like this one, from *Henry the Fourth, Part One*, Act I, Scene 3:

> Worcester:                              You start away
>                     And lend no ear unto my purposes.
>                     Those prisoners you shall keep.
> Hotspur:                                        Nay, I will! That's flat!
>                     He said he would not ransom Mortimer,
>                     Forbade my tongue to speak of Mortimer,
>                     But I will find him when he lies asleep,
>                     And in his ear I'll hollo 'Mortimer.'

First, look at Hotspur's name for an acting note. He's quick, hot, easily inflamed, and "spurs" into action. Then, notice that Worcester's last line counts six beats, and Hotspur's first line counts five—making eleven. Aside from the punctuation (two exclamation marks on a single line), Shakespeare gives you another acting note in Hotspur's extra beat, saying:

> "Cut Worcester off! Your patience is at an end, and you slice off the last beat in his line with your first beat. That will *begin* your fury. I give you even more fierceness to play with by the repetition of the name "Mortimer." But it all begins with that first, silencing cut-off, "Nay, I will!" where you crush Worcester's last beat with your first word."

With these eleven-beats-in-dialogue, Shakespeare tells you that the conversation between characters (question/answer, exchange of thought) is so fast, furious, excited, or important that they *literally* cut each other off. Try, subtly, to keep your dialogue to ten beats per line by speaking your first word even as the other character is finishing his last word.

A lot of teachers and directors probably think I'm being rigid with these "rules," but all I'm interested in is the *playing* of the text, not overblown rhythmic analysis; these rules *play well*. They make your text *physical* and *immediate,* and your time onstage must be exacting and ferocious. Shakespeare's text is to be *heard,* and he knows what he's doing with these extra beats. You just have to listen closely enough, and trust him, to hear his directions.

When you try to keep iambic pentameter together, and when you observe these extra beats, you actually set yourself free as an actor. Shakespeare has done most of the work for you, but what he has left for you to fill in is liberating. Tinkering with these tiny beats is where you express your creativity.

Just *where* you cleave out a beat with interruption is up to you, but with eleven-beats-in-dialogue, always ask yourself—

Are the characters...

- *Arguing?*
- *Biting* at each other?
- *Desperately* trying to *break through* to each other?
- *Finishing* each other's *thoughts?*
- *Panicked* and *raw, clawing for answers?*

You decide.

## Does Shakespeare Ever Tell Us to Slow Down in the Verse?

Yes.

When Shakespeare wants you to slow down, or take a few pauses in the verse, he writes *a couple of lines in succession with fewer than ten beats.* I think you notice this most often when a character is speaking to a king (or some other aristocratic figure) in a non-emergency situation. In this case, Shakespeare is telling you, "Don't interrupt or slice into each other's lines. Listen, take note, and respond."

Like in this text from *Henry the Fourth, Part Two,* Act II, Scene 4:

| | |
|---|---|
| Warwick: | Many good morrows to your majesty! |
| King: | Is it good morrow, lords? |
| Warwick: | 'Tis one o'clock, and past. |
| King: | Why, then, good morrow to you all, my lords. |
| | Have you read o'er the letters that I sent you? |
| Warwick: | We have, my liege. |

King:        Then you perceive the body of our kingdom
             How foul it is, what rank diseases grow,
             And with what danger, near the heart of it.

These shorter lines are not shared. If Shakespeare had wanted you to split lines, he would have written:

King:        Is it good morrow, lords?
Warwick:                                 'Tis one o'clock
             And past.

These are more simple, straight-to-the-point conversations. Warwick doesn't take the full ten beats on all of his lines out of respect for the king. Shakespeare's note to the king here is, "Be brief and immediate—I want your curtness to set up a tension with Warwick. Don't offer up to share your line, just speak your thought tersely."

His note to Warwick is, "Pay homage to your king by greeting him with a full flourish of ten beats. Afterwards, show deference, and only respond with a short, exact answer. You know what's coming, so get to the point—be humble and direct. You know that the situation needs you to wait."

When you see big sections of verse in which there are fewer than ten beats and no shared lines, just play:

Question. Answer. Respond.

Obviously, you play the lines with the tension the situation requires, but there's no need for swiftness of thought. Slow down and wait, building the tension for whatever reason; play your thoughts bluntly.

However, when you notice a *single* line that counts fewer than ten beats in an otherwise *full iambic text*, this is another very important hidden direction about the use of "short lines."

## What About Short Lines?

Just as you will encounter longer-than-usual lines, you will also come across abnormally short lines, still within the verse form, and sticking out like a hitchhiker's thumb. Short lines flag you down and give you a very strong acting note.

What, specifically, they mean will depend on the play, your character, your action, and the situation. The best way to uncover these hidden directions is to look at a couple of very clear examples. Here, we have Cleopatra from *Antony and Cleopatra*, Act IV, Scene 15, holding the dying Mark Antony in her arms. She says:

> Noblest of men, woo't die?
> Hast thou no care of me? Shall I abide
> In this dull world, which in thy absence is
> No better than a sty? O, see, my women,
> *(Antony dies)*
> The crown o' the earth doth melt. My lord!
> O, wither'd is the garland of the war,
> The soldier's pole is fall'n: young boys and girls
> Are level now with men; the odds is gone,
> And there is nothing left remarkable
> Beneath the visiting moon.
> *(Swoons)*

Let's look at the last two lines:

> And there is nothing left remarkable
> Beneath the visiting moon.

The rhythm of the first line is remarkably slow and regular. And it is a perfect ten beats. Fine. But, "Beneath the visiting moon." only has seven beats. *Where are the last three beats?*

> Beneath the visiting moon (beat) (beat) (beat).

Shakespeare writes in a stage direction after this line: "*Swoons.*" Simple. He's given you three beats to swoon. Shakespeare's hidden direction is, "Don't start fainting on "beneath," and don't faint on the first line of the next character's speech. Faint after you say, "moon." I have given you *exactly* three beats to faint."

How you swoon on those three beats is up to you, but your action must *fill* those three beats, and *only* those three beats. It must be a *full* action—as full as words. Use your imagination. Here are two over-the-top examples to get your mind working. You could play:

- Beneath the visiting moon (stagger once) (collapse) (sigh).
- Beneath the visiting moon (buckle) (right yourself) (collapse).

How you swoon is your choice, but fill in those three beats with action. Now, let's take a look at the fifth line of this text. Cleopatra says:

The crown o' the earth doth melt. My lord!

Only nine beats. Has Shakespeare made a mistake? No, he gives you another stage direction, and it's up to you to fill it; you *must fill in that missing beat,* either through an action, or in the way you use the words:

- The crown o' the earth doth melt. (gasp) My lord!
- The crown o' the earth doth melt. My...(reaching out to hold him)...lord!
- The crown o' the earth doth melt. My *lo-oord!* (A cry of great longing)

Any strong action can work—but you must fill in that one beat.

And here, from *Julius Caesar,* Act III, Scene 1, is another clear example of filling in those missing beats with action:

| | |
|---|---|
| Cinna: | O Caesar. |
| Caesar: | Hence! Wilt thou lift up Olympus? |
| Decius: | Great Caesar. |
| Caesar: | Doth not Brutus bootless kneel? |
| Casca: | Speak hands for me. |
| | *(They stab Caesar—Casca first, Brutus last.)* |
| Caesar: | *Et tu, Brute?*—Then fall Caesar. |
| | *(Dies.)* |
| Cinna: | Liberty! Freedom! Tyranny is dead! |
| | Run hence, proclaim, cry it about the streets! |

Notice the fifth line (Casca's). He says:

Speak hands for me.

Only four beats. Now look at Shakespeare's written stage direction: "They stab Caesar—Casca first, Brutus last." There are six missing beats between Casca's line and that stage direction. Easy: Shakespeare gives you *exactly six beats* to attack Caesar. Fewer than six beats wouldn't have a dramatic impact on the audience; any more than six beats would hold up the play too much (it's only Act III, remember). Look at the sixth line (Caesar's):

Et tu, Brute?—Then fall Caesar.

Only eight beats, followed by Shakespeare's note: "Dies." You have two missing beats on which to die. No more, no less. How you die is up to you, but think:

- *Et tu, Brute?*—Then (struggle to breathe)...fall (writhe)... Caesar.
- *Et tu, Brute?*—Then (clutch your gaping wound)...(see the blood)...fall Caesar.
- *Et tu, Brute?*—Then fall Caesar (wheeze) (collapse).

I think the best choice would be for Caesar to die completely *on* his beats; the conspirators would take two beats to register his death before shouting, "Liberty!"

Listen very closely for these missing beats. The more you practice scanning for them with your eyes and ears, the more apparent they become. It doesn't take long to get to the stage where you can pick up a text, read it over once, and notice all of Shakespeare's little acting notes. By paying attention to his subtle rhythms, missing beats, and written stage directions, you will quickly become attuned to his whispered directions.

## When Missing Beats Indicate a Mini-Conclusion

You'll find a lot of missing beats in verse that seem *non-action oriented*. One character is speaking to another (with no stabbing, beating, or dying going on), and—all of a sudden—he has an abnormally short line in the middle of his text: like Othello, in Act I, Scene 3:

Othello:     Her father loved me, oft invited me;
Still questioned me the story of my life
From year to year—the battles, sieges, fortunes
That I have passed.
I ran it through, even from my boyish days
To th' very moment that he bade me tell it.
Wherein I spoke of most disastrous chances,
Of moving accidents by the flood and field;

Look at his fourth line, "That I have passed." We only have four beats there. Why did Shakespeare leave us hanging like that?

This is an example of using an irregularly short line to make a mini-conclusion. It's not a full conclusion because we haven't come to the end of the speech yet. But Othello speaks only these four short beats on a ten beat line in order to separate one part of his speech from the next; it is a brief wrap-up before launching into the next important section. There are several things you can do with these kinds of lines:

- Use a few beats of silence to let your previous thoughts "sink in" to the listeners.
- Use a few beats of silence to shift gears entirely, changing your rhythm and tone.
- Use a few beats of laughter, rage, tears, etc.
- Use a few beats to gather yourself together (collect your emotions or thoughts) in a high-powered scene.
- Fill in those missing beats with physical action. Choose your action carefully and deliberately.

Whatever you choose, make sure that you use this opportunity Shakespeare gives you to *really make a mini-conclusion*, separating the old, spoken thought from the fresh, unspoken new one. Here's another good example from *Love's Labour's Lost*:

Berowne:     And I, forsooth, in love!
I, that have been love's whip,
A very beadle to a humorous sigh,
A critic, nay, a night-watch constable,
A domineering pedant o'er the boy,
Than whom no mortal so magnificent.

Shakespeare gives you two short lines right at the beginning. The first line has only six beats, and stands on its own as a mini-conclusion. Berowne, abstaining from love, is shocked, outraged, amused, confused, and completely, furiously baffled by his feelings. You have four missing beats with which to fill his mini-conclusion. You might try:

- And I (two beats of: *"Me?* Of *all* people?! Can you believe it, audience?! You, sir? You, madam?"), forsooth, in LOVE??! (Two beats of shocked laughter.)
- And I, forsooth, in love! (Four beats of hysterical, mocking, *concluding* laughter.)
- And I, forsooth—*in love*!! (Complete outrage. Play this line as though this was the *only* thing you were going to say. A "full" mini-conclusion. Then surprise us by continuing your speech.)

Choose good, full action, or make a strong mini-conclusion, and then go on to Berowne's next line, which is another mini-conclusion with only six beats. Try:

- I, that have been love's whip (action which says, "No, no—I can't take it anymore! I'm finished, folks!")
- I, that have been love's whip (four beats of pouting, which says, "That's it, folks! I'm screwed!")
- *I* (this is the funniest thing I've ever heard!), that have been (double over in laughter)—LOVE'S WHIP (uncontainable hilarity; explode with mocking laughter)!

Only when you have made your mini-conclusion can you launch into the next section of Berowne's petulant and self-mocking speech.

Use these mini-conclusions to *fully explore your thoughts*, and *then to put an end to them*. Take the necessary fill-in beats to examine the full impact of the line, to make a discovery or judgment with the line, and then to change direction for your next thought.

You'll notice mini-conclusions in *dialogue* as well. Take this part of *Much Ado About Nothing*, Act IV, Scene 1, for example:

| | |
|---|---|
| Leonato: | Sweet Prince, why speak not you? |
| Pedro: | What should I speak? |
| | I stand dishonored that have gone about |
| | To link my dear friend to a common stale. |
| Leonato: | Are these things spoken, or do I but dream? |
| John: | Sir, they are spoken, and these things are true. |
| Benedick: | This looks not like a nuptial. |

| | |
|---|---|
| Hero: | 'True'! O God! |
| Claudio: | Leonato, stand I here? |
| | Is this the Prince? Is this the Prince's brother? |
| | Is this face Hero's? Are our eyes our own? |

Hero and Claudio are in the middle of their wedding, but Claudio has just accused his fiancée of screwing around behind his back and losing her virginity to another. Of course, this accusation comes as the most tremendous shock and horror—the crowd is uniformly baffled, confused, outraged and furious. *All* react powerfully (except for Benedick, who gives his glib line).

Notice how "clean" the verse is, except for Claudio's seven beat line, "Leonato, stand I here?" A clear note from Shakespeare, saying, "I've given you three beats let the idea sink in. Let shock and anger register with the crowd."

He gives you these mini-conclusions in dialogue for a reason. You must use these short lines to let an idea, emotion, discovery, etc., *sink in* to the onstage listeners (and the audience). Your character takes these moments to *affect a change in his partner(s), his audience, or himself.* Any good theatre director *must* be sensitive to these mini-concluding beats, and use them. *This* is where the cast reacts with dumb silence, with recognition of danger, or with the digestion of a new thought, experience, or perspective.

All in all, it doesn't really matter *how* you make a mini-conclusion. Just notice that Shakespeare gives you strong opportunities here to change tones, to affect change, and to bring one problem or argument to a small conclusion before launching into a greater thought. Use these missing beats well.

## Hidden Directions in Words

This is a little extension of something I mentioned in our *King Lear* example.

Shakespeare gives you both acting and character notes in the *types of words* he chooses. Fundamentally, he uses three sounds:

- blunt, strong (mainly monosyllabic) Saxon noises
- delicate, intelligent (mainly polysyllabic) Latin-based words
- some combination of the two

It may seem redundant to point this out, as the melding of Saxon and Latin speech is intrinsic to the English language itself. But it's important to keep this in mind as you begin to uncover Shakespeare's hidden directions, because you will notice purposeful groupings of these words together, which in turn will give you very clear character descriptions.

English is a bastard language, chaotically fused together with the skill of a half-wit cobbler, and without clear order. The Saxon part of our language comes from the viscera: barbaric, in touch with the elements, immediate, powerful, and onomatopoeic. When you see a whole section of text filled with these kinds of words, Shakespeare is giving you clear character notes.

- This character is *"on fire."*
- This character has become *"base," "harsh,"* or *"belligerent."*
- This character is *"immediate"* and *"direct."*
- This character is *"enraged," "hungry," "animalistic."*
- This character is now at his/her very *"center,"* his/her *"core."*

The Latin-based part of our language comes from a sense of refinement and intellect. It is led by the "higher" part of our character, and is used to express courtliness, thoughtfulness, intelligence, and diplomacy—softer stuff. When you see text crammed with these kinds of words, Shakespeare's direction is obvious:

- This character is *"using his brain."*
- This character is more *"cool."*
- This character is exploring *"higher thoughts."*
- This character is displaying *"lordly,"* or *"kingly"* qualities.

And when you see the overall mixing of these two types of words, your character is more balanced, more full, more together, and a more complete part of society. The character exists in the "normalcy" of his expression, or is in a more "balanced" frame of mind.

Of course, this is just a basic sketch. There's no definite scale here—Shakespeare writes both instinctively and thoughtfully. But it's interesting to notice how our language works, and how it worked particularly well in its formative days. When we are more animalistic, we use short, curt sounds. Think *rip, stab, fuck, tear, kill* and *cry*. When we're "polite," we use longer syllables, which take more time and more thought *affection, discipline, symmetric* and *harmonious.*

So how will this affect your acting? You think about that for a while, and begin to answer these questions for yourself. Here are a few good examples:

Cleopatra (Act V, Scene 2) is almost out of her mind with fiery passion. Listen to the kinds of words she uses here:

i.                              Where are thou, death?
                     Come hither, come: come, come, and take a queen
                     Worth many babes and beggars!

ii.                     Sir, I will eat no meat, I'll not drink, sir—
                     If idle talk will once be necessary—
                     I'll not sleep neither.

Notice the desperate, immediate qualities of "come," "take," "death," "eat," "drink," "meat." Notice also the hissing, snaky qualities of "sir," "once," "necessary," "sleep." You can think of Cleopatra in these moments as a kind of dragon-lady, at the very core and center of her being. Later on, Cleopatra describes herself as "fire and air;" this is her "fire."

Every word in the second text is important: *there are ten equal stresses on the line.* Every word here gets an equal amount of weight, which tells you something about how to deliver that line.

Compare these with the words she uses shortly after this, when she is in the presence of Caesar, Proculeius, Gallus, and Maecenas. Here, she is forced to be courtlier, and to use her "higher" self.

    O Caesar, what a wounding shame is this,
    That thou vouchsafing here to visit me,
    Doing the honor of thy lordliness
    To one so meek, that mine own servant should
    Parcel the sum of my disgraces by
    Addition of his envy.

Here, the words are less meaty. Cleopatra uses "vouchsafing," "lordliness," "parcel," "disgraces," "addition"—refined, courtly, diplomatic words. She is no longer the dragon, but the lady; this is her "air."

Notice how few words are stressed in these lines. The full thoughts are more important than each individual word. "To one so meek, that mine own servant should/Parcel the sum of my disgraces by/Addition of his envy" rolls off the tongue as a single entity. When you have fewer stresses like this, Shakespeare is telling you to speak the full thought as a whole. *Your immediacy is in the completion of your thought, and not in the muscle of each moment.*

Now compare Cymbeline (from the play *Cymbeline*) with Lear. Both are kings, and though both live in very different circumstances, both are living through a highly impassioned, fiery situation. What can you tell about their characters from these two snippets of text?

| | |
|---|---|
| Cymbeline: | O rare instinct! |
| | When shall I hear all through? This fierce abridgment |
| | Hath to it circumstantial branches, which |
| | Distinction should be rich in. |
| Lear: | Howl, howl, howl! O, you are men of stones. |
| | Had I your tongues and eyes, I'ld use them so |
| | That heaven's vault should crack. She's gone forever. |
| | I know when one is dead, and when one lives. |
| | She's dead as earth. |

How these sounds and words inform your acting is pretty obvious. Speak Cymbeline's text out loud a few times. Really use those elegant words and shape his full thought. Let it trip off your tongue. Exaggerate for the moment, and notice what this does to your body.

Now speak Lear's five lines. Use those long, open vowels and those sometimes thudding, sometimes sharp consonants. Notice what this does to your body.

## How Do I Find the "Internal Rhythm" of My Character?

This is a bit hard to explain on paper. It's even harder to find by simply reading Shakespeare with your eyes, and not listening to him with your ears. But the more you practice out loud, the more your eyes and ears will become one.

The best I can do with typed-out words is to say this to you:

- To find the internal rhythm of your character, look to the external—namely the written words. Speak each individual word out loud. Then speak the full thought out loud. Listen to the vowels and consonants very closely. Are your vowels long and open? For example: "Aww! Oh! Oooh! Eeee! Ow! Ire! Eeerr!" Or are they short, clipped ones, like: "i, a, u"?
- Are your consonants sharp and crisp, or soft, wispy ones? Compare "Ta! Da! La! Pa! Ka!" with "th, ssshh, wh (as in "who"), llll, mmmm."
- Really exaggerate the sounds you hear in your practice. Notice whether the words are thudding Saxon sounds, or rational polysyllabic Latin words. Notice if they're sensuous, longer, tasting sounds, or explosive, barbaric noises.

Blow all your words out fully, and go completely over the top in your practice. Listen to the texture of those words. Speak them all together in a full thought, and notice the *rhythm* of that thought. Does it gallop off the tip of your tongue, the consonants tinkling out like wind chimes? Or does the phrase punch and slug its way out, barking, halting, hulking? Or is it a combination of the two? Exaggerate what you hear, and listen, until it unlocks a connection.

*Notice what these phrases and sounds do to your body.*

You may also find the internal rhythm of your character by simply looking at how many stressed or unstressed beats are in a line. If you have a lot of quick, stressed, cracking syllables in a text, or single lines that seem to flow without major stresses, chances are your character is quick, hot-tempered, excited, and flying through his or her text for some very heightened reason. Take a look at Hotspur from *Henry the Fourth, Part One*, Act I, Scene 3. Read it out loud to yourself, and notice how the rhythm sparkles and crackles with lots of tiny stressed beats and whole lines that fly quickly off the tongue:

My liege, I did deny no prisoners.
But I remember, when the fight was done,
When I was dry with rage and extreme toil,
Breathless and faint, leaning upon my sword,
Came there a certain lord, neat, and trimly dress'd,
Fresh as a bridegroom; and his chin new reap'd
Show'd like a stubble-land at harvest-home;
He was perfumed like a milliner;
And 'twixt his finger and his thumb he held
A pouncet-box, which ever and anon
He gave his nose and took't away again;
Who therewith angry, when it next came there,
Took it in snuff; and still he smiled and talk'd,
And as the soldiers bore dead bodies by,
He call'd them untaught knaves, unmannerly,
To bring a slovenly unhandsome corse
Betwixt the wind and his nobility.
With many holiday and lady terms
He question'd me; amongst the rest, demanded
My prisoners in your majesty's behalf.
I then, all smarting with my wounds being cold,
To be so pester'd with a popinjay,
Out of my grief and my impatience,
Answer'd neglectingly I know not what,
He should or he should not; for he made me mad
To see him shine so brisk and smell so sweet
And talk so like a waiting-gentlewoman
Of guns and drums and wounds—God save the mark!—
And telling me the sovereign'st thing on earth
Was parmaceti for an inward bruise;
And that it was great pity, so it was,
This villanous salt-peter should be digg'd
Out of the bowels of the harmless earth,
Which many a good tall fellow had destroy'd
So cowardly; and but for these vile guns,
He would himself have been a soldier.
This bald unjointed chat of his, my lord,

> I answer'd indirectly, as I said;
> And I beseech you, let not his report
> Come current for an accusation
> Betwixt my love and your high majesty.

Compare this with Cleopatra's text from *Anthony and Cleopatra*, Act V, Scene 2:

> Give me my robe, put on my crown; I have
> Immortal longings in me: now no more
> The juice of Egypt's grape shall moist this lip:
> Yare, yare, good Iras; quick. Methinks I hear
> Antony call; I see him rouse himself
> To praise my noble act; I hear him mock
> The luck of Caesar, which the gods give men
> To excuse their after wrath: husband, I come:
> Now to that name my courage prove my title!
> I am fire and air; my other elements
> I give to baser life. So; have you done?
> Come then, and take the last warmth of my lips.
> Farewell, kind Charmian; Iras, long farewell.

Notice how slow and sensuous the rhythm is? Particularly the first two lines, where every word, every syllable is stressed. Ten beats out of ten are stressed:

> *Give me my robe, put on my crown; I have*
> *Im-mor-tal long-ings in me: now no more*

This gives you an obvious, strong internal rhythm. Slow down, taste each beat fully, and savor every sound and moment.

And two last things to think about:

1. When a character is being direct, practical and down-to-earth (unmusical), Shakespeare will give you very little "poetry." Like this text of Henry the Fifth's (Act III, Scene 3):

> Open your gates. Come, uncle Exeter,
> Go you and enter Harfleur; there remain

And fortify it strongly 'gainst the French.
Use mercy to them all. For us, dear uncle,
The winter coming on, and sickness growing
Upon our soldiers, we will retire to Calais.

And this, from Act III, Scene 6:

We are in God's hands, brother, not in theirs.
March to the bridge. It now draws toward night.
Beyond the river we'll encamp ourselves,
And on tomorrow bid them march away.

2. When a character is given more to "high thoughts," when he is being philosophical, less frank and open, more reflective and insightful, and viewing the world with less immediacy and with more "musical" passivity, Shakespeare gives you more "poetry." One of the best examples is Richard II—the golden-tongued king. Listen to this text from Act III, Scene 3:

For well we know no hand of blood and bone
Can gripe the sacred handle of our scepter,
Unless he do profane, steal, or usurp.
And though you think that all, as you have done,
Have torn their souls by turning them from us
And we are barren and bereft of friends,
Yet know, my master, God omnipotent,
Is mustering in his clouds on our behalf
Armies of pestilence, and they shall strike
Your children yet unborn and unbegot
That lift your vassal hands against my head
And threat the glory of my precious crown.
Tell Bolingbroke, for yon methinks he stands,
That every stride he makes on my land
Is dangerous treason. He is come to ope
The purple testament of bleeding war.
But ere the crown he looks for live in peace,
Ten thousand bloody crowns of mothers' sons
Shall ill become the flower of England's face,

Change the complexion of her maid-pale peace
To scarlet indignation, and bedew
Her pastor's grass with faithful English blood.

And this from Act IV, Scene 1:

O that I were a mockery king of snow,
Standing before the sun of Bolingbroke
To melt myself away in water drops!

Now we come to some of the greatest of all Hidden Directions. Some of the most important, the most useful, and the most-overlooked acting notes you will ever find from Shakespeare can be found in Overruns.

## Overruns

When I first *explain* Overruns to actors, I always get the same reaction: scrunched-up faces, shaking heads, and immediate refusal. "How dare you suggest such an 'obstacle' to an actor's 'freedom' and 'interpretation' of a line?!" And then the "buts" come in. "But what about...but that means...but, but, but." I hear every argument in the book against the idea of Overruns.

That is, until I *play* an example of using the Overrun, compared with not using it. Then the light bulbs click, and the naysaying stops cold. When the first brave actor tries an Overrun, and uses it with purpose—heads nod, smiles form, and the Hallelujah Chorus pipes in right on cue: "Ohhhh." After that, I insist that lazy verse-speaking be crushed underfoot like a mealy-mouthed cockroach. Overruns are easy to dimiss and often overlooked. Do so at your peril, as they will improve your playing dramatically.

## What Is an Overrun?

We have discussed verse and prose, we have touched on Shakespeare's Hidden Directions, and we have learned the importance of punctuation in Shakespeare's text. But what happens when you come to the *end of your verse line...and find no punctuation there to guide you*? You will often see a comma, a period, a semi or full colon at the end of your ten beats—but just as often you are left with a blank. What to do, what to do...

Since we are somewhat familiar with Cleopatra's text, let's use it again:

Antony:               ...Now my spirit is going.
                    I can no more.
Cleopatra:            Noblest of men, woo't die?
                    Hast thou no care of me? Shall I abide
                    In this dull world? which in thy absence is
                    No better than a sty? O, see, my women,
                    The crown o' th' earth doth melt. My lord!
                        *(Antony dies)*
                    O, wither'd is the garland of the war,
                    The soldier's pole is fall'n: young boys and girls
                    Are level now with men; the odds is gone,
                    And there is nothing left remarkable
                    Beneath the visiting moon.

Here we go.

Most of Cleopatra's lines are *end-stopped*. That is to say, they end in punctuation: you have a question mark, a few commas, and an exclamation mark. But her 2nd, 3rd, 7th, and 9th lines have nothing at the end. We're just left hanging there.

One line is "run over" into the next. This is an Overrun. So, should you just continue speaking one line right into the next? After all, you might think to yourself, "It's the same thought. Shakespeare just ran out of room at the end of the line."

Should you play it as:

                    Noblest of men, woo't die?
Hast thou no care of me? Shall I abide in this dull world?
Which in thy absence is no better than a sty?
O, see, my women,
The crown o' th' earth doth melt. My lord!
O, wither'd is the garland of the war,
The soldier's pole is fall'n: young boys and girls are level now with men;
The odds is gone,
And there is nothing left remarkable beneath the visiting moon.

Even though it's the end of the line, *it's still all one thought*. So why not *play* it as one full thought? Right?
Wrong.

> *If Shakespeare had wanted you to play one full thought unbroken by punctuation, he would have written it in prose.*

But he *chose to* write it in verse. And then he just...leaves an empty space there at the end of the line. How do you play it?

It's all one thought! Yes. Even though one line is "run-over" without punctuation into the next, it *is* all one thought. But that little blank spot at the end of the line without punctuation *means something*. It speaks as loudly as punctuation.

Observing these Overrun lines are *vital* to good Shakespeare playing; and most directors don't even know about them. When Shakespeare gives you a line (in verse, not in prose) with no punctuation at the end, he is giving you a very important stage direction: *Hold this thought.*

There are two ways to do this:

1. Hold the *last word* in the line for a moment (in order to discover, decide, or disclose your next line). Pay *special attention* to this last word. I call this (for lack of imagination) a *Holding Overrun*.

—or—

2. Use that last word to *propel you into the next line with more vigor*. I call this one a *Trampoline Overrun*.

Confused?
Don't be.
Let's look to Cleopatra, for our example of:

## Overrun #1: The *Holding Overrun*

| Antony: | ...Now my spirit is going. |
| | I can no more. |
| Cleopatra: | Noblest of men, woo't die? |
| | Hast thou no care of me? Shall I abide |

> In this dull world? which in thy absence is
> No better than a sty? O, see, my women,
> The crown o' th' earth doth melt. My lord!
>     (*Antony dies*)
> O, wither'd is the garland of the war,
> The soldier's pole is fall'n: young boys and girls
> Are level now with men; the odds is gone,
> And there is nothing left remarkable
> Beneath the visiting moon.

Remember: this is the most tender and heart-wrenching moment in the play. Antony is dying in Cleopatra's arms, and they have finally reconciled themselves to each other and to their fates; all thoughts of anger and betrayal are gone, as they hold each other for the last time.

The first thing you notice is that Antony's last line, "I can no more," has only four beats. Cleopatra's first line, "Noblest of men, woo't die?" has six. As we learned earlier, there is *no interruption* between the thoughts, and Cleopatra's first word picks up exactly where Antony leaves off. She asks, "Would die?"

The second line is where we meet the first Overrun. Cleopatra asks:

> Hast thou no care of me? Shall I abide

But with no punctuation after "abide."

Shakespeare is whispering an important stage direction in your ear. He is saying:

"This thought is important! Hold it! Hold "abide"!"

As an exercise now, speak the line. Hold five beats after you speak the word "abide" before going on to "In this dull world?"

> Hast thou no care of me? Shall I abide *(1...2...3...4...5)*
> In this dull world?

Feels strange, doesn't it?

You're probably thinking, "What's the point of that?" or "This feels so contrived!"—so let me explain:

You can never forget that you, the actor, are playing *to an audience*. If you were in the Globe Theatre, your Cleopatra would probably be downstage center, very close to the crowd, holding Antony in her arms. You're being watched by some three thousand people—a huge crowd just below and in front of you, people up and to your left, people directly opposite and above (looking down at you), folks up and to your right—all peering carefully, listening, and concentrating on this moving scene. By holding the word "abide" for a moment, Cleopatra is making an *awful moment of discovery*.

(This bleeds a little bit into the "Three Dynamic D's" that I'll teach you in the next Chapter. Don't flip over to that section just yet; stay with these Overruns first.)

Cleopatra sees the crowd, slowly taking in each face. Then she realizes for the first time that the world is dull, that most people are awful, boring, lifeless, ugly, and that there is no point to life without Antony. She makes eye contact with as much of the audience as she can, noticing for the first time their shabby dress, their mediocre lives, and the overall futility of life.

Now, play the line with all this in mind.

> Hast thou no care of me? Shall I abide...

*...Hold it!* Make an *awful moment of discovery. Realize where you are*, look at the people gaping at you; see their poverty-stricken faces and threadbare clothes. *Ask yourself* mentally "Do I really want to live..."

> In this dull world?

You see how holding the word "abide" for a moment—letting it hang in the air as you make your terrible discovery of the next line—really fuels, "In this dull world?"

Speak these four words with an *awful realization*:

> "In...this...dull...world?"

Each word is a poisonous, terrible recognition. Shakespeare gives you good, strong "d" and "l" sounds in "dull" and "world." Use them.

And onto the next Overrun:

Which in thy absence is...

...*Hold it!* Make an *awful moment of decision.* Your world has crumbled, and you *realize for the first time* that life without Antony is...

No better than a sty.

*Awful conclusion.* Speak this line with *finality.*

There is no Overrun for the next few lines, but let's work through the text:

O, see, my women,
The crown 'o th' earth doth melt. My lord!

First, use that "O" as a real shock sound, or to breathe you into "see." Second, Shakespeare has given you a few commas to play with. Breathe between them. *Order* or *invite* your women to "see." Don't forget to stretch out the two-beat "My lord!" into three beats, in order to fill the ten beats. Take your time.

Next:

O, wither'd is the garland of the war,

Beautiful thought. Take your time with it. Let your "O"-sigh *breathe you into the line.* Notice the perfection of this iambic rhythm. Notice the two whining "w"s.

And where is the next Overrun? You got it:

The soldier's pole is fall'n: young boys and girls...

...*Hold it! Make your discovery*—that young boys and girls...

Are level now with men; *(breathe)* The odds is gone,

And your final Overrun:

And there is nothing left remarkable...

*...Hold it!* Make a *discovery* or a *decision*. Shakespeare also asks you to hold it *because Cleopatra is about to faint.* Right here, she begins to lose strength...

Beneath the visiting moon.

And then your three beats to faint on. Simple.

Delicately and gently, Shakespeare asks you to use these Overruns—in order to guide one thought into the next—by *holding* them. Use your Overruns *well*. Discover them, breathe with them, and allow them to inform your playing.

Go back over this text a few times, and really practice these Overruns; make new discoveries. Hold them longer than you think you should. Milk them for all they're worth (during your practice). When you have exercised sufficiently, go on to the next little example of Richard's, from *Richard III*, Act I, Scene 2:

Teach not thy lip such scorn; for it was made
For kissing, lady, not for such contempt.

In *Henry the Fourth, Part Three*, Richard murdered Anne's father-in-law, King Henry. In this play, he decides that he will become king, by hook or by crook, and part of the execution of this plan involves marrying Anne. Here in the tomb, while Anne cries over her father-in-law's rotting corpse, Richard shimmies in, full of false repentance. He charms her, and woos her. First, Anne has a little lashing-out at him...and then accepts his proposal! Your Richard must be powerfully magnetic, and must use the most convincing false penance. *Using the Overrun will help you suck Anne into your charm.* Just before these two lines, Anne gave Richard the snidest, most disgusted look of contempt, curling her lip and sneering.

Notice the Overrun on the first line. Shakespeare gives you no punctuation, and therefore gives you a clear stage direction:

"Catch her, charm her, seduce her—with my Overrun!"

Give it a try.

Teach not thy lip such scorn; for it was made...

...*Hold it! Discover* Anne's lips; *draw her in with your pause, discover your seductive power*, and *discover your next thought*. Hold her with "made." Confuse her, and let her become a bit fearful—make her ask herself, "Made for what? What's he going to do? Is he going to kill me or rape me?" And then give your conclusion:

For kissing, lady, not for such contempt.

By holding "made" and using that brief pause to fuel your next line, you draw Anne into you. You will frighten her, and intrigue her. You will catch the audience too. As you hold "for it was made" they will ask themselves, "Made for what? What's that rat-bastard going to do now?" You hold their ear, and set them on the edge of their seats.

Notice the perfectly placed commas in the second line. Use them.

For kissing, *(hold her with your comma. Now use "lady" seductively, or snidely. Choose to use that particular word)* lady, *(hold her again, and make her wait for your next words)* not for such contempt.

This kind of "Holding Overrun" is *held momentarily*. Not excessively milked, but *used*. Listen to the Overrun; play around and discover what you can do with it. When you hold it and allow it to gently ease you into the next line, *you will uncover your motivation through the line itself*:

- Why does Richard hold his thought like that? Because he is drawing Anne into his seduction.
- Why does Cleopatra hold her thoughts like that? Because she is discovering the true horror of the world without Antony for the first time—discovering that time itself is turned upside down now that Antony is dead.

You can hold an Overrun for the briefest instant, just barely pinching the audience's ear, or, you can use it for many long seconds, holding a crowd breathless in your thought. It's up to you. But use them, use them; use them for all they're worth.

## Overrun #2: The *Trampoline Overrun*

The first type of Overrun *holds* thought and attention. This second type does the *opposite*.

Sometimes, you'll find an Overrun that makes absolutely no sense to hold on to. Listen closely, and you may hear that it actually *ruins* the sense of the full thought. This Overrun is used to *explode you into your next line* with extra power. It is a *bounce* into your next line—a *lift* on the last word so that you can land more solidly onto the next full thought.

This "Trampoline Overrun" requires no long pause, no holding of thought—just an extra "oomph" on the last word with the briefest split-second pause. You use this kind of Overrun either to launch you a) onto the *first word or two* of the next line with more attack, or, b) onto the *full phrase* of the next line with more attack.

There is no rule regarding *how* to trampoline your thought, or whether you should bite into the first word or two of the next line, or the whole line itself. But if you listen closely to your text, you will feel it out. The best way to start sensing how to bite down on the Trampoline Overrun is by playing with examples:

1. Here's Richard again, from *Henry VI, Part III*, Act V, Scene 6:

> What? Will the aspiring blood of Lancaster
> Sink in the ground? I thought it would have mounted.
> See how my sword weeps for the poor king's death.
> O may such purple tears be always shed
> From those who wish the downfall of our house.
> If any spark of life be yet remaining,
> Down, down to hell, and say I sent thee thither,
>
> > *(Stabs him again.)*
>
> I, that have neither pity, love, nor fear.
> Indeed 'tis true that Henry told me of,
> For I have often heard my mother say
> I came into the world with my legs forward.
> Had I not reason, think ye, to make haste

And seek their ruin that usurped our right?
The midwife wonder'd, and the women cried,
'O, Jesus bless us! He is born with teeth!'
And so I was; which plainly signified
That I should snarl and bite and play the dog.
Then, since the heavens have shaped my body so,
Let hell make crook'd my mind to answer it.
I have no brother, I am like no brother;
And this word 'love,' which greybeards call divine,
Be resident in men like one another,
And not in me. I am myself alone.
Clarence, beware. Thou keep'st me from the light;
But I will sort a pitchy day for thee;
For I will buzz abroad such prophecies
That Edward will be fearful of his life;
And then, to purge his fear, I'll be thy death.
King Henry and the prince his son are gone.
Clarence, they turn is next, and then the rest,
Counting myself but bad till I be best.
I'll throw thy body in another room
And triumph, Henry, in thy day of doom.

Pick out the Overruns. Now, practice this monologue with my direction:

What? Will the aspiring blood of *Lancaster* (hold it for a split-second. Launch *into*)
*Sink* (really bite into this word.) in the ground? I thought it would have mounted.
See how my sword weeps for the poor king's death.
O may such purple tears be always *shed* (hold it for a split-second. Attack *into*)
*From those who wish the downfall of our house.*
If any spark of life be yet remaining,
Down, down to hell, and say I sent thee thither,
    (Stabs him again.)
I, that have neither pity, love, nor fear.
Indeed 'tis true that Henry told me of;
For I have often heard my mother *say* (hold it for two seconds. Relish *your next line*)
*I came into the world with my legs forward.*
Had I not reason, think ye, to make *haste* (hold it for a split-second. Launch *into*)

*And seek their ruin that usurped our right?*
The midwife wondered, and the women cried,
'O, Jesus bless us! He is born with teeth!'
And so I was; which plainly *signified* (hold it for a split-second. Enjoy)
*That I should snarl and bite and play the dog.*
Then, since the heavens have shaped my body so,
Let hell make crook'd my mind to answer it.
I have no brother, I am like no brother;
And this word 'love,' which greybeards call divine,
Be resident in men like one another,
And not in me. I am myself alone.
Clarence, beware. Thou keep'st me from the light;
But I will sort a pitchy day for thee;
For I will buzz abroad such *prophecies* (hold for two seconds. Discover)
*That Edward will be fearful of his life;*
And then, to purge his fear, I'll be thy death.
King Henry and the prince his son are gone.
Clarence, they turn is next, and then the rest,
Counting myself but bad till I be best.
I'll throw thy body in another *room* (hold it. Rejoice, *and* bite *into*)
*And triumph,* Henry, in thy day of doom.

2. Here's Hotspur again, from *Henry the Fourth, Part One*, Act IV, Scene 3:

The king is kind, and well we know the king
Knows at what time to promise, when to pay.
My father and my uncle and myself
Did give him that same royalty he wears;
And when he was not six-and-twenty strong,
Sick in the world's regard, wretched and low,
A poor unminded outlaw sneaking home,
My father gave him welcome to the shore;
And when he heard him swear and vow to God
He came but to be Duke of Lancaster,
To sue his livery and beg his peace,
With tears of innocence and terms of zeal,
My father, in kind heart and pity moved,

Swore him assistance, and performed it too.
Now when the lords and barons of the realm
Perceived Northumberland did lean to him,
The more and less came in with cap and knee;
Met him in boroughs, cities, villages,
Attended him on bridges, stood in lanes,
Laid gifts before him, proffer'd him their oaths,
Gave him their heirs as pages, followed him
Even at the heels in golden multitudes.
He presently, as greatness knows itself,
Steps me a little higher than his vow
Made to my father, while his blood was poor,
Upon the naked shore at Ravenspurgh;
And now, forsooth, takes on him to reform
Some certain edicts and some strait decrees
That lie too heavy on the commonwealth;
Cries out upon abuses, seems to weep
Over his country's wrongs; and by this face,
This seeming brow of justice, did he win
The hearts of all that he did angle for;
Proceeded further—cut me off the heads
Of all the favorites that the absent king
In deputation left behind him here
When he was personal in the Irish war.

## Taste these Overruns, following my pointers:

The king is kind, and well we know the *king (launch. Hold it for a split-second. Land on)*
*Knows* at what time to promise, when to pay.
My father and my uncle and *myself (launch. Hold it for a split-second. Bite into)*
*Did give him* that same royalty he wears;
And when he was not six-and-twenty strong,
Sick in the world's regard, wretched and low,
A poor unminded outlaw sneaking home,
My father gave him welcome to the shore;
And when he heard him swear and vow to God *(launch. Hold it for a second.*
     *Land on a mini-conclusion)*
*He came but to be Duke of Lancaster,*

To sue his livery and beg his peace,
With tears of innocence and terms of zeal.
My father, in kind heart and pity moved,
Swore him assistance, and performed it too.
Now when the lords and barons of the *realm* (hold it for a split-second. Land on)
*Perceived Northumberland did lean to him,*
The more and less came in with cap and knee;
Met him in boroughs, cities, villages,
Attended him on bridges, stood in lanes,
Laid gifts before him, proffer'd him their oaths,
Gave him their heirs as pages, followed *him* (hold it two seconds. Bite into)
*Even at the heels* in golden multitudes.
He presently, as greatness knows itself,
Steps me a little higher than his *vow* (hold it for a split-second. Land on)
*Made to my father*, while his blood was poor,
Upon the naked shore at Ravenspurgh;
And now, forsooth, takes on him to *reform* (hold it for two seconds. Land on)
*Some certain edicts* and some strait *decrees* (hold it for a second. Make a strong
      mini-conclusion)
*That lie too heavy on the commonwealth;*
Cries out upon abuses, seems to *weep* (hold it for a split-second. Launch into)
*Over his country's wrongs*; and by this face,
This seeming brow of justice, did he *win* (hold it for a split-second. Chew)
*The hearts of all* that he did angle for;
Proceeded further—cut me off the *heads* (really launch off this word and bite into)
*Of all the favorites* that the absent *king* (hold it for a second. Use the next two
      words carefully)
*In deputation* left behind him *here* (Launch off this word, and make a strong conclusion)
*When he was personal in the Irish war.*

Practice these two monologues over and over again carefully, using the little indicators I gave you. In the privacy of your bedroom or living room, really fly off the last word in the line with energy. Bring that Overrun up a semi or full-tone, and see if this helps shape your continuing thought with more vitality. Go over the top with it at first, and then carefully bring the Overruns back down to reality, using them as energy-boosters. When you get used to just using the last word on the line as a launching pad to trampoline you into your next line, then play around a bit with different ways to use the "landing words" or "landing phrases." The way you use the Overrun is completely up to you.

But use it, and use it well.

## How Do I Know Whether to Use the Holding Overrun or the Trampoline Overrun?

You won't know until you actually play around with the text. Try holding the last word for several beats, and notice whether it helps you unlock your next line. If not, try bouncing off the last word in order to fuel your next line with more power. Experiment, be flexible, and have fun with these Overruns.

You might notice, however, that a scene or monologue possesses a very slow, somber or sensuous rhythm. This is a good indicator that your Overruns may be equally slow, and thus of the "holding" variety. If your text has a quick, fire-cracking tempo, chances are your Overruns will be an extension of this, and will "trampoline" or explode you into your next lines. Be sensitive to your text and to its rhythm.

## Will I Ever Find *Both* Holding and Trampoline Overruns within a Single Monologue?

Yes, of course. Within a single monologue you will find both kinds of Overruns mixed in together. If you reread Richard and Hotspur, you will be able to see where a Holding Overrun may be used in place of a Trampoline Overrun, and vice-versa. Titus gives us a good example of this (from *Titus Andronicus, Act V, Scene 2*):

> Come, come, Lavinia; look, thy foes are bound.
> Sirs, stop their mouths, let them not speak to me,
> But let them hear what fearful words I utter.
> O villains, Chiron and Demetrius!
> Here stands the spring whom you have stain'd with mud,
> This goodly summer with your winter mix'd.
> You killed her husband, and for that vile *fault* (You have a choice here. Depending
>      on how you want to play the scene, you can hold it in order to build the tension and draw out
>      the villains' suffering—or, trampoline onto the next line with bite and fury.)

Two of her brothers were condemned to death,
My hand cut off and made a merry jest;
Both her sweet hands, her tongue, and that more *dear* (Trampoline off the
    *word up a semi-tone—get through "Than hands or tongue" quickly, and land on "spotless*
    *chastity" with vengeance. Use this trampolined "dear" as a barbed threat.)*
Than hands or tongue, her spotless chastity,
Inhuman traitors, you constrained and forced.
What would you say if I should let you speak?
Villains, for shame you could not beg for grace.
Hark, wretches, how I mean to martyr you.
This one hand yet is left to cut your *throats* (Trampoline off the word, and use
    *the energy to fuel you straight through to the next Overrun.)*
Whiles that Lavinia 'tween her stumps doth *hold* (Holding Overrun, for sure.
    *Take three or more beats to play with the villains, and torture them with tension.)*
The basin that receives your guilty blood.
You know your mother means to feast with me,
And calls herself Revenge, and thinks me mad.
Hark, villains, I will grind your bones to dust,
And with your blood and it I'll make a paste,
And of the paste a coffin I will rear,
And make two pasties of your shameful heads,
And bid that strumpet, your unhallowed dam,
Like to the earth, swallow her own increase.
This is the feast that I have bid her to,
And this banquet she shall surfeit on;
For worse than Philomel you used my daughter,
And worse than Progne I will be revenged.
And now prepare your throats. Lavinia, come,
Receive the blood; and when that they are dead,
Let me go grind their bones to powder *small* (You choose here. You can hold the
    *tension again, after this long, quicker section, or you can trampoline onto the next full line.)*
And with this hateful liquor temper it;
And in that paste let their vile heads be baked.
Come, come, be every one *officious* (Trampoline off this one up a semi-tone and
    *match your pitch with "banquet." Use "officious" and "banquet" together merrily.)*
To make this banquet, which I wish may *prove* (Hold it. Discover the next line, or
    *use "prove" to drip out the next line with revenge or celebration.)*

More stern and bloody than the Centaurs' feast.
> *He cuts their throats.*
So, now bring them in, for I'll play the *cook (Your choice here. Try both, and see*
> *how each one unlocks the next line for you.)*
And see them ready against their mother comes.

## Banging It into Your Head

All in all, I want you to learn the following from these Overrun exercises:

- In verse, you will come across a line ending in no punctuation whatsoever. This line is "run-over" into the next.
- This "Overrun" is there for a reason. If Shakespeare had wanted one line simply extended into the next with no significant attention paid to it, he would have written it in prose.
- You must pay attention to this Overrun, and use it, either by holding it, or by trampolining off it into the next line.
- Experiment and play around with lines ending in Overruns. Discover why they are over-run, and how this can inform your playing.

## What Overrun Lines Are Not

Overruns are never a single, unbroken thought that continues regardless of the verse form. They're not:

Noblest of men, woo't die? Shall I abide in this dull world?
Which in thy absence is no better than a sty?

—or—

What? Will the aspiring blood of Lancaster sink in the ground? I
thought it would have mounted.

Overruns are single thoughts, broken by (and attention paid to) the final word in one line that informs and fuels the further thought.

Noblest of men, woo't die? Shall I abide *(Overrun)*
In this dull world? Which in thy absence is *(Overrun)*
No better than a sty.

—and—

What? Will the aspiring blood of Lancaster *(Overrun)*
Sink in the ground? I thought it would have mounted.

Remember your Overruns, and don't get lazy. Use this new tool well, and it will reward you many times over.

# GOOD PHRASING AND BAD PHRASING = GOOD BREATH AND BAD BREATH!

Let's go very slowly with this section.

Good phrasing is probably the most important thing you will learn as you unlock the techniques of playing Shakespeare well. And I have to reiterate—like many other fundamental ingredients to good classical acting—good phrasing is overlooked too often in contemporary productions. Good phrasing will improve not only your classical work, but will give you an edge in contemporary productions, and in life.

I'll bet that most of you have never heard a director talk about the importance of phrasing something well. I know you've heard about objectives, intentions, actions, emotional recall, sense memory, and the usual litany, but let's add on something more interesting than all that—let's give you another tool.

Phrasing is one of the old-timers' skills, and, like observing Overruns and playing arguments, it's *almost* a relic of the past. But not quite—that's why you have me around.

Good acting is not about *you* feeling the emotions of your character (although some actors do this instinctively, or as a result of their experience, etc.), but about *making the audience feel*. Concern yourself only with moving your listeners, and instilling an emotional and intellectual response *in them*. One of the best ways to do this is to phrase your text well. A small technical (and artistic) thing like phrasing has a monumental impact on the audience.

In life, saying what you need to say with clarity, with conviction, with power, and with eloquence helps you in many ways. Regardless of your feelings or fears, if you understand what it is you need to say you will be understood. If you are understood, your words will evoke an intelligent and emotional response from the listener. If you are confused about what you want to say, if you hem, haw, stutter, or speak indirectly, you will not be understood, and your words will have no impact on the listener other than confusion, irritation, and perhaps even pity.

When you learn to phrase Shakespeare's text well, you may want to score it, as a musician scores his sheet music. A good flutist, for example, will score his papers with notes, reminding him where to breathe, where to take a little pause, where to soften his playing, and where to fire it up. It's the same with the beginning stages of your Shakespeare playing. Mark into your text *where* to breathe, how *long* a breath to take, where Shakespeare gives you *sharp little consonants*, and where he gives you *long, open, vowels*. Once you get used to good phrasing, you will no longer need notes: you will be able to pick up his text and just play.

Let me introduce you to good phrasing.

## What Is Phrasing?

Very simply, phrasing is *the way you express your thought in words*. It sounds easy enough, but good phrasing is sadly absent in the yap-yap of life. Say you have an idea, an image, or a thought to communicate to somebody else. In theory, you would shape that thought into words and speak it. But we have a lot of problems nowadays getting our thoughts across clearly and concisely; expressing larger images and ideas in a round and communicable way is pretty foreign to those of us born in the latter part of the twentieth century. We're used to clipped images, scrappy sound-bites, clap-trap advertising, and thus we've become mentally distracted and less familiar with simple, full, round thought, and its utterance.

The word "phrasing" is almost completely out of fashion, and, as a result, is kind of dusty—*perceived* as an erstwhile and rusty way of thinking. But I think good phrasing should be taught in school as part of the regular curriculum. It is as vital a part of functioning society as reading, writing, rudimentary math, basic physical well-being and a cultural perspective. And yet, in the education of tomorrow's leaders, thinkers, workers, and artists, the training of the spoken thought is as overlooked and shapeless as the whetting of original and dynamic minds. The family dinner and its attendant conversation has become a thing of the past, and social discourse is a dying art. Simply put: for a generation, *genuine communication* has become more and more difficult to find.

I'm almost off my soapbox, bear with me.

Good phrasing is *not about diction, nor is it about accent or vocal agility*. It's simpler, and yet somehow more difficult for today's actor to learn. Good phrasing is about one thing: *how to shape your thought and then speak it*. And while it is important in life, it is absolutely essential to good classical acting.

Despite the explosion of information exchange, we have a harder time really communicating well with each other today than ever before. Why? Because we are rarely taught how to speak, how to phrase a thought, how to get to the point when we need to, and how to explore an exchange of image or wit between each other.

Our primary obstacle to effective communication lies in the fact that communication is a skill like any other—cooking, dance, geometry, literature, or baseball—and must be taught in order to be learned. For example, when I was a drama student (waaaaay back in the mid-'90s), I worked in a coffee shop. And I'd hear people say things like the following all the time:

> "Uh, yeah...hi...how ya doing? You got any, like...um...gimme a...you know, a large...um, no...maybe, yeah okay. And, like, um...I think I'll take...can I have one of those?"

How can we follow what anyone else is saying when we hem and haw and umm ourselves into confusion? I would much rather hear this:

> "How you doing? Gimme a large coffee. And I'll take one of those."

Breathe, focus, and say what you need to say.

## What Does This Have To Do with Shakespeare?

When you play Shakespeare's text, you never have a chance to bumble and mutter and take pauses in the wrong places. You will ruin your speech and ruin the play.

With Shakespeare's text, *good phrasing has everything to do with breath*. You must breathe only *when* he allows you to, *where* he allows you to, for *as long* as he allows you to. You must be able to carry complex and inspiring images through your breath to the audience's ear. The shape and power of his words, the rhythm of his thought, and the flow of ideas and images are entirely connected to the actor's breath.

## So When Do I Breathe?

You breathe only when there is a significant change in thought. A good general rule of thumb is to breathe only on a note of punctuation.

Why?

When there is a note of punctuation, there is a change in thought, the furthering of an argument, a new idea, the building of an image, and so on.

Shakespeare's thoughts have an arc and shape uninterrupted by the actor's own peculiarities, breathing patterns, or nervousness. His thoughts and breath are shaped specifically. You must maintain the integrity of Shakespeare's rhythm by breathing only in the right places. If you muck up his rhythm by adding your own breaths and pauses, then his arguments, images, and actions lag—and your playing suffers. Unless, of course, there is a good dramatic reason to take a pause, which you must choose conscientiously. His text relies not on the actor's interpretation and individuality, but on honoring the thoughts themselves. Sometimes his text relies heavily on short, sharp intakes of breath when a character is excited, impassioned, quick in thought, terrified, etc. Sometimes his text relies on a strong first breath that arcs over an intricate idea or thought, and is uninterrupted through a complex set of images.

*Where* you breathe is as important as the *entirety of the text itself.*

## Breath, Breath, and More Breath

I want you to pay very close attention to these practices, and to take your time working through them until you fully understand how to phrase well.

I give you a piece of Friar Laurence's text from *Romeo and Juliet*, Act III, Scene 3. Read it out loud and breathe where I tell you. Go slow, and take your time with your breath; notice how it ends one thought and shapes the next. The column on the left contains breaths in the right places; the column on the right contains breaths in the wrong places (how a beginning actor might play the speech). Breathe through them both, and notice the difference:

| Good Phrasing = Good Breath | Bad Phrasing = Bad Breath |
|---|---|
| Hold thy desperate hand. (breathe) | Hold thy (breathe) desperate hand. |
| Art thou a man? (breathe) Thy form cries out thou art; (breathe) | Art thou a man? Thy form cries out (breathe) thou art; |
| Thy tears are womanish, thy wild acts denote | Thy tears are womanish, thy wild (breathe) acts denote |
| The unreasonable fury of a beast. (breathe) | The unreasonable fury of a beast. |
| Unseemly woman in a seeming man! (breathe) | Unseemly woman in (breathe) a seeming man! |
| And ill-seeming beast in seeming both! (breathe) | And ill-seeming beast in seeming (breathe) both! |
| Thou hast amazed me. (breathe) By my holy order, | Thou hast amazed me. By my (breathe) holy order, |
| I thought thy disposition better tempered. (breathe) | I thought thy disposition (breathe) better tempered. |
| Hast thou slain Tybalt? (breathe) Wilt thou slay thyself? (breathe) | Hast thou slain Tybalt? Wilt (breathe) thou slay thyself? |
| And slay the lady that in thy life lives, | And slay the lady that in (breathe) thy life lives, |
| By doing damned hate upon thyself? (breathe) | By doing damned hate (breathe) upon thyself? |
| Why railest thou on thy birth, the heaven, and earth? (breathe) | Why railest thou (breathe) on thy birth, the heaven, and earth? |
| Since birth and heaven and earth, all three do meet | Since birth and (breathe) heaven and earth, all three do meet |
| In thee at once; (breathe) which thou at once wouldst lose. | In thee at once; which thou (breathe) at once wouldst lose. |

Hear the difference? In the "Good Phrasing" column, you breathe only on a final note of punctuation. You keep your thought together within one breath and breathe only when there is a significant change in thought. Good phrasing is intimately connected to breathing only at the right place.

In the "Bad Phrasing" column, you breathe randomly, whenever you feel like it. The thought is interrupted, the image weakened, and you are unable to sustain your idea. Bad phrasing is intimately connected to random, undisciplined breathing.

Speak the text in the "Good Phrasing" column again, paying very close attention to how your breath ends one full thought and shapes the new one to come. Speak the text in the "Bad Phrasing" column again, and note the breaking and disconnecting of your thought.

Got it? Now let's move forward.

## What About Commas, Colons, Semi-colons, and Other Notes of Punctuation?

Remember our sketch guideline from the Prose chapter?

- A *period* is a full stop, or a full breath. It separates one full idea from a new one.
- A *comma* is a half-stop, or half-breath. It adds on to an existing idea, detaching momentarily from a full thought in order to build on it or to offer a new insight. It is also a mini-change in direction from one thought to another.
- A *colon* is a full stop, or full breath (slightly shorter than a period). You can use it to change direction entirely within the structure of one full thought, or to make a dramatic conclusion to that thought.
- A *semi-colon* is a half-stop, or half-breath (longer than a comma). You can use it to make a mini-conclusion before the full stop of a period.

You can break these "rules" when you get proficient. But right now, to help you shape your phrasing, let's hold ourselves to this sketch guideline.

A comma gives you the opportunity to catch a "cheat" breath. Later on, you will use this cheat breath, not only to refill your aching lungs, but to change direction within a thought, to further fuel a thought, to build on your thought, or to offer a new insight to your thought. But for this exercise, just get used to catching cheat breaths. At the moment, I don't mark any semi-colons—we'll come to those later.

> Hold thy desperate hand. (breathe)
> Art thou a man? (breathe) Thy form cries out thou art;
> Thy tears are womanish, (cheat) thy wild acts denote
> The unreasonable fury of a beast. (breathe)
> Unseemly woman in a seeming man! (breathe)
> And ill-beseeming beast in seeming both! (breathe)
> Thou hast amazed me. (breathe) By my holy order, (cheat)
> I thought thy disposition better tempered. (breathe)
> Hast thou slain Tybalt? (breathe) Wilt thou slay thyself?(breathe)
> And slay thy lady that in thy life lives, (cheat)
> By doing damned hate upon thyself? (breathe)
> Why railest thou on thy birth, (cheat) the heaven, (cheat) and earth? (breathe)
> Since birth and heaven and earth, (cheat) all three do meet
> In thee at once; which thou at once wouldst lose. (breathe)

No, you don't need all those cheat breaths. You don't need to breathe three times on the 12th line, for example: "Why railest thou on thy birth, (cheat) the heaven, (cheat) and earth? (breathe)" If you breathe all three times in this sentence, you chop it up too much.

When you have these kinds of lists, you want to keep them together, and build them up a semi-tone at a time on one breath.

Do it again. Use your full-stop breath to bring a full, conclusive stop to one thought. Breathe, and begin a new, fresh thought. Use your cheat breaths to fuel your continuing thought. Snatch in your breath, and use it to pour gasoline on the fire. Each time you take a cheat breath, use it to renew your thought and keep the sentence moving forward, with more energy:

> Hold thy desperate hand. (Conclude. Breathe. Start a new thought)
> Art thou a man? (Ask the question. Breathe. Start a new thought) Thy form cries out thou art;
> Thy tears are womanish, (cheat—more energy!) thy wild acts denote

The unreasonable fury of a beast. (Conclude. Breathe. New thought)
Unseemly woman in a seeming man! (Conclude. Breathe. New thought)
And ill-beseeming beast in seeming both! (Conclude. Breathe. New thought)
Thou hast amazed me. (Conclude. Breathe. New thought) By my holy order,
(cheat—more energy!)
I thought thy disposition better tempered. (Conclude. Breathe. New thought)
Hast thou slain Tybalt? (Ask the question. Breathe. New thought) Wilt thou slay
thyself? (Ask the question. Breathe. New thought)
And slay thy lady that in thy life lives, (cheat—more energy!)
By doing damned hate upon thyself? (Ask the question. Breathe. New thought)
Why railest thou on thy birth, (cheat—up a semi-tone—more energy!) the heaven,
(cheat—up a semi-tone—more energy!) and earth? (Ask the question. Breathe. New thought)
Since birth and heaven and earth, (cheat—more energy!) all three do meet
In thee at once; (Conclude) which thou at once wouldst lose.

You're beginning to phrase well. Now, let's try a second exercise—we can always rely on Mark Antony for good examples. Again, you should work slowly. First, I give you only your full-stop breaths. Breathe only on them. Our Friar Laurence speech was easy; his full thoughts didn't require all that much lung-power. With Mark Antony, you will need deeper breaths, and more control. I want you to begin to notice how to phrase a full and complete thought without your cheat breaths; later we'll play with cheats, and I'll teach you a little more about their use. You will have no trouble with your breathing in the first part of the speech, but the second part will stretch and exercise you. Push yourself. The more you practice broadening your thoughts over a full set of lungs, the easier it becomes.

O, pardon me, thou bleeding piece of earth,
That I am meek and gentle with these butchers! (Breathe!)
Thou art the ruins of the noblest man
That ever lived in the tide of times. (Breathe!)
Woe to the hand that shed this costly blood! (Breathe!)
Over thy wound now do I prophesy
(Which, like dumb mouths, do ope their ruby lips
To beg the voice and utterance of my tongue),
A curse shall light upon the limbs of men; (Breathe!)

Domestic fury and fierce civil strife
Shall cumber all the parts of Italy; (Breathe!)
Blood and destruction shall be so in use
And dreadful objects so familiar
That mothers shall but smile when they behold
Their infants quartered with the hands of war,
All pity choked with custom of fell deeds; (Breathe!)
And Caesar' spirit, ranging for revenge,
With Ate by his side come hot from hell,
Shall in these confines with a monarch's voice
Cry 'Havoc!' and let slip the dogs of war,
That this foul deed shall smell above the earth
With carrion men, groaning for burial. (Breathe, if you haven't passed out yet!)

## Please Let Me Take a Cheat Breath!

Feel the lungpower and discipline you need to get through a long, complex image or thought on one full breath? Now you're shaping good phrasing.

Is that all you get? A few, paltry breaths on which to play all these thoughts? Not necessarily, but I want you to exercise your lungs and carry long thoughts on a single breath. Practice this again and again. Get used to the strength and effort it takes.

Now, let's be a little more realistic.

This time, I give you your cheat breaths. Use these quick, half-breaths to fuel your further thought. Use your breath to reenergize, or to further develop your image. Remember, a cheat breath is just that—a quiet, quick snatch of breath to keep you going over the sustained speech. You won't need them all, but practice taking them in anyway.

O, (cheat) pardon me, (cheat) thou bleeding piece of earth, (cheat)
That I am meek and gentle with these butchers! (breathe)
Thou art the ruins of the noblest man
That ever lived in the tide of times. (breathe)
Woe to the hand that shed this costly blood! (breathe)
Over thy wound now do I prophesy
(Which, (cheat) like dumb mouths, (cheat) do ope their ruby lips

To beg the voice and utterance of my tongue), (cheat)
A curse shall light upon the limbs of men; (breathe)
Domestic fury and fierce civil strife
Shall cumber all the parts of Italy; (breathe)
Blood and destruction shall be so in use
And dreadful objects so familiar
That mothers shall but smile when they behold
Their infants quartered with the hands of war, (cheat)
All pity choked with custom of fell deeds; (breathe)
And Caesar' spirit, (cheat) ranging for revenge, (cheat)
With Ate by his side come hot from hell, (cheat)
Shall in these confines with a monarch's voice
Cry 'Havoc!' and let slip the dogs of war, (cheat)
That this foul deed shall smell above the earth
With carrion men, (cheat) groaning for burial. (exhale)

See, it's not so bad when you can sneak a breath in between the larger thoughts. What I want you to learn, as you practice these breathing exercises over and over again, is to really allow your deeper breaths to shape your larger thought. Sneak in a cheat breath on a comma (when there is a significant mini-pause), or when you absolutely need a fresh breath.

## "Shifting Gears" Exercise

When you shift gears in your car, the engine kicks itself into a different function, a higher cycle, and a renewed effort. It reboots itself to use more strength to move faster, or less strength to move more slowly; it takes on a new task. And you notice the sound of your engine changing with its function; its pitch and tone changes. Your car moves differently, responds differently to each new gear.

That's what you can do with your full breaths and cheat breaths. Shifting gears in your car is a good image to use for phrasing. With your change in thought (each comma, period, semi-colon, colon, or slash mark) comes a change in tone. And just as you shift gears in a car to kick yourself forward or to slow down, you use these notes of punctuation to change direction and refuel your speech.

Let's work a bit more with the commas. I give you the same speech again, but this time I want you to use the cheat-commas to really

- change direction,
- shift gears,
- use a new intonation,
- change pitch,
- fire through,
- slow down,
- bite into,
- lighten up,
- hammer home,
- suggest, or
- refuel each new thought.

At the moment, don't worry about *how* you speak each new thought, just as long as it's *different* from your previous thought. Shout, scream, lighten, gently dab, refuel each new thought—whatever. Just make sure your new thought is different from your old one.

- For every comma cheat breath: a slight change, keeping the thought moving forward.
- For every full stop breath: a completely new direction and a totally new intonation.

And for the sake of this exercise, we'll consider your semi-colons as full stops. Play around with pitch, use your highest, lowest, and everything-in-between tones. Have fun with it.

O, (change direction!) pardon me, (shift gears!) thou bleeding piece of earth,
    (change direction and fuel)
That I am meek and gentle with these butchers! (Breathe! Completely new tone)
Thou art the ruins of the noblest man
That ever lived in the tide of times. (Breathe! Completely new tone)
Woe to the hand that shed this costly blood! (Breathe! Completely new tone)
Over thy wound now do I prophesy
(Which, (change direction! It's a sub-thought) like dumb mouths, (change direction) do
ope their ruby lips

To beg the voice and utterance of my tongue), (change direction! continue your prophesy, use the same tone you left "now do I prophesy" on)

A curse shall light upon the limbs of men; (breathe! Really fuel your curse! Higher gear)

Domestic fury and fierce civil strife

Shall cumber all the parts of Italy; (breathe! Refuel your curse! Higher gear)

Blood and destruction shall be so in use

And dreadful objects so familiar

That mothers shall but smile when they behold (hold this Overrun, and then continue on the same breath)

Their infants quartered with the hands of war, (quick cheat and shift gears)

All pity choked with custom of fell deeds; (breathe! Completely new, low tone)

And Caesar' spirit, (change direction) ranging for revenge, (shift gears)

With Ate by his side come hot from hell, (change direction and really fuel this next part)

Shall in these confines with a monarch's voice

Cry 'Havoc!' and let slip the dogs of war, (shift gears lower, preparing for conclusion)

That this foul deed shall smell above the earth

With carrion men, (new, final thought) groaning for burial.

Good. Notice how you reach for your full breath to stretch a long, complex thought, and how you use your cheat breath to kick a new gear and change direction on a mini-thought. Here are Antony's main thoughts:

- Antony *begs* Caesar's pardon for being so "meek and gentle with these butchers."
- Antony *reassures* Caesar's corpse that he is the "ruins of the noblest man/That ever lived in the tide of times."
- Antony *threatens* the hand that shed Caesar's blood.
- Antony *prophesies* over Caesar's bloody wounds.
- Antony *discovers* that Caesar's stab wounds are like "dumb mouths" which open "their ruby lips/To beg the voice and utterance" of his tongue.
- Antony *proclaims* a curse upon "the limbs of men."
- Antony *describes* and *tastes* this curse: "Domestic fury and fierce civil strife/Shall cumber all the parts of Italy."
- Antony *bathes in* his curse. There will be "blood and destruction," "dreadful objects so familiar" (swords, machines of

war), that mothers will smile when they see their infants chopped up with the hands of war.

- Antony *relishes* his curse. "All pity choked with custom of fell deeds."
- Antony *is completely taken over* by his curse. Caesar's spirit will come hot from hell, looking for revenge, with Ate (goddess of mischief) by his side.
- Antony *exalts* in his curse. "Shall in these confines with a monarch's voice/Cry 'Havoc!' and let slip the dogs of war."
- Antony *comes back* to Caesar's murder: "this foul deed shall smell above the earth/With carrion men, groaning for burial."

Allow each little part of Antony's speech to be informed by a change in direction, a new intonation, and a fresh breath. Every thought is new, and builds on its previous thought. Once you finish one thought—it's gone; it's dead; you never have to go back to it. So use a completely new tone for each new thought.

In the end, how you play this speech is up to you and your director. But these basic rules of good phrasing will help unlock the speech's potential. Below, I give you a few suggestions for each new thought and each new breath. I know it's a paltry sketch compared with what you can do if you really use your imagination and good phrasing—along with the character's fury—but notice how your full-stop breath *concludes*, and how your cheat breath stokes the fire and keeps the speech moving forward. Don't allow your cheat breath to slow you down or to drop your energy, but keep it moving forward, building, blazing.

O, (stay on this "O" for a while. Use it to take in the sight of Caesar's dead body, taste his death, realize your situation, and stoke the fire of rage inside your belly. Now change direction) pardon me, (mean it. Beg Caesar's pardon. Now shift gears) thou bleeding piece of earth, (allow a momentary sorrow. For the first time, you see your leader as a piece of meat. Now change direction)

That I am meek and gentle with these butchers! (Full fury at your own impotence! You've been too gentle. Explode on *"these butchers!"* Breathe. Completely new tone)

Thou art the ruins of the noblest man

That ever lived in the tide of times. (Full realization, and full sorrow. The man you loved and honored above all others is now a rotting corpse, a "ruins." You pay tribute to his nobility. Breathe! Completely new tone)

Woe to the hand that shed this costly blood! (Real threat. Brace yourself for
revenge. Breathe! Completely new tone)

Over thy wound now do I prophesy (make it a *real* prophecy. Take in his wound, and
use it as a kind of Bible to swear on.)

(Which, (realize what these wounds are like. Change direction) like dumb mouths, (see
the image—change direction) do ope their ruby lips

To beg the voice and utterance of my tongue), (strong image. Use it. Caesar's
wounds are like silent mouths, opening their ruby lips to beg a curse from Antony's tongue.
Realize this image. Change direction)

A curse shall light upon the limbs of men; (breathe! Really fuel your curse!)

Domestic fury and fierce civil strife

Shall cumber all the parts of Italy; (breathe! Pour gasoline on the fire of your curse!
Enjoy the following images of your curse. Relish the idea that your revenge will have its day!
Change tone)

Blood and destruction shall be so in use

And dreadful objects so familiar

That mothers shall but smile when they behold

Their infants quartered with the hands of war, (small mini-conclusion. Bounce,
choking to)

All pity choked with custom of fell deeds; (breathe! Now come to Caesar's spirit.
Savor it, wish for it, enjoy it! Completely new tone)

And Caesar' spirit, (celebrate this whole new image. Threaten the audience with it, taste it,
warn the world, enjoy this potential destruction! Change direction) ranging for
revenge, (use those two "r"s to rev you up. Shift gears)

With Ate by his side come hot from hell, (refuel and let the fire burn! Enjoy a
vengeful madness! Let loose! Love the thought of Caesar and Ate crawling up from hell to
wreak revenge on their enemies! Change direction)

Shall in these confines with a monarch's voice

Cry 'Havoc!' and let slip the dogs of war, (explode on 'Havoc!' Love all this! Adore
those dogs of war, and shift gears; winding down, and coming back to earth)

That this foul deed shall smell above the earth

With carrion men, (new, final thought which brings you sorrow and disgust) groaning
for burial.

## Mixing Overruns and Phrasing

Salisbury from *Henry the Sixth, Part Two* (Act III, Scene 3) does-
n't give you a real lung-stretcher, but he gives you a good exam-

ple of shifting gears with punctuation and with Overruns. Here, you use your Overruns in the same way as punctuation. As always, read it out loud once before I give you your cheat breaths and changes in direction. Note for yourself where there is a change in thought and a fresh intake of breath:

> Sirs, stand apart. The king shall know your mind.
> Dread lord, the commons send you word by me,
> Unless Lord Suffolk straight be done to death
> Or banished fair England's territories,
> They will by violence tear from him your palace
> And torture him with grievous ling'ring death.
> They say, by him the good Duke Humphrey died;
> They say, in him they fear your highness' death;
> And mere instinct of love and loyalty—
> Free from a stubborn opposite intent,
> As being thought to contradict your liking—
> Makes them thus forward in his banishment.
> They say, in care of your most royal person,
> That if your highness should intent to sleep
> And charge that no man should disturb your rest
> In pain of your dislike or pain of death,
> Yet, notwithstanding such a strait edict,
> Were there a serpent seen with forked tongue
> That slily glided towards your majesty,
> It were but necessary you were waked,
> Lest, being suffered in that harmful slumber,
> The mortal worm might make the sleep eternal.
> And therefore do they cry, though you forbid,
> That they will guard you, whe'r you will or no,
> From such fell serpents as false Suffolk is;
> With whose envenomed and fatal sting
> Your loving uncle, twenty times his worth,
> They say is shamefully bereft of life.

The stakes in this speech are high, so blaze through it as though life and death are on the line. Suffolk and Warwick have entered the presence of the King with their weapons drawn.

Salisbury is trying to diffuse the situation, and warn the King of his impending danger. He is focused and serious, counseling Henry of the danger of this snake, Suffolk. Make your points as sharply and clearly as a dagger's edge. I give you your thoughts in this section, and then your breaths in the next section. Use your breath to shape these thoughts well—don't get flabby!

Sirs (first thought), stand apart (second thought). The king shall know
your mind. (New thought)
(To the King, and those in your immediate surroundings)
Dread lord, (new thought) the commons send you word by me, (new thought)
Unless Lord Suffolk straight be done to death (new thought/Overrun)
Or banished fair England's territories, (new thought)
They will by violence tear from him your palace (new thought/Overrun)
And torture him with grievous ling'ring death. (New thought)
They say, (new thought) by him the good Duke Humphrey died; (new thought)
They say, (new thought) in him they fear your highness' death; (new thought)
And mere instinct of love and loyalty—(new thought)
Free from a stubborn opposite intent, (new thought, but a sub-thought of the above)
As being thought to contradict your liking—(new thought, still a sub-thought)
Makes them thus forward in his banishment. (New thought)
They say, (new thought) in care of your most royal person, (new thought)
That if your highness should intent to sleep (new thought/Overrun)
And charge that no man should disturb your rest (new thought/Overrun)
In pain of your dislike or pain of death, (new thought)
Yet, (new thought) notwithstanding such a strait edict, (new thought)
Were there a serpent seen with forked tongue (new thought/Overrun)
That slily glided towards your majesty, (new thought)
It were but necessary you were waked, (new thought)
Lest, (new thought) being suffered in that harmful slumber, (new thought)
The mortal worm might make the sleep eternal. (New thought)
And therefore do they cry, (new thought) though you forbid, (new thought)
That they will guard you, (new thought) whe'r you will or no, (new thought)
From such fell serpents as false Suffolk is; (new thought)
With whose envenomed and fatal sting (new thought/Overrun)
Your loving uncle, (new thought) twenty times his worth, (new thought)
They say is shamefully bereft of life. (New thought)

Now you have all your fresh, new thoughts. Yes, some thoughts are sub-thoughts, and some thoughts are continuations of their previous thoughts (Overruns), but for the sake of this exercise:

- don't worry too much about meter and rhythm
- take a pause with each new thought
- breath anew on each new thought
- make each new thought different from the one before
- use a new intonation on each thought

Above all, *discover* each new thought. Imagine you have never seen or heard this speech before, and take your time relishing and discovering your next lines. Once you have practiced this a few times, then move on to the next section. I give you your cheat breaths, and your full breaths. Change direction with each breath. Take your time and explore:

Sirs, (cheat) stand apart. (Breathe) The king shall know your mind. (Breathe)

Dread lord, (cheat) the commons send you word by me, (cheat)

Unless Lord Suffolk straight be done to death (hold it! New idea next line)

Or banished fair England's territories, (cheat)

They will by violence tear from him your palace (hold it! New idea next line)

And torture him with grievous ling'ring death. (Breathe)

They say, (cheat) by him the good Duke Humphrey died; (breathe)

They say, (cheat) in him they fear your highness' death; (breathe)

And mere instinct of love and loyalty—(new idea coming up—shift gears)

Free from a stubborn opposite intent, (cheat)

As being thought to contradict your liking—(new idea coming up—shift gears)

Makes them thus forward in his banishment. (Breathe)

They say, (cheat) in care of your most royal person, (cheat)

That if your highness should intent to sleep (hold it! New idea next line)

And charge that no man should disturb your rest (hold it! New idea next line)

In pain of your dislike or pain of death, (cheat)

Yet, (cheat) notwithstanding such a strait edict, (cheat)

Were there a serpent seen with forked tongue (hold it! New idea next line)

That slily glided towards your majesty, (cheat)

It were but necessary you were waked, (cheat)

Lest, (cheat) being suffered in that harmful slumber, (cheat)

The mortal worm might make the sleep eternal. (Breathe)
And therefore do they cry, (cheat) though you forbid, (cheat)
That they will guard you, (cheat) whe'r you will or no, (cheat)
From such fell serpents as false Suffolk is; (breathe)
With whose envenomed and fatal sting (hold it! New idea next line)
Your loving uncle, (cheat) twenty times his worth, (cheat)
They say is shamefully bereft of life.

## But All in All, It's All up to You

These exercises are for you to use to cut your teeth. When you breathe life into your speech, you certainly don't need to cheat after *every* comma, or take a good, long, deep breath after *every* full stop. But do pay attention to these two speeches we've looked at. What I want to get out of you is this:

- Notice your commas. Use them to refuel you and to change direction.
- Notice your full stops. Use them to end one train of thought, breathe, and start a new train of thought.
- Really try and shift gears with each new note of punctuation.
- And, above all, *don't breathe or pause when you have no punctuation* (except for your Overruns). *Keep all thoughts, enveloped by punctuation, together. Breathe only when you have your cheats or your full stops.*

## Do I Need To Take *All* Those Cheat Breaths?

Of course not. It doesn't matter if you decide not to breathe on a cheat comma, as long as you *use the comma to change direction.* In fact, taking *every* cheat available is not a good idea. It will chop up your speech too much. *You* choose when you want to breathe. *You* decide how to refuel, as long as it is on a note of punctuation and maintains the integrity of good phrasing. Be sensitive to Shakespeare's text. Listen closely to its rhythm, to its urgency or slow pace, and make your choices.

For example, you may decide to play the last part of Antony's speech on a single breath. And if you have the lungs for it, it can work beautifully—as long as you keep stoking the fire through each comma. Try it on a single breath now, but use the commas to push Antony's fury forward, biting into each new thought, building and building.

Fill up your lungs, and go:

> And Caesar's spirit, ranging for revenge,
> With Ate by his side come hot from hell,
> Shall in these confines with a monarch's voice
> Cry 'Havoc!' and let slip the dogs of war,
> That this foul deed shall smell above the earth
> With carrion men, groaning for burial.

Pretty tough to get it all out on one breath, but not impossible. Practice and experiment.

## Pounding It into Your Skull Until You're Sick of Me

Okay, a couple more examples just to carve everything into your brain permanently. Same as before: read it over first to yourself, carefully. I'll give you an example of bad phrasing, which no one ever wants to hear. Then, good phrasing. Here, Tullus Aufidius gives us his homoerotic speech from *Coriolanus*, Act IV, Scene 5:

> O Marcius, Marcius!
> Each word thou hast spoke hath weeded from my heart
> A root of ancient envy. If Jupiter
> Should from yond cloud speak divine things,
> And say 'Tis true,' I'd not believe them more
> Than thee, all-noble Marcius. Let me twine
> Mine arms about thy body, whereagainst
> My grained ash an hundred times hath broke,
> And scarr'd the moon with splinters. Here I clip
> The anvil of my sword, and do contest
> As hotly and as nobly with thy love
> As ever in ambitious strength I did
> Content against thy valor. Know thou first,
> I loved the maid I married; never man
> Sighed truer breath. But that I see thee here,

Thou noble thing, more dances my rapt heart
Than when I first my wedded mistress saw
Bestride my threshold. Why, thou Mars, I tell thee,
We have a power on foot; and I had purpose
Once more to hew thy target from thy brawn,
Or lose mine arm for't. Thou hast beat me out
Twelve several time, and I have nightly since
Dreamt of encounters 'twixt thyself and me.
We have been down together in my sleep,
Unbuckling helms, fisting each other's throat,
And waked half dead with nothing. Worthy Marcius,
Had we no other quarrel else to Rome, but that
Thou art thence banished, we would muster all
From twelve to seventy, and, pouring war
Into the bowels of ungrateful Rome,
Like a bold flood o'erbeat. O, come, go in,
And take our friendly senators by th' hands,
Who now are here, taking their leave of me,
Who am prepared against your territories,
Though not for Rome itself.

## Bad Phrasing

Try this breathing. Notice how poorly structured it is. Listen to how taking breaths in the wrong places ruins the flow of thought. If I ever hear you do this, I'll hunt you down:

O (breathe) Marcius, Marcius!
Each word thou hast spoke hath (cheat) weeded from my heart
A root of ancient envy. If (breathe) Jupiter
Should from yond (cheat) cloud speak divine things,
And say 'Tis true,' I'd not believe (cheat) them more
Than thee, all-noble (cheat) Marcius. Let me twine
Mine arms (breathe) about thy body, whereagainst
My grained ash an hundred (cheat) times hath broke,
And scarr'd the moon (cheat) with splinters. Here I clip
The anvil of my sword, and do contest

As hotly (breathe) and as nobly with thy love
As ever in (cheat) ambitious strength I did
Content against thy (cheat) valor. Know thou first,
I loved (breathe) the maid I married; never man
Sighed truer breath. But that I see thee here,
Thou noble thing, more (cheat) dances my rapt heart
Than when I first my wedded mistress saw
Bestride my threshold. Why, thou Mars, I tell thee,
We have a (breathe) power on foot; and I had purpose
Once more to hew thy target (cheat) from thy brawn,
Or lose mine arm for't. Thou hast beat me out
Twelve several time, and I have nightly (cheat) since
Dreamt of encounters 'twixt thyself and me.
We have been down together in my sleep,
Unbuckling (breathe) helms, fisting each other's throat,
And waked half dead with nothing. Worthy (cheat) Marcius,
Had we no other quarrel else to Rome, but that
Thou art thence (breathe) banished, we would muster all
From twelve to seventy, and, pouring (cheat) war
Into the bowels of ungrateful Rome,
Like a bold (cheat) flood o'erbeat. O, come, go in,
And take our friendly senators by th' hands,
Who now (breathe) are here, taking their leave of me,
Who am prepared against your territories,
Though not (cheat) for Rome itself.

Ugly, ugly, ugly. Tuneless, shapeless, breathless. That's what undisciplined and unskilled actors sound like.

Below, I give you a suggestion. I try to keep the arc and shape of Shakespeare's thoughts together, and to maintain the flow of images by breathing only when there is a reason to. You may not shape this speech the same way. That's fine; but do breathe only when there is time and reason to.

Listen:

O Marcius, (beat—taste the word) Marcius!
Each word thou hast spoke hath weeded from my heart (beat)
A root of ancient envy. (Breathe) If Jupiter (trampoline)

Should from yond cloud speak divine things, (cheat)
And say 'Tis true,' (beat) I'd not believe them more (trampoline)
Than thee, (beat—taste the phrase) all-noble Marcius. (Breathe) Let me twine
    (trampoline)
Mine arms about thy body, (cheat and *fuel*) whereagainst
My grained ash an hundred times hath broke,
And scarred the moon with splinters. (Breathe) Here I clip (trampoline)
The anvil of my sword, (beat) and do contest (trampoline)
As hotly and as nobly with thy love (trampoline)
As ever in ambitious strength I did (beat)
Content against thy valor. (Breathe) Know thou first, (beat)
I loved the maid I married; (cheat and beat) never man (trampoline)
Sighed truer breath. (Breathe) But that I see thee here, (beat and *fuel*)
Thou noble thing, (beat) more dances my rapt heart (trampoline)
Than when I first my wedded mistress saw (beat)
Bestride my threshold. (Breathe) Why, (cheat and *really fuel*) thou Mars,
    (cheat) I tell thee,
We have a power on foot; (let it linger a short beat) and I had purpose (trampoline)
Once more to hew thy target from thy brawn, (cheat and fuel)
Or lose mine arm for't. (Breathe) Thou hast beat me out (beat...relish the next word)
Twelve several time, (beat) and I have nightly since (beat...confess)
Dreamt of encounters 'twixt thyself and me. (Breathe)
We have been down together in my sleep, (fuel)
Unbuckling helms, (fuel *again*) fisting each other's throat, (*really* fuel)
And waked half dead with nothing. (Breathe...taste) Worthy Marcius, (cheat)
Had we no other quarrel else to Rome, (fuel) but that (trampoline)
Thou art thence banished, (fuel) we would muster all (trampoline)
From twelve to seventy, (beat) and, (fuel) pouring war (trampoline—*really fuel!*)
Into the bowels of ungrateful Rome, (*burn!*)
Like a bold flood o'erbeat. (Breathe...collect yourself) O, (beat) come, go in,
And take our friendly senators by th' hands,
Who now are here, (cheat...suggest) taking their leave of me, (cheat)
Who am prepared against your territories,
Though not for Rome itself.

Hear the difference? Good phrasing helps shape your performance more than any other tool you may learn.

## Sex Breath

Shakespeare wasn't a Puritan, so I'm not going to be coy with these examples. This stuff is just too fascinating to pussyfoot around.

I told you a few pages ago that Aufidius's speech was homo-erotic. Therefore, you have to phrase it to play up its sexiness. (Don't worry, there's a female orgasm in a couple of pages, too.) I told you Shakespeare's pen was finely tuned to a huge breadth of human experience—not just the war, love, court stuff—but the breath of sex, too.

Listen:

Aufidius meets his enemy, Coriolanus, for the first time. He meets his match—the only man who can *best* him, and the only man who can *help* him. Listen to not only the obvious, written sexual images, but to the breath and pulsing underneath the text:

> O Marcius, Marcius!

The very first words that come out of Aufidius's mouth are open, slow, sensual sounds. Breathe through the "O" with an open, slow throat. Taste the name Marcius's both times. Notice the seductive hissing "mm" "ahr" "sh" and "sss." This introduces the whole speech, so use it.

> Let me twine
> Mine arms about thy body, whereagainst
> My grained ash an hundred times hath broke,
> And scarr'd the moon with splinters.

Except for "whereagainst," every word has only one or two syllables. Eat these sounds and use them with the phrase's purposeful, forward-moving, heart-strong rhythm. Play it all on *one breath*, and notice how the whole phrase falls out of the mouth. Notice how everything pops out, *lifting* up "broke," and *falling* on the repetition of "s" in "scarr'd" and "splinters," which fall perfectly on the iambic beat. The phrase *sets* Aufidius, and makes his heart beat more quickly, and more passionately.

> Know thou first,
> I loved the maid I married; never man
> Sighed truer breath. But that I see thee here,
> Thou noble thing, more dances my rapt heart
> Than when I first my wedded mistress saw
> Bestride my threshold. Why, thou Mars

The written image is obviously sexual. But listen more closely: "Know thou" to "truer breath" is quick-clipped, straight facts, a little oath to get the stuff about his wife *out of the way* before moving in for the sex. Now listen to how "But that I see thee here," slows everything down as he takes in Coriolanus's presence again. Those "eee" sounds in "see," "thee," and "here" *decelerate* you as you get ready to pounce on, or taste *"Thou noble thing."* These three words are celebratory and sensuous. "More dances" to "threshold" speeds you right up again, matching Aufidius's heartbeat. Listen to how many hissing, or seductive "sss" and "sh" sounds you have in that little phrase. They're wooing, or trying-to-soothe cooing sounds. Use them as such. Next, discover or rejoice in the slow, admiring, sexy, "thou Mars."

> and I have nightly since
> Dreamt of encounters 'twixt thyself and me.
> We have been down together in my sleep,
> Unbuckling helms, fisting each other's throat,
> And waked half dead with nothing. Worthy Marcius

Well, now. Aufidius *corners* and *locks* onto Coriolanus with "and I have nightly since/Dreamt of encounters 'twixt thyself and me." And next comes the part where you really have to *choose your breaths carefully*, using your comma rules, because this goes *really fast* and with *real sexual intensity*. You have one, long *phrase-thrust* with "We have been down together in my sleep," and a fast cheat breath. Race through the first three words. You really don't have much in the phrase until the word "down," which hits the first strong beat as Aufidius *pushes*, and then catches a fast breath. You have a *short thrust* with "Unbuckling helms," and another snatch breath. You have *another thrust*, more intense, with "fisting each other's throat" and then a longer, drawing-in cheat breath before your *orgasm* on "And waked half dead with nothing." Now, *a full stop*. You take a full breath to recover before the *post-climactic* "Worthy Marcius" with those softer, sensuous sounds.

And listen to the choice of words: "down together in my sleep," "unbuckling" and "fisting."

Interesting? I think so. And guess what. You've just combined phrasing with rhythm.

Next up, we have Juliet, with her own orgasm. This is a fantastic example of open breath and phrasing from *Romeo and Juliet*, Act III, Scene 2:

Gallop apace, you fiery-footed steeds,
Towards Phoebus' lodging: such a wagoner
As Phaethon would whip you to the west,
And bring in cloudy night immediately.
Spread thy close curtain, love-performing night,
That runaway's eyes may wink and Romeo
Leap to these arms, untalk'd of and unseen.
Lovers can see to do their amorous rites
By their own beauties; or, if love be blind,
It best agrees with night. Come, civil night,
And learn me how to lose a winning match,
Play'd for a pair of stainless maidenhoods:
Hood my unmann'd blood, bating in my cheeks,
With thy black mantle; till strange love, grown bold,
Come, night; come, Romeo; come, thou day in night;
For thou wilt lie upon the wings of night
Whiter than new snow on a raven's back.
Come, gentle night, come, loving, black-brow'd night,
Give me my Romeo; and, when he shall die,
Take him and cut him out in little stars,
And he will make the face of heaven so fine
That all the world will be in love with night
O, I have bought the mansion of a love,
But not possess'd it, and, though I am sold,
Not yet enjoy'd: so tedious is this day
As is the night before some festival

> To an impatient child that hath new robes
> And may not wear them. O, here comes my nurse,
> And she brings news; and every tongue that speaks
> But Romeo's name speaks heavenly eloquence.

This one is really fun. Tune in your ears because your orgasm is perfectly shaped.

First, you have:

> Gallop apace, you fiery-footed steeds,
> Towards Phoebus' lodging: such a wagoner
> As Phaethon would whip you to the west,
> And bring in cloudy night immediately.
> Spread thy close curtain, love-performing night,
> That runaway's eyes may wink and Romeo
> Leap to these arms, untalk'd of and unseen.

Hungry, overpowering *excitement* in the first four lines. The speech starts on a strong, stressed beat with the *demanding,* rhythmic sound of *gallupupace*. Really bite into this noise, and notice how it propels you forward. Then she jumps right into "f" "f" "f" "f" and "w" "w" "w" with "fiery-footed," "Phoebus," "wagoner," "Phaethon," "would," "whip," "west." Those are *incredibly fast, eager* sounds. Phrase it like this:

*Go, go, go!!!*     Gallop apace, you fiery-footed steeds,
                           Towards Phoebus' lodging: (breathe. And *go, go, go!!!*)
                                       such a wagoner
                           As Phaethon would whip you to the west,

It flies so fast, your heart races—as only a fourteen-year-old girl's can. And then Juliet concludes with the *demanding* "gimme" of:

> And bring in cloudy night immediately.

You have to slow down with this line, because the consonants and vowels force you to. She demands the word "immediately." And then the more paced, slower:

Spread thy close curtain, love-performing night,

with the obvious sexual imagery. Note not only the reference in "Spread thy close curtain," but the opening "rrreeaahhh" in "spread" and those two coy "c" "c" sounds that follow it. And then:

Come, civil night,

with the *demand,* "Come." This word comes right after "Lovers can see to do their amorous rites/By their own beauties; or, if love be blind,/It best agrees with night." which is delicate, reflective, and—above all—justifying. Juliet *justifies* her sexual hunger with the phrase, using those little "b" sounds, and then decides, hungrily, "Come." Then she softens it up (perhaps surprised at her own sexual passion) with the word "civil" and the soft whisper of the sounds "civil night." Think I'm going too far with the "come"? Just wait a few more phrases.

And learn me how to lose a winning match,
Play'd for a pair of stainless maidenhoods:
Hood my unmann'd blood, bating in my cheeks,
With thy black mantle; till strange love, grown bold,

In-your-face sexual imagery. Notice how "stainless maidenhoods" slows the phrase down as she tastes the sounds before the one-or-two syllable "Hood my unmann'd blood, bating in my cheeks,/With thy black mantle." Strong Saxon sounds—primal, strong, open. She steels herself, pouncing on the word, "*bold*" and then:

Come, night; come, Romeo; come, thou day in night;

Three 'come's on one line. Powerful, hungry, orgasmic sounds and rhythm. Phrase it like this:

Demand: Come, night; (Breathe. Plead) come, Romeo; (open up those vowels and taste the "o" "mmm" "eeeo" with real sexual hunger. Now demand) come, (cheat breath. Admire and praise with) thou day in night;

This is *really* strong stuff. Now, after that raw, open, sexual phrase you have the hyper-romantic:

> For thou wilt lie upon the wings of night
> Whiter than new snow on a raven's back.

which is so pretty it's almost sorrowful. You still have one or two syllables in each word here, so Juliet is still in a primal place. She just softens her hunger up a moment with this desperately romantic phrase before:

> Come, gentle night, come, loving, black-brow'd night,
> Give me my Romeo;

The *complete orgasm* phrase.

You have two more hungry "comes" again followed by a "loving." The first "come" is the strongest, followed by the softening "gentle night." Then, the opening, joyous "come" and "loving" and then hungry "black-brow'd night." Phrase it like this:

> *Come,* (cheat) gentle night, (longer cheat) *come,* (cheat) *loving,* (cheat)
> *black-brow'd night* (cheat)

Lots of panting here, as Juliet's breathing gets shorter and more gasping. Notice how you have a bit more time between the first "come" and the second. Then, only one breath between the second "come" and "loving." One *tiny* breath after "loving," then *no breath at all* in the ravenous "black-brow'd night" as Juliet is a split-second away from orgasm.

Then, the exploding orgasm on:

> Give me my Romeo;

with those open, strong vowels "eeee" "eye" and "oh" "eeee" "oh." Every word is important, and the rhythm strong and even. Note the three sensuous "mmmm"s. Go over the top with it right now:

> *Give meee mmyyyy Roommmeeeeooooohhhh!!!*

Juliet discovers this rhythm, these vowels, these breaths, for the first time. It's a first-time, open, youthful, joyous orgasm. But wait, you have a semi-colon right after. Enough time to collect *some* breath and change direction—but not enough time to get over what happened before. You have the post-orgasmic, giddy, body-on-fire, lush and laughing:

> and, when he shall die,
> Take him and cut him out in little stars,
> And he will make the face of heaven so fine
> That all the world will be in love with night

which comes down, down, down, and is full of fantasy and joy and discovery.

And don't forget the play on words there, "when he shall die." Not only foreshadowing the play, but "die" meaning orgasm. The French call it "petit mort" or "little death." So, not only when Romeo dies, but when he orgasms, explode him into the sky, "take him and cut him out in little stars."

There's more.

Now Juliet realizes it's just a daydream. She comes back to reality, and her orgasmic excitement turns to impatience and petulance—she wants the real thing, not the fantasy.

> O, I have bought the mansion of a love,
> But not possess'd it, and, though I am sold,
> Not yet enjoy'd: so tedious is this day
> As is the night before some festival
> To an impatient child that hath new robes
> And may not wear them.

Listen to the petulant, wanting words: "bought," "possess'd it," "sold," "enjoy'd," "tedious," "impatient," "child."

A *well-shaped*, and *full* female orgasm.

Think of Audifius's sex breath: shorter, more thrusting, more to the point. He relishes a bit in the beginning, locks onto his target, and then uses stronger, quicker consonants. Juliet is more excited, and more open. She uses wider vowels mixed with strong consonants. She takes more time to get to her climax, but the result is stronger and more explosive, with highly romantic post-orgasmic sentiments.

## Am I Reading Too Much into It?

No.

It's all there, if you open your ears and really get in synch with the rhythm, vowels, consonants, and phrasing. You don't need to burden yourself with finding out what Juliet's objective is, or what her actions are. It's all right there. She's *hungry* for a blissful, new experience—and she has one. Aufidius wants to *seduce* Coriolanus into a course of action, and he does. Simple.

So, do you *play* the sex stuff? Well, that's up to you and your director. But it's underneath and all over the text. I would use it subtly, underscoring, and suggesting. But I'd also play *moments* of it blatantly. It depends on what you want for the scene.

## Rumbling and Squeaking

Before we finish off our phrasing work, I want to give you a very important exercise. This will help you change pitch and tone; it'll help you musically, though I hesitate to use the word. I don't want you to start singing Shakespeare's text like turn-of-the-century actors did. And believe me, they did. Try to find an old recording of Sarah Bernhardt playing "To be or not to be"—you'd think she was in the opera. But *do* listen to recordings of Olivier, Gielgud, and especially Richard Burton. Though their old-time clipped accents may seem a bit prissy and delicate, listen to how they change pitch and tone, and how they phrase; how swift their playing is, but how they relish the important thoughts. Their changes in pitch and tone are remarkable.

This exercise should help you break up tonal monotony and unlock changes of pitch. Before you say you aren't at all a monotone person, let me tell you that most of us in North America are pretty monotone, without realizing it. We usually speak everything on one tone. Or, we speak in the minor key, as opposed to the major key. You've got to listen to *good* music, and practice hitting clear tones and semi-tones. Listen to opera and classical music. Or Frank Sinatra—pay attention to how he *phrases* his songs, and how he hits his notes with clean precision without sliding and warbling. Stay away from the minor key inflections in your voice, and that means trying to avoid absorbing the doleful sounds of grunge music, and most of the plaintive wail of the '90s stuff. Even rap has its problems. Though you can learn a lot about rhythm and breath from rap, it's been my experience that actors who listen to nothing but rap end up pretty tuneless—they seem to have the hardest time with Shakespeare in the beginning because they're used to poetry and cadence without tune.

So, work this exercise:

First, find your lowest tone. Let go a "haaaaaaaa" sound in your deepest range—really scrape and go as low as you can, without whispering. Find the cleanest, clearest, bottom note. Mark that as 1.

Now find your highest tone. Let go a "haaaaaaaa," really reaching up there. Find the highest note you can, without going into falsetto. I want a clean, natural high sound. Mark that as 5.

Now go back to 1. "Haaaaaaaa" again. Come up a few tones, and mark a 2. Come up a few tones from there, and mark a 3. Come up again, a few tones under your 5, and mark a 4. Now go up to 5 and make sure that it's your highest sound.

Got it?

*Now, go through each word in the text, slowly. Exaggerate completely, and speak the word with the tone I mark.* (The poem appears in both numbered and unnumbered versions just for the sake of your eyes. You may want to read it through first and then begin your practice.)

I[3] shall[1] lack[4] voice[5]. The[1] deeds[5] of[2] Co[4] rio[1] la[3] nus[5]
Should[1] not[5] be[2] ut[4] ter'd[1] fee[5] bly[1]. It[3] is[4] held[5]
That[1] va[5] lor[3] is[2] the[2] chief[4] est[2] vir[3] tue[4], and[5]
Most[4] dig[5] ni[4] fies[3] the[2] ha[4] ver[1]. If[4] it[1] be[5],
The[1] man[5] I[3] speak[2] of[4] can[5] not[1] in[4] the[2] world[5]
Be[2] sin[5] gly[4] coun[5] ter[4] poised[1]. At[3] six[5] teen[5] years[5],
When[1] Tar[4] quin[2] made[3] a[1] head[3] for[2] Rome[4], he[4] fought[5]
Be[1] yond[5] the[3] mark[4] of[1] o[5] thers[1]: our[3] then[2] dic[4] ta[2] tor[5],
Whom[1] with[2] all[5] praise[4] I[3] point[1] at[3], saw[4] him[2] fight[5],
When[3] with[2] his[1] A[3] ma[1] zo[4] nian[2] chin[5] he[1] drove[3]
The[1] bris[4] tled[2] lips[4] be[3] fore[5] him[1]: he[3] be[1] strid[5]

An$^1$ o'er$^4$ press'd$^3$ Ro$^4$ man$^1$ and$^2$ i'$^3$ th'$^1$ con$^4$ sul's$^1$ view$^5$
Slew$^4$ three$^5$ o$^3$ ppo$^4$ sers$^1$; Tar$^5$ quin's$^3$ self$^5$ he$^3$ met$^1$,
And$^2$ struck$^5$ him$^1$ on$^3$ his$^2$ knee$^4$. In$^3$ that$^5$ day's$^5$ feats$^5$,
When$^3$ he$^2$ might$^1$ act$^3$ the$^1$ wo$^3$ man$^2$ in$^3$ the$^1$ scene$^4$,
He$^1$ proved$^3$ best$^5$ man$^5$ i'$^5$ th'$^1$ field$^5$, and$^3$ for$^4$ his$^1$ meed$^5$
Was$^3$ brow$^4$-bound$^3$ with$^2$ the$^2$ oak$^1$. His$^3$ pu$^4$ pil$^1$ age$^3$
Man$^3$-en$^2$ ter'd$^1$ thus$^4$, he$^3$ waxed$^2$ like$^2$ a$^1$ sea$^3$,
And$^1$ in$^4$ the$^3$ brunt$^2$ of$^1$ se$^5$ ven$^1$ teen$^5$ ba$^5$ ttles$^1$ since$^5$
He$^1$ lurch'd$^3$ all$^5$ swords$^5$ of$^4$ the$^3$ gar$^2$ land$^1$. For$^4$ this$^3$ last$^5$,
Be$^1$ fore$^4$ and$^1$ in$^3$ Co$^2$ rio$^1$ les$^4$, let$^3$ me$^2$ say$^4$,
I$^3$ can$^4$ not$^2$ speak$^3$ him$^2$ home$^1$. He$^2$ stopp'd$^4$ the$^1$ fli$^4$ ers$^5$;
And$^3$ by$^4$ his$^1$ rare$^5$ e$^3$ xam$^4$ ple$^1$ made$^3$ the$^1$ co$^4$ ward$^3$
Turn$^2$ ter$^5$ ror$^1$ in$^4$ to$^2$ sport$^5$. As$^1$ weeds$^4$ be$^1$ fore$^4$
A$^1$ ves$^3$ sel$^2$ un$^3$ der$^1$ sail$^4$, so$^5$ men$^4$ o$^1$ bey'd$^5$
And$^1$ fell$^5$ be$^4$ low$^3$ his$^2$ stem$^1$: his$^3$ sword$^5$, death's$^3$ stamp$^5$,
Where$^1$ it$^2$ did$^3$ mark$^5$, it$^3$ took$^5$. From$^1$ face$^3$ to$^2$ foot$^5$
He$^3$ was$^2$ a$^1$ thing$^4$ of$^1$ blood$^5$, whose$^1$ e$^3$ very$^2$ mo$^3$ tion$^5$
Was$^3$ timed$^5$ with$^4$ dy$^3$ ing$^2$ cries$^5$. A$^1$ lone$^5$ he$^3$ en$^4$ ter'd$^5$
The$^3$ mor$^5$ tal$^3$ gate$^1$ of$^1$ th'$^1$ ci$^3$ ty$^5$, which$^3$ he$^1$ pain$^5$ ted$^3$
With$^2$ shun$^4$ less$^3$ des$^2$ ti$^2$ ny$^1$; aid$^5$ less$^3$ came$^1$ off$^5$,
And$^3$ with$^4$ a$^1$ sud$^3$ den$^2$ re$^3$ in$^2$ force$^4$ ment$^3$ struck$^5$
Co$^5$ rio$^4$ les$^2$ like$^4$ a$^1$ pla$^5$ net$^1$. Now$^4$ all's$^3$ his$^5$,
When$^3$, by$^1$ and$^1$ by$^3$, the$^1$ din$^3$ of$^1$ war$^3$ gan$^2$ pierce$^4$
His$^3$ rea$^5$ dy$^1$ sense$^5$; then$^1$ straight$^5$ his$^3$ dou$^4$ bled$^1$ spi$^4$ rit$^5$
Re$^4$ quick$^4$ en'd$^4$ what$^1$ in$^1$ flesh$^5$ was$^3$ fa$^4$ ti$^3$ gate$^5$,
And$^1$ to$^5$ the$^2$ bat$^5$ tle$^4$ came$^3$ he$^2$; where$^1$ he$^4$ did$^3$
Run$^2$ reek$^5$ ing$^1$ o'er$^4$ the$^3$ lives$^4$ of$^1$ men$^5$, as$^1$ if$^5$
'Twere$^3$ a$^2$ per$^1$ pe$^4$ tual$^3$ spoil$^5$: and$^1$ till$^3$ we$^2$ call'd$^5$
Both$^5$ field$^5$ and$^1$ ci$^3$ ty$^2$ ours$^4$, he$^2$ ne$^4$ ver$^2$ stood$^5$
To$^1$ ease$^3$ his$^2$ breast$^4$ with$^3$ pan$^5$ ting$^1$.

I shall lack voice. The deeds of Coriolanus
Should not be utter'd feebly. It is held
That valor is the chiefest virtue, and
Most dignifies the haver. If it be,
The man I speak of cannot in the world
Be singly counterpoised. At sixteen years,
When Tarquin made a head for Rome, he fought
Beyond the mark of others: our then dictator,

Whom with all praise I point at, saw him fight,
When with his Amazonian chin he drove
The bristled lips before him: he bestrid
An o'erpress'd Roman and i' th' consul's view
Slew three opposers; Tarquin's self he met,
And struck him on his knee. In that day's feats,
When he might act the woman in the scene,
He proved best man i' th' field, and for his meed
Was brow-bound with the oak. His pupil age
Man-enter'd thus, he waxed like a sea,
And in the brunt of seventeen battles since
He lurch'd all swords of the garland. For this last,
Before and in Corioles, let me say,
I cannot speak him home. He stopp'd the fliers;
And by his rare example made the coward
Turn terror into sport. As weeds before
A vessel under sail, so men obey'd
And fell below his stem: his sword, death's stamp,
Where it did mark, it took. From face to foot
He was a thing of blood, whose every motion
Was timed with dying cries. Alone he enter'd
The mortal gate of th' city, which he painted
With shunless destiny; aidless came off,
And with a sudden reinforcement struck
Corioles like a planet. Now all's his,
When, by and by, the din of war gan pierce
His ready sense; then straight his doubled spirit
Requicken'd what in flesh was fatigate,
And to the battle came he; where he did
Run reeking o'er the lives of men, as if
'Twere a perpetual spoil: and till we call'd
Both field and city ours, he never stood
To ease his breast with panting.

Go ahead and sing the thing if you need to. Hit these tones specifically, and on the right syllable. This should help you break up any monotony and guide you to hitting good tones at the right time.

Notice that most of the Overruns are marked with a 5. Hit these higher tones and discover how that helps you hold or trampoline into the next thought. Notice what kind of excitement you can build for the audience by using higher tones to hold their attention, and lower tones to help conclude the thought. Play around with this exercise over and over again. And when you've got it into your system, bring everything down to reality. Speak each thought, keeping the tone-shifts, but making them more realistic.

## How Does This Help?

Apart from beginning to loosen you up, allowing you to express Shakespeare's thoughts with variety, tune, and tonal-precision, using these kinds of higher and lower notes will help you with the swift exchanges of thought that I refer to as "wit-play."

Take a look at Rosalind and Celia again:

| | |
|---|---|
| Celia: | Why, cousin! why, Rosalind! Cupid have mercy! Not a word? |
| Rosalind: | Not one to throw at a dog. |
| Celia: | No, thy words are too precious to be cast away upon curs; throw some of them at me; come, lame me with reasons. |
| Rosalind: | Then there were two cousins laid up; when the one should be lamed with reasons and the other mad without any. |
| Celia: | But is all this for your father? |
| Rosalind: | No, some of it is for my father's child. O, how full of briers is this working-day world! |
| Celia: | They are but burrs, cousin, thrown upon thee in holiday foolery: if we walk not in the trodden paths our very petticoats will catch them. |
| Rosalind: | I could shake them off my coat: these burrs are in my heart. |
| Celia: | Hem them away. |
| Rosalind: | I would try, if I could cry 'hem' and have him. |
| Celia: | Come, come, wrestle with thy affections. |
| Rosalind: | O, they take the part of a better wrestler than myself! |

| Celia: | O, a good wish upon you! you will try in time, in despite of a fall. But, turning these jests out of service, let us talk in good earnest: is it possible, on such a sudden, you should fall into so strong a liking with old Sir Rowland's youngest son? |
|---|---|
| Rosalind: | The duke my father loved his father dearly. |
| Celia: | Doth it therefore ensue that you should love his son dearly? By this kind of chase, I should hate him, for my father hated his father dearly; yet I hate not Orlando. |
| Rosalind: | No, faith, hate him not, for my sake. |
| Celia: | Why should I not? doth he not deserve well? |
| Rosalind: | Let me love him for that, and do you love him because I do. Look, here comes the duke. |

In wit-play, and all crackling dialogue, a character latches onto *one specific word* or *idea* thrown at them by their scene partner. They then throw back another word or idea, bouncing specifically off the original idea. Like a tennis match, you have to keep it up—sharp, light and quick. You have to send and receive with excitement and flow. And you have to *match tones*. Why? Because you have to keep your complicated thought-strands clear for the audience. The only way you'll do this is to *highlight the specific phrase or word that you're bandying about, with tone.*

Let's use our tone-numbering exercise in this scene. I'll highlight the word or group of words being played with, and match them specifically with the sender and receiver. Match the word with the exact tone. Move from the left column to the right, matching word and tone specifically. Then move back to the left (for the next idea), keeping it up, and in synch.

| Celia | Rosalind |
|---|---|
| *not*$^3$ a *word*$^5$? | *not*$^5$ *one*$^3$ to throw at a *dog*$^5$ |
| thy *words*$^3$ are too precious to be cast away upon *curs*$^5$ | |
| *throw*$^3$ some of them at *me*$^5$; come, *lame*$^3$ me with *reasons*$^2$ | then there were *two*$^5$ cousins *laid*$^3$ up; when the one should be lamed with *reasons*$^3$ and the *other*$^5$ mad without *any*$^2$ |
| But is all this for your *father*$^5$? | No, some of it is for my father's *child*$^5$. |

| Celia |
|---|
| |
| They are but *burrs*[3] |
| *our very petticoats will catch them*[3] |

| Rosalind |
|---|
| O, how full of *briers*[3] is this working-day world! |
| |
| *I could shake them off my coat*[3] |

Continue the rest on your own now. Match the "hems," match the "wrestlers," match the "loved his son" with the "hated his father." Match the wit-play in tone, be sharp and specific with your vocal highlighter.

# SHAKESPEARE IN THREE-D

So far I've been hinting at, and getting you used to the idea of the Three Dynamic D's. I've slipped a couple of them in here and there, so the concept should be scratching away somewhere in the back of your brain. The Three Dynamic D's will help you make choices and breathe life into your text, without forcing you to fret over "actions."

## I Don't Need "Actions"?

Nah. Shakespeare's text is muscular and active by its nature; it is alive and energetic. The moment you engage yourself in the act of speaking the text, you *become* physical. Your body will be as involved with Shakespeare's ideas as your mind and emotions.

And yet, actors are forever fretting over monologues that they consider inactive. They often don't know what to "do" onstage—don't know which actions to pick, and then get frustrated when their actions don't work. The usual result is that an actor will shout out a monologue with red-faced, spit-flying bluster; sob out a speech in a haze of weepiness; or hop around the stage in a manic frenzy of clumsy clowning. And (sigh), new actors often decide that there isn't much to do with a monologue, give the lower lip a quiver, and *emote*.

Let's try to steer you away from the nebulous stuff, shall we? Relax. Shakespeare always gives us active, often visceral thoughts that engage the audience. You don't always have to pick actions for monologues. In fact, sometimes choosing actions will complicate and dilute the text too much. In order to lift the writing off the page and into active argument, all you need do is apply the Three Dynamic D's:

**Disclosure      Discovery      Decision**

I know, I know: it sounds like one of those formulaic acting "codes." But it's not. It's easy.

Shakespeare gives your character a monologue. Ultimately, your character has a problem that needs to be worked out, a plan to share with the audience, or a revelation that needs to considered. Remember the definition of a classical monologue. You work this monologue out *with the audience* by either:

*Disclosing* a thought    *Discovering* a thought    or *Deciding* a thought

When your character speaks with the audience, you share your thoughts, your plan, your problem. I hope you don't come onstage with your argument ready and intact—it's boring if you blather something you already know or something you've already worked out perfectly.

*Through the act of speaking the monologue,* your character will *decide* a course of action, *discover* new ideas or possibilities, *disclose* (and sometimes *solve*) a dilemma, *deliberate* a problem, or *determine* a way out of his situation. Sometimes, you will reveal some truths and insights about life. Remember, too, that you weigh the pros and cons of a particular situation or dilemma, and *decide* on a course of action *right then and there.*

Everything is shared with the audience. Nothing is private. Soliloquies aren't "for you." Ever. Got it?

It's up to you to decide which D to use on a line; you can choose any one you want for any line. But often you'll find that one D doesn't work as well as another for a particular line, so play around and experiment. Through trial and error, you'll find which one works.

Confused? Don't be.

Here's Viola to help us Discover, Decide or Disclose, from *Twelfth Night*, Act II, Scene 2:

> I left no ring with her: what means this lady?
> Fortune forbid my outside have not charm'd her!
> She made good view of me; indeed, so much,
> That sure methought her eyes had lost her tongue,
> For she did speak in starts distractedly.
> She loves me, sure; the cunning of her passion

Invites me in this churlish messenger.
None of my lord's ring! why, he sent her none.
I am the man: if it be so, as 'tis,
Poor lady, she were better love a dream.
Disguise, I see, thou art a wickedness,
Wherein the pregnant enemy does much.
How easy is it for the proper-false
In women's waxen hearts to set their forms!
Alas, our frailty is the cause, not we!
For such as we are made of, such we be.
How will this fadge? my master loves her dearly;
And I, poor monster, fond as much on him;
And she, mistaken, seems to dote on me.
What will become of this? As I am man,
My state is desperate for my master's love;
As I am woman, —now alas the day! —
What thriftless sighs shall poor Olivia breathe!
O time! thou must untangle this, not I;
It is too hard a knot for me to untie.

Before we begin, I should note for you that Viola is about fourteen years old. She was in a shipwreck, and was cast ashore on the beaches of Illyria, a country she finds very strange. She goes on to disguise herself as a boy called Cesario, and became the manservant of Duke Orsino (with whom she promptly falls in love). Orsino, in turn, is in love with Olivia, and has sent Viola/Cesario to deliver affections of his love. Olivia falls for Viola/Cesario, and sends her one of her own rings via Malvolio (an arrogant, puritanical servant), as a token of love. Malvolio tosses this ring down at Viola's feet and storms off in a huff; of course, he has the hots for Olivia, too. Poor Viola is caught in the middle. And that's where we start.

Now, let's apply the three D's.

For right now, play only the D's I suggest. Afterwards, you can fiddle around with the speech. When you have a good grasp on the Three D's, you can experiment, finding which one works for you, and for the monologue. You'll find the right one.

I'm going to add my own punctuation here to help you uncover your Three D's:

I left no ring with her: what means this lady?

Remember, this line is not for you, it's for the audience. So fill us in.
*Disclose* your thought to us:

I left no ring with her.

Plain and simple disclosure. Speak directly to the audience, as if to say, "Look here, folks: I left no ring with her. What the hell is going on?"

—or—

*Decide*, forcefully:

I left no ring with her!

Look at the ring, look at Malvolio tromping off, pasty-footed, and *decide* once and for all, "I left no ring with her!"
Got it? Let's continue:
*Ask* us the question, plain and direct:

What means this lady?

Slowly, *Discover* the reality:

Fortune forbid my...outside have not...charmed her! (Note the exclamation mark.)

*Decide*:
She made good view of me; (decide "Yep—she did indeed!")

*Discover:*

> indeed...so much...
> That sure...methought her eyes has lost her tongue...
> For she did speak in starts distractedly. (End on an "Oh, no!" note.)

*Decide:*

> She loves me sure;

*Disclose:*

> the cunning of her passion
> Invites me in this churlish messenger.

*Disclose:*

> None of my lord's ring! (*Really* disclose this to the audience, person to person.)

*Decide:*

> Why—he sent her none.

*Discover:*

> *I...am...the man:*

*Disclose:*

> if it be so,

*Decide:*

> as 'tis,

*Discover:*

> Poor lady...

*Disclose:*

she were better love a dream. (And *mean* it. You genuinely feel sorry for Olivia.)

*Decide:*

Disguise, I see, thou *art* a wickedness,
Wherein the pregnant enemy does much.

(When Viola was younger, someone probably told her, "Don't ever dress up and pretend you're somebody else. Disguise is a wickedness 'wherein the pregnant enemy does much'." —an old-time expression. Here, she *agrees*, and *decides* it's true.)

*Discover:*

How easy is it...for the proper-false...
In women's waxen hearts...to set their forms!

(Viola discovers for the first time how easy it is for liars and deceivers to imprint themselves in women's malleable hearts.)

*Decide:*

Alas, our frailty is the cause, not we!

*Disclose:*

For such as we are made of, such we be.

(Again, this is probably an old saying, repeated to Viola many times when she was young. Here, she discloses it to the audience and, once more, agrees.)

*Ask us:*

How will this fadge?

("Fadge" means "turn out." So Viola asks the audience, simply and directly, "How will this turn out?")

*Disclose:*

my master loves her dearly;

*Disclose:*

And I, poor monster, fond as much on him:

(This disclosure is a bit slow and sorrowful. Use those commas to *discover* "poor monster.")

*Discover:*

And she...mistaken...seems to dote...on me!

*Ask us:*

What will become of this?

*Decide:*

As I am man—
My state is desperate for my master's love;

*Discover:*

As I am woman,

*Disclose:*

—now alas the day!—

*Discover:*

What thriftless sighs shall poor Olivia breathe!

*Disclose:*

O time!

(Now you really call out to Time here. Not an expression, but you really try to make Time hear your voice, pleadingly, or with accusation and anger.)

*Decide:*

thou must untangle this, not I;

*Decide:*

> It is too hard a knot for me to untie.
>
> (Before Viola runs offstage, weeping and confused, she decides that it us up to Time and Fate to untangle everything. She decides she is too helpless and powerless to do anything. Use those delicate little words "me to untie.")

Easy.

Suddenly, by applying these Three D's, you begin the lift the ideas off the page and into active argument. No worrying about choosing the right actions—no pulling at your hair, wondering: "But what do I *do*?" Shakespeare does so much for you already, you need do very little. As long as you communicate the thoughts clearly to the audience, the audience will follow you. Apply the Three D's, and your playing becomes active and alive.

## Mix 'n' Match

I've given you a little chart to practice with. All the thoughts in Viola's text are listed under the Discover, Disclose, and Decide headings. Play each one of the thoughts with a different D, and see what works. You'll often find that a thought can be played all three ways. In these cases, it's up to you to make the final choice as to which one you choose in performance. Play around, be flexible—mix and match these thoughts around, like a jigsaw puzzle. Play *each thought with each D fully*, and notice what works and what doesn't. Keep each D fresh and new.

| Discover | Disclose | Decide |
|---|---|---|
| I left no ring with her | if it be so | she made good view of me |
| she did speak in starts distractedly | Fortune forbid my outside have not charm'd her! | none of my lord's ring! why, he sent her none |
| if it be so | she loves me, sure | poor lady, she were better love a dream |
| indeed, so much | how easy is it for the proper-false in women's waxen hearts to set their forms | for such as we are made of, such we be |
| I am the man | | I left no ring with her |
| as 'tis | my master loves her dearly | I am the man |
| alas, our frailty is the cause, not we! | | alas, our frailty is the cause, not we! |
| sure methought her eyes had lost her tongue | | |

| Discover | Disclose | Decide |
|----------|----------|--------|
| the cunning of her passion invites me in this churlish messenger | as I am man, my state is desperate for my master's love | she loves me, sure |
| my master loves her dearly | what thriftless sighs shall poor Olivia breathe! | my master loves her dearly |
| now alas the day | she made good view of me | sure methought her eyes had lost her tongue |
| as I am woman | as I am woman | as I am man, my state is desperate for my master's love |
| none of my lord's ring! why, he sent her none | as 'tis | o time! |
| as I am man, my state is desperate for my master's love | and I, poor monster, fond as much on him; and she, mistaken, seems to dote on me | Fortune forbid my outside have not charm'd her! |
| what thriftless sighs shall poor Olivia breathe! | it is too hard a knot for me to untie | now alas the day |
| Fortune forbid my outside have not charm'd her! | I left no ring with her | as I am woman |
| she loves me, sure | she did speak in starts distractedly | how easy is it for the proper-false in women's waxen hearts to set their forms |
| how easy is it for the proper-false in | poor lady, she were better love a dream | what thriftless sighs shall poor Olivia breathe! |
| women's waxen hearts to set their forms | now alas the day | thou must untangle this, not I |
| and I, poor monster, fond as much on him; and she, mistaken, seems to dote on me | the cunning of her passion invites me in this churlish messenger | as 'tis |
| o time! | for such as we are made of, such we be | it is too hard a knot for me to untie |
| thou must untangle this, not I | o time! | indeed, so much |
| disguise, I see, thou art a wickedness, wherein the pregnant enemy does much | sure methought her eyes had lost her tongue | disguise, I see, thou art a wickedness, wherein the pregnant enemy does much |
| poor lady, she were better love a dream | thou must untangle this, not I | if it be so |
| she made good view of me | disguise, I see, thou art a wickedness, wherein the pregnant enemy does much | she did speak in starts distractedly |
| for such as we are made of, such we be | none of my lord's ring! why, he sent her none | the cunning of her passion invites me in this churlish messenger |
| it is too hard a knot for me to untie | indeed, so much | and I, poor monster, fond as much on him; and she, mistaken, seems to dote on me |
| What means this lady? | I am the man | |

## Are the Three D's Applicable to *All* Monologues?

Mostly, yes. Although you will find some monologues to be primarily a series of Discoveries, or a series of Disclosures without much Decision; a series of Decisions without much Discovery, and so on. These kinds of monologues are usually storytelling ones—speeches in which one character simply tells another character a story, a dream he or she had, a conversation overheard, or a revelation that struck him. In these cases...*just tell us the story*. Simple. But keep the story fresh and edgy by *trying* to apply all the Three D's.

Even in these storytelling monologues, you will usually have a culmination or a conclusion that ends on a final Decision, or a last Disclosure. As we discovered (or as I disclosed) earlier, Shakespeare's monologues are arguments (even the storytelling variety). And an argument is only interesting if a character has not already memorized every pro, con, and conclusion, and if he makes the arguments on the spot—fresh, alive, thunderstruck. *Discover* these new insights, *Decide* your pros and *Disclose* your cons. Or *Decide* your insights, *Discover* your pros, and *Decide* your cons. Or *Disclose*...and on and on; you get the point. Keep it alive and fresh.

## Can I Switch D's within One Line?

Yes, yes, yes. The more variety you can spice up your monologue with, the better. Try to choose one D for one full thought, and another D for the next full thought. And pay close attention to where there is a *change in thought within one single line,* and switch D's if it makes sense to. If you can turn on a dime, you will keep your speech dynamic.

Clarence gives us a monologue now that combines storytelling, a series of (mainly) Discoveries, and turning-on-a-dime switches. From *Richard III*, Act I, Scene 4, we find Clarence locked up in the tower. He's not doing so hot, and he tells the Jail-Keeper:

| | |
|---|---|
| Clarence: | O, I have passed a miserable night, |
| | So full of fearful dreams, of ugly sights, |
| | That, as I am a Christian faithful man, |
| | I would not spend another such a night |

Though 'twere to buy a world of happy days—
So full of dismal terror was the time.

Keeper: What was your dream, my lord? I pray you tell me.

Clarence: Methoughts I had broken from the Tower
And was embarked to cross to Burgundy,
And in my company my brother Gloucester,
Who from my cabin tempted me to walk
Upon the hatches: thence we looked toward England
And cited up a thousand heavy times,
During the wars of York and Lancaster,
That had befall'n us. As we paced along
Upon the giddy footing of the hatches,
Methought that Gloucester stumbled, and in falling
Struck me (that thought to stay him) overboard
Into the tumbling billows of the main.
O Lord! methought what pain it was to drown!
What dreadful noise of waters in mine ears!
What sights of ugly death within mine eyes!
Methoughts I saw a thousand fearful wracks;
A thousand men that fishes gnawed upon;
Wedges of gold, great anchors, heaps of pearl,
Inestimable stones, unvalued jewels,
All scatt'red in the bottom of the sea:
Some lay in dead men's skulls, and in the holes
Where eyes did once inhabit, there were crept
(As 'twere in scorn of eyes) reflecting gems,
That wooed the slimy bottom of the deep
And mocked the dead bones that lay scatt'red by.

Keeper: Had you such leisure in the time of death
To gaze upon these secrets of the deep?

Clarence: Methought I had; and often did I strive
To yield the ghost; but still the envious flood
Stopped in my soul, and would not let it forth
To find the empty, vast, and wand'ring air,
But smothered it within my panting bulk,
Who almost burst to belch it from the sea.

Keeper: Awaked you in this sore agony?

Clarence: No, no, my dream was lengthened after life.
O, then, began the tempest to my soul!

I passed (methought) the melancholy flood,
With that sour ferryman which poets write of,
Unto the kingdom of perpetual night.
The first that there did greet my stranger soul
Was my great father-in-law, renowned Warwick,
Who spake aloud, 'What scourge for perjury
Can this dark monarchy afford false Clarence?'
And so he vanished. Then came wand'ring by
A shadow like an angel, with bright hair
Dabbled in blood, and he shrieked out aloud,
'Clarence is come—false, fleeting, perjured Clarence,
That stabbed me in the fields by Tewkesbury:
Seize on him, Furies, take him unto torment!'
With that (methoughts) a legion of foul fiends
Environed me, and howled in mine ears
Such hideous cries that with the very noise
I, trembling, waked, and for a season after
Could not believe but that I was in hell,
Such a terrible impression made my dream.

Shakespeare has given you some pretty beefy images to play with here. Notice not only the language, but also the rhythm of the speech. Shakespeare sprinkles in tiny, soft consonants when he wants the tempo quick, and long open vowels to slow down the more macabre images. Listen to the rhythm closely as you speak. And remember that Clarence is not only telling his story for the first time, but reliving it. Go.

*Discover:*

O

(As strange as it may sound, really discover this "O." Clarence is remembering his dream here—the hairs on the back of his neck are tingling at the memory; his blood flows cold. Use this sound as a real discovery.)

*Disclose:*

I have passed a miserable night.

(Tell the Keeper, plain and direct, about your night.)

*Discover:*

So full of fearful dreams, of ugly sights,

(Remember your dream again; remember how it left you frosty, and rediscover the horror.)

*Decide:*

That, as I am a Christian faithful man,
I would not spend another such a night
Though 'twere to buy a world of happy days—

(Decide this thought strongly. By your faith, you will never spend another night like that. Not for anything!)

*Discover:*

So full of dismal terror was the time.

(Feel the hair tingling at the back of your neck as you rediscover last night's vision.)

*Disclose:*

Methoughts I had broken from the Tower
And was embarked to cross to Burgundy
And in my company

(Very matter-of-fact. Fill the Keeper in on your dream.)

*Discover:*

my brother Gloucester

(Discover the interesting fact that your rotten brother, Gloucester, was in your dream. Give the word "Gloucester" some extra weight as you see him, smell him and hear him again.)

*Disclose:*

Who from my cabin tempted me to walk
Upon the hatches: thence we looked toward England
And cited up a thousand heavy times,
During the wars of York and Lancaster,
That had befall'n us.

(Collect yourself from the image of Gloucester as evil, and disclose the facts to the Keeper. Relive the experience with a grudging camaraderie between you and your brother. See England again for the first time, listen to those old stories you and your brother shared.)

*Discover:*

As we paced along
Upon the giddy footing of the hatches,

(See your dream again with more detail. Discover what happened. Notice how quickly "upon the giddy footing of the hatches" trips off the tongue. Shakespeare is telling you to Discover all of this quickly, with a new energy.)

*Rediscover with more energy:*

Methought that Gloucester stumbled, and in falling
Struck me (that thought to stay him) overboard

(Relive it all; rediscover it with more energy and animation. "Struck" is a good, strong word. Use it.)

*Discover with horror:*

Into the tumbling billows of the main.

(This is horrible for Clarence. He is drowning *again*, in his memory, and he rediscovers what happened. See those tumbling billows, taste the salt water. Notice "tumbling billows" opens and pops your mouth—it *sounds* bubbly and sea-like. Use these words to slow your thought right down.)

*Rediscover and relive it all:*

O Lord! methought what pain it was to drown!
What dreadful noise of waters in mine ears!
What sights of ugly death within mine eyes!

(See it all again for the first time. Hear the noise and rush of drowning. Relive the nightmare. Notice the good, long, open vowels in "O...Lord...pain...drown." Slooooowwwwww down your rhythm as you sink meter by meter into the sea, choking. Notice that "what pain it was to drown" goes short-*long*-short-*long*-short-*long*. It's like pumping your brakes on an icy street in winter.)

(Now, here's where you can switch on a dime. Use the long, "O Lord!"—then switch. With the quick "methought" send that over to the Keeper as a Disclosure, then switch back to discover and reliving with the word "what." Switch...switch. It breaks up the drama with a little light moment.)

*Refuel your Discovery:*

Methoughts I saw a thousand fearful wracks;
A thousand men that fishes gnawed upon;
Wedges of gold, great anchors, heaps of pearl,
Inestimable stones, unvalued jewels,
All scatt'red in the bottom of the sea:

(See it all again—the dazzling beauty, the sickening ugliness; relive it all again. You can Disclose some of it to the Keeper, then sweep back into Discovery. Notice the quick, sharp vowels in this section: the sounds alone are exciting. Use them to infuse your *energetic Discovery*. Notice the delicate rhythm Shakespeare gives you in the last line, slow, then very quick: "Aawwllll-*dabba-dabba-dabba-dabba-da*." Use it.)

## *Disclose:*

> Some lay in dead men's skulls, and in the holes
> Where eyes did once inhabit, there were crept
> (As 'twere in scorn of eyes) reflecting gems,
> That wooed the slimy bottom of the deep
> And mocked the dead bones that lay scatt'red by.

(*Share* all this with the Keeper. Don't keep your Discoveries to yourself! Disclose them to him. Scare him; entice him with the grisly stuff and the images of magnificent gems. Be sensitive to the sounds of the words, "reflecting... gems...wooed...slimy...deep... mocked...bones." Use these words to whet the Keeper's appetite.)

## *Disclose:*

> Methought I had; and often did I strive
> To yield the ghost;

(Now that you've sucked the Keeper into your nightmare, just answer his question, plain and direct.)

## *Discover:*

> but still the envious flood
> Stopp'd in my soul, and would not let it forth
> To find the empty, vast, and wand'ring air,
> But smothered it within my panting bulk,
> Who almost burst to belch it from the sea.

(Explore your dream again. Switch from Disclosure to your new Discovery. Notice the quick, desperate rhythm in this text. Use the good "st," "so," "smu" sounds in "stopped," "soul," and "smothered" to bring on a renewed panic. Note the plosive, gasping b's in "bulk, burst, belch" as Clarence gasps for air, reliving his nightmare. Use these sounds.)

## *Decide:*

> No,

(Snap this quick decision at the Keeper.)

## *Disclose:*

> no,

(Turn on a dime. Reassure the Keeper with this word. Let him know there's more horror for him to enjoy.)

*Discover:*

> my dream was lengthened after life.
> O, then, began the tempest to my soul!
> I passed (methought) the melancholy flood,
> With that sour ferryman which poets write of,
> Unto the kingdom of perpetual night.

(Slip back into your horrible dream world again, slowly tasting and rediscovering the earth-shattering reality. Let the "O" slow you down again. Taste each word. Shakespeare gives you some slow, soft sounds here to linger on: "tempest, soul, melancholy, flood, sour." Listen closely to the rhythm of the last line, "Unto the kingdom of perpetual night." It's delicate and haunting. As Clarence discovers this kingdom again, taste each consonant.)

*Rediscover with more energy:*

> The first that there did greet my stranger soul
> Was my great father-in-law, renowned Warwick,
> Who spake aloud, 'What scourge for perjury
> Can this dark monarchy afford false Clarence?'

(See Warwick again; listen to his majestic voice.)

*Disclose:*

> And so he vanished.

(Your Keeper should be either petrified or thoroughly enjoying himself by now. Refer back to him; tantalize him by Disclosing this thought to him. Or scare him by breathing and shushing this line out like a whip-lash.)

*Discover:*

> Then came wand'ring by
> A shadow like an angel, with bright hair
> Dabbled in blood, and he shrieked out aloud,
> 'Clarence is come—false, fleeting, perjured Clarence,
> That stabbed me in the fields by Tewkesbury:
> Seize on him, Furies, take him unto torment!'

(Discover the d's and b's in "dabbled in blood." Notice how you taste and bounce the words. Then, as you hear this horrific voice again, use the good "s" and "f" and "t" sounds Shakespeare gives you to really bite and spit this thought out. "Shrieked," "Clarence," "false," "fleeting," "stabbed," "fields," "Tewkesbury," "seize," "furies," "take," "torment" are primal, vengeful spit-words. Rediscover this shrill, bloody angel with terror.)

*Discover:*

> With that (methoughts) a legion of foul fiends
> Environed me, and howled in mine ears
> Such hideous cries that with the very noise

(Keep seeing and Discovering. Then, on a dime)

*Disclose:*

> I, trembling, waked,

(Use this Disclosure to snap back into reality. Share these thoughts with the Keeper, and ground yourself.)

*Decide:*

> and for a season after
> Could not believe but that I was in hell,
> Such a terrible impression made my dream.

(This is your coming-down-off-the-high phrase. You also make your final Decision or conclusion. *Decide* to shake off the nightmare.)

You have a lot of Discoveries here, but you can still make it active and colorful by spicing in some Disclosure and Decision. Play around and switch D's, testing each line. Discover whichever one works best, then use it fully. You really don't need too much analysis of objective and action with Shakespeare. He's already done ninety-five percent of your work for you.

You might get stuck on a few obscure monologues, and wrack your brain trying to figure out which D's to use. And when you get stuck, you can do your objective/action work. I'll help you with that in our "Shakespeare Jambalaya."

I leave you with two monologues you can practice with on your own. Choose your own Disclosure, Discovery, and Decision:

Sebastian, from *Twelfth Night*, Act IV, Scene 2:

> This is the air; that is the glorious sun;
> This pearl she gave me, I do feel't and see't;
> And thought 'tis wonder that enwraps me thus,

Yet 'tis not madness. Where's Antonio then?
I could not find him at the Elephant;
Yet there he was, and there I found this credit,
That he did range the town to seek me out.
His counsel now might do me golden service;
For though my soul disputes well with my sense
That this may be some error, but no madness,
Yet doth this accident and flood of fortune
So far exceed all instance, all discourse,
That I am ready to distrust mine eyes
And wrangle with my reason that persuades me
To any other trust but that I am mad,
Or else the lady's mad. Yet, if 'twere so,
She could not sway her house, command her followers,
Take and give back affairs and their dispatch
With such a smooth, discreet, and stable bearing
As I perceive she does. There's something in't
That is deceivable. But here the lady comes.

### And Juliet, from *Romeo and Juliet*, Act IV, Scene 3:

Farewell! God knows when we shall meet again.
I have a faint cold fear thrills through my veins
That almost freezes up the heart of life.
I'll call them back again to comfort me.
Nurse!—What should she do here?
My dismal scene I needs must act alone.
Come, vial.
What if this mixture do not work at all?
Shall I be married then tomorrow morning?
No, no! This shall forbid it. Lie thou there.
*(Lays down a dagger.)*
What if it be a poison which the friar
Subtly hath minist'red to have me dead,
Lest in this marriage he should be dishonored
Because he married me before to Romeo?
I fear it is; and yet methinks it should not,

For he hath still been tried a holy man,
How if, when I am laid into the tomb,
I wake before the time that Romeo
Come to redeem me? There's a fearful point!
Shall I not then be stifled in the vault,
To whose foul mouth no healthsome air breathes in,
And there die strangles ere my Romeo comes?
Or, if I live, is it not very like
The horrible conceit of death and night,
Together with the terror of the place—
As in a vault, an ancient receptacle
Where for this many hundred years the bones
Of all my buried ancestors are packed;
Where bloody Tybalt, yet but green in earth,
Lies fest'ring in his shroud; where, as they say,
At some hours in the night spirits resort—
Alack, alack, is it not like that I,
So early waking—what with loathsome smells,
And shrieks like mandrakes torn out of the earth,
That living mortals, hearing them, run mad—
O, if I wake, shall I not be distraught,
Environed with all these hideous fears,
And madly play with my forefathers' joints,
And pluck the mangled Tybalt from his shroud,
And, in this rage, with some great kinsman's bone
As with a club dash out my desp'rate brains?
O, look! methinks I see my cousin's ghost
Seeking out Romeo, that did spit his body
Upon a rapier's point. Stay, Tybalt, stay!
Romeo, I come! this do I drink to thee.
*(She falls upon her bed within the curtains.)*

## PART THREE

# SHARPEN YOUR TEETH

# SHAKESPEARE JAMBALAYA

Well, you've tasted a good part of the techniques of playing Shakespeare well. We went straight to the meaty practices, and now it's time to stir in a whole bunch of little things—tiny problems, tools, suggestions, and small, revealing insights.

## Mixing in Objectives and Actions

At the beginning of the book, we scrapped the idea of objectives, intentions, actions, and the rest of it. Now it's time to bring them back.

There are as many different ways to unlock intentions and objectives in a scene as there are directors and teachers. But first, I want to redefine the word "intention;" it's too weak for me. I don't really care what an actor's intention is in a scene—I want to know what your *objective* is and what you do, *actively*, to obtain it.

When you look at a scene or monologue, you want to ask yourself a few important questions:

- What do I *need* from this other character or these other characters?
- What do I *need* from the situation?
- What will I *do* in order to obtain what I need?

These are good, strong, basic questions to ask yourself in order to kick your acting into high-gear. Remember, you *act*; you *do*.

First of all, I don't care what *you* feel in a scene. I want the *audience* to feel; I don't care if you're thinking about your scene, or thinking about painting your toenails, as long as you move the audience. The way you do this is to make bold, vigorous choices.

Second, the way you phrase your search for an objective is very important. There's a big difference between what you *want* and what you *need*—in life, as onstage. When you're onstage, I don't give a rat's ass what you *want*. I need to see what you *need*. And when you put your attention on the other person, when you say, "I need *you* to (...)," you lift your playing out of yourself and make the interplay more dynamic by focussing more on your scene partner.

Third, when you need something, you *do* things to achieve your objective, either subtle or overt. You will choose strong actions that support your objective in a scene. This will be our "objaction."

So imagine now you're one character, and you have a scene with another character. Let's phrase our "objaction" work like this:

"I need you to (...). Therefore I will (...) you with this line."

"I need you to (...)" is your *objective*. "Therefore I will (...) you with this line" is your *action*.

For example, suppose you want to *seduce* the other character. That's a start, but phrase your objective more dynamically. Put your attention on the other character:

I need you to *go to bed with me*.

It becomes more practical. And when you want to go to bed with someone, you:

- *charm* them
- *suggest* to them
- *humor* them
- *soothe* them
- *trick* them
- *flatter* them
- *force* them

These are all possibilities *in life*. They may or may not be true *for you*, but they are certainly true for some people, somewhere in the world. Keep compiling your list and then decide which best fits your character:

- *seduce* them
- *make verbal love* to them
- *threaten* them
- *woo* them

And so on. Go ahead and keep adding to the list on your own. As long as you make strong, active choices, you'll find enough of these *actions* to pepper throughout the scene. So now you can go through your scene like this:

> "I need you to *go to bed with me.*
> Therefore, I will *charm* you with this line."

> "I need you to *go to bed with me.*
> Therefore, I will *humor* you with this line."

> "I need you to *go to bed with me.*
> Therefore, I will *flatter* you with this line."

Keep on going down the list.

How does this work with Shakespeare? Let me give you a simple example that you're familiar with already:

O, pardon me, thou bleeding piece of earth,
That I am meek and gentle with these butchers!
Thou art the ruins of the noblest man
That ever lived in the tide of times.
Woe to the hand that shed this costly blood!
Over thy wound now do I prophesy
(Which, like dumb mouths, do ope their ruby lips
To beg the voice and utterance of my tongue),
A curse shall light upon the limbs of men;
Domestic fury and fierce civil strife
Shall cumber all the parts of Italy;
Blood and destruction shall be so in use
And dreadful objects so familiar
That mothers shall but smile when they behold
Their infants quartered with the hands of war,
All pity choked with custom of fell deeds;
And Caesar' spirit, ranging for revenge,
With Ate by his side come hot from hell,

Shall in these confines with a monarch's voice
Cry 'Havoc!' and let slip the dogs of war,
That this foul deed shall smell above the earth
With carrion men, groaning for burial.

What is Mark Antony's objective? You make up your own mind now, but let me offer a suggestion. Since Mark Antony's first line is "O, pardon me"... it makes sense that he wants Caesar's forgiveness. So,

"I need you to *forgive* me."

And when you need someone to forgive you, what do you do?
- *beg* them
- *plead* with them
- *vow* to them
- *praise* them
- *flatter* them
- *soothe* them
- *attack* their enemies for them
- *cry* for them

And so on. Now here's the trick: keep *everything* we've worked on already—Overruns, phrasing, visceral language—everything. *Just add your objective and actions.*

"I need you to forgive me.
Therefore, I will *beg* you with this line:"

O, pardon me, thou bleeding piece of earth,

"I need you to forgive me.
Therefore, I will *attack your enemies* for you with this line:"

That I am meek and gentle with these butchers!

"I need you to forgive me.
Therefore, I will *praise* you with this line:"

Thou art the ruins of the noblest man
That ever lived in the tide of times.

"I need you to forgive me.
Therefore, I will *swear* to you with this line:"

Woe to the hand that shed this costly blood!

"I need you to forgive me.
Therefore, I will *vow* (deeper than *swear*) to you with this line:"

Over thy wound now do I prophesy

"I need you to forgive me.
Therefore, I will *cry* for you with this line:"

(Which, like dumb mouths, do ope their ruby lips
To beg the voice and utterance of my tongue),

"I need you to forgive me.
Therefore, I will *vow* to you with this line:"

A curse shall light upon the limbs of men;
Domestic fury and fierce civil strife
Shall cumber all the parts of Italy;
Blood and destruction shall be so in use
And dreadful objects so familiar
That mothers shall but smile when they behold
Their infants quartered with the hands of war,
All pity choked with custom of fell deeds;

"I need you to forgive me.
Therefore, I will *soothe* you with this line:"

And Caesar' spirit, ranging for revenge,

"I need you to forgive me. Therefore, I will *vow, plead, attack,
beg,* everything at once for you with this line:"

With Ate by his side come hot from hell,
Shall in these confines with a monarch's voice
Cry 'Havoc!' and let slip the dogs of war,

"I need you to forgive me.
Therefore, I will *promise* you with this line:"

> That this foul deed shall smell above the earth
> With carrion men, groaning for burial.

Keep in mind what you *need* and what you *actively will do with a line in order to achieve that end* with all your scenes and monologues. This, plus the techniques you learned in Part Two, will really set you on fire.

## Irony

Contrary to what some intellectual snobs may think, North Americans can play irony beautifully, thank you very much. There's irony everywhere in the world—we just have slightly different styles and intonations when we use it. The main stumbling block for young actors is the substitution of *sarcasm* for irony.

We use sarcasm in order to trash somebody—to put them down. You take a weakness, a situation, a phrase the other person just uttered, and twist it around in order to mock or destroy them. This is not irony. Be careful of using sarcasm in Shakespeare. There isn't a lot of it.

Irony is used to *teach* or instruct a person, very subtly. By saying one thing, you point out another, more telling, bit of truth. Remember Antony speaking about Brutus in *Julius Caesar*? Remember how many times he said, "Brutus is an honorable man"? That's irony. He repeats the phrase over and over again, each time getting his little dig in there, and meaning exactly the opposite. I'll highlight the irony for you; mean the opposite. Start very subtly, and with each subsequent dig, uncover more and more in-your-face obviousness:

> Friends, Romans, countrymen, lend me your ears;
> I come to bury Caesar, not to praise him.
> The evil that men do lives after them;
> The good is oft interred with their bones;
> So let it be with Caesar. The *noble Brutus*

Hath told you Caesar was ambitious:
If it were so, it was a grievous fault,
And grievously hath Caesar answer'd it.
Here, under leave of Brutus and the rest—
*For Brutus is an honorable man;*
*So are they all, all honorable men—*
Come I to speak in Caesar's funeral.
He was my friend, faithful and just to me:
But Brutus says he was ambitious;
*And Brutus is an honorable man.*
He hath brought many captives home to Rome
Whose ransoms did the general coffers fill:
Did this in Caesar seem ambitious?
When that the poor have cried, Caesar hath wept:
Ambition should be made of sterner stuff:
Yet Brutus says he was ambitious;
*And Brutus is an honorable man.*
You all did see that on the Lupercal
I thrice presented him a kingly crown,
Which he did thrice refuse: was this ambition?
Yet Brutus says he was ambitious;
*And, sure, he is an honorable man.*
I speak not to disprove what Brutus spoke,
But here I am to speak what I do know.
You all did love him once, not without cause:
What cause withholds you then, to mourn for him?
O judgment! thou art fled to brutish beasts,
And men have lost their reason. Bear with me;
My heart is in the coffin there with Caesar,
And I must pause till it come back to me.

There are smaller flecks of irony in the speech, but just concentrate on the repetition of "honorable." Mean the opposite every time. Slip it in subtly a few times, and then hammer it towards the end; make sure the crowd knows what you're *really* saying.

Antony is a master orator. He asks rhetorical questions, and sets up answers that the crowd already knows. He makes his point through rhetoric and irony. Practice this speech. Lead us into your logic, tease us with the rhetoric, and *instruct* us with your irony. Don't put Brutus down—rather, *teach* us that he is the opposite of "honorable."

You'll find a lot of irony in Shakespeare, so get used to it with this speech.

## The Problem with "O"

This is a sticking point with me. I hear these little o's and they poke at me like cartoon devils.

You have a lot of these pesky o's in Shakespeare. What are they? Well, let me tell you what they're *not*. They're rarely a prim, proper "O." Go ahead and stick out your lips like you're holding a big grape between them. Now pop out the tiniest little "o" you can. "O."

Please don't play that in performance. These o's are almost never the tidy, cutesy, choir-boy-lipped sound that we so often hear in irritating Shakespeare performances. So what are they?

They're *the sound you make before you utter your next thought.*

Sometimes before we start a thought, we have to take in our surroundings, our fellow characters, the situation, the depth or confusion of the event, or a surprise of joy. Sometimes, our words aren't quite formulated because of the complexity of the thought we're about to speak. So that "O" sound is the noise you make before you speak your thought. You sort of breathe, slide, or jump with it.

Open your mouth and throat now, and breathe out a long, slow, whispered "ohhhhhhhhhhhhhh." Now give an exclamation "oh!" Try "ack," "omph," "arrrrrgh," "mmmmph"—anything. Any sound you need to make to breathe you into your next thought is fine! As long as you don't give the audience an empty, meaningless, grape-lipped, little "o."

## The Problem of Accent

Please, please—oh please—use *your own accent* when you play Shakespeare. It's a good idea to work at acquiring the standard accent of the region you call home. (This is not to say that you need to learn a hoity-toity upper class accent, merely to point out that some communities have such a thick patois that main-stream audiences may not be able to understand you.) Just use your own standard accent, wherever you come from (unless your director wants a specific accent for a very specific reason). All the time, I hear actors tearing Shakespeare apart with a messed-up British sound, and I can't stand to listen to them. I have to stop them mid-audition and ask them to use their own accent. Then they get all confused, and everything goes to hell. Just be who you are.

## Sentiment vs. Sentimentality

Shakespeare's work is filled with sentiment, but rarely is it senti-mental. There's a big difference.

Real sentiment is *real emotion*. A *real* feeling in a *real* situation. It's truthful, open, muscular, and honest. Sentimentality is the weepy, false stuff of the nineteenth century. Drippy, "poetic," and namby-pamby. You won't find that much in Shakespeare. So, whatever you do, don't weaken your text by layering maudlin sentimentality on top of it.

## Caesura

A caesura is a *natural pause* or beat in your *line of verse*. It's a lit-tle heartbeat from one mini-thought to another mini-thought. Read Sonnet 18, and see if you can notice the little pause from one thought to another, line-by-line:

> Shall I compare thee to a summer's day?
> Thou art more lovely and more temperate:
> Rough winds do shake the darling buds of May,
> And summer's lease hath all too short a date:
> Sometime too hot the eye of heaven shines,
> And often is his gold complexion dimm'd;
> And every fair from fair sometime declines,
> By chance or nature's changing course untrimm'd;
> But thy eternal summer shall not fade
> Nor lose possession of that fair thou owest;
> Nor shall Death brag thou wander'st in his shade,

When in eternal lines to time thou growest:
So long as men can breathe or eyes can see,
So long lives this and this gives life to thee.

## Find it?

Shall I compare thee (caesura) to a summer's day?
Thou art more lovely (caesura) and more temperate:
Rough winds do shake (caesura) the darling buds of May,
And summer's lease (caesura) hath all too short a date:
Sometime too hot (caesura)) the eye of heaven shines,
And often is his gold complexion (caesura) dimm'd;
And every fair (caesura) from fair sometime declines,
By chance (caesura) or nature's changing course untrimm'd;
But thy eternal summer (caesura) shall not fade
Nor lose possession (caesura) of that fair thou owest;
Nor shall Death brag (caesura) thou wander'st in his shade,
When in eternal lines to time (caesura) thou growest:
So long as men can breathe (caesura) or eyes can see,
So long lives this (caesura) and this gives life to thee.

So what do you do with it? Well, it's up to you. First, notice *where* the caesura is. Next, notice that you *can* take the tiniest mini-beat with it if you want: in order to help *uncover the next thought*, to *think it out*, to *discover, decide, disclose* it, or to *keep the listener engaged*. These caesuras can be tiny or big, so be careful with them. You certainly don't have to use them, or use them all the time, but the *choice* is there. Think the text through, and figure out how you might play the caesuras (I'm exaggerating a bit for you here; you needn't play the exaggeration in performance):

Shall I compare thee (beat. Hmm, what shall I compare thee to? A horse? Nah. A mug of beer? Nah. A rotten sock? Nah. How about) to a summer's day?

(All the other poets in town are comparing their girlfriends to a summer's day—I'm not going to use their cliché. I'm way more inventive than that. So, shall I compare thee to a summer's day—like they would? No way! Because)

Thou art more lovely (beat. Let me assure you, dear) and more temperate:
Rough winds (beat. What about them? What do they do?) do shake the darling buds of May,

And summer's lease (beat. What about summer's lease? What's the matter with it?) hath
    all too short a date:
Sometime too hot (beat. What's too hot? Ah) the eye of heaven shines,
And often is his gold complexion (beat. What happens to his complexion?) dimm'd;
And every fair (beat. What happens?) from fair sometime declines,
By chance (beat. Hmm...that bloody nature, whose course I despise) or nature's
    changing course untrimm'd;
But thy eternal summer (beat. What about it? It) shall not fade
Nor lose possession (beat. Lose possession of what?) of that fair thou owest;
Nor shall Death brag (beat. What will Death brag?) thou wander'st in his shade,
When in eternal lines to time (beat. What? What will happen in these eternal lines to
    time?) thou growest:
So long as men can breathe (beat. Only that long? How about longer?) or eyes
    can see,
So long lives this (beat. And then what happens? Let me conclude with something she'll
    never forget) and this gives life to thee.

## Masculine and Feminine Endings

A *masculine* ending refers to a line of verse ending in a *stressed* syllable. Like:

O for a Muse of fire, that would a*scend*

Masculine endings give a punch, or a lift-off the end of the line. They keep the ear engaged, waiting for the next line to begin. Or, they conclude the line with strong finality. Like this:

Come not between the dragon and his *wrath.*

A *feminine* ending refers to a line of verse ending in an *unstressed syllable.* Like:

Or if you will, to speak more proper*ly,*

where that "ly" falls off the end of the line.

A *feminine* ending more often refers to a line ending in an *extra, unstressed beat,* like:

To be, or not to be—that is the ques*tion;*

Feminine endings leave the line trailing off, weakly. You can use them to suggest hesitancy, or a falling off of thought. Though we learned not to trail off at the end of a line in verse-speaking, here, the syllable naturally dies out.

Associative terms are not politically correct and are used here merely to differentiate the two types of endings. Verse-terms associate a strong punch with being masculine and a weak faltering as being feminine.

## Making Sounds Work

Be really sensitive to Shakespeare's text, because he often gives you the *sound of the mood or thought-pattern you're playing with*. Read this speech of Henry V's, from Act I, Scene 2:

We are glad the Dauphin is so pleasant with us;
His present and your pains we thank you for:
When we have match'd our rackets to these balls,
We will, in France, by God's grace, play a set
Shall strike his father's crown into the hazard.
Tell him he hath made a match with such a wrangler
That all the courts of France will be disturb'd
With chases. And we understand him well,
How he comes o'er us with our wilder days,
Not measuring what use we made of them.
We never valued this poor seat of England;
And therefore, living hence, did give ourself
To barbarous licence; as 'tis ever common
That men are merriest when they are from home.
But tell the Dauphin I will keep my state,
Be like a king and show my sail of greatness
When I do rouse me in my throne of France:
For that I have laid by my majesty
And plodded like a man for working-days,
But I will rise there with so full a glory
That I will dazzle all the eyes of France,
Yea, strike the Dauphin blind to look on us.
And tell the pleasant prince this mock of his

Hath turn'd his balls to gun-stones; and his soul
Shall stand sore charged for the wasteful vengeance
That shall fly with them: for many a thousand widows
Shall this his mock mock out of their dear husbands;
Mock mothers from their sons, mock castles down;
And some are yet ungotten and unborn
That shall have cause to curse the Dauphin's scorn.
But this lies all within the will of God,
To whom I do appeal; and in whose name
Tell you the Dauphin I am coming on,
To venge me as I may and to put forth
My rightful hand in a well-hallow'd cause.
So get you hence in peace; and tell the Dauphin
His jest will savour but of shallow wit,
When thousands weep more than did laugh at it.
Convey them with safe conduct. Fare you well.

Right before this, the Dauphin's Ambassador presented Henry with a case full of tennis balls—mocking him, and suggesting that he's just a little sporty boy, and not a man. It's the final straw: Henry decides what he has to do, and gives this speech to Ambassador, full of threat and relishing.

In the first two lines of the speech, Shakespeare gives you three p's to play with in "pleasant," "present," and "pains." These plosive sounds give you a little punch, allowing you to scare the Ambassador, and to imitate the sound of sport.

Now, notice this section:

And tell the pleasant prince this mock of his
Hath turn'd his balls to gun-stones; and his soul
Shall stand sore charged for the wasteful vengeance
That shall fly with them: for many a thousand widows
Shall this his mock mock out of their dear husbands;
Mock mothers from their sons, mock castles down;

He tastes those p's again with "pleasant prince." But what else do you notice? Henry says the word "mock" five times in six lines. Punch that word out of your mouth, really use the "ock" well, and launch into it with a quick "m." Mock, mock, mock. What does that sound like?

It's the *sound* of tennis balls. Hear those Wimbledon matches in your mind: mock, pock, pock, pock, as the balls are slammed with the rackets. Notice the repetition of "mock mock" in the fifth line? Henry sends those tennis balls straight back to the Ambassador in his sound and his intention, threatening and mocking with the word itself.

Clever.

Now, read the Chorus from the same play, in Act IV:

> Now entertain conjecture of a time
> When creeping murmur and the poring dark
> Fills the wide vessel of the universe.
> From camp to camp through the foul womb of night
> The hum of either army stilly sounds,
> That the fixed sentinels almost receive
> The secret whispers of each other's watch:
> Fire answers fire, and through their paly flames
> Each battle sees the other's umber'd face;
> Steed threatens steed, in high and boastful neighs
> Piercing the night's dull ear, and from the tents
> The armourers, accomplishing the knights,
> With busy hammers closing rivets up,
> Give dreadful note of preparation:
> The country cocks do crow, the clocks do toll,
> And the third hour of drowsy morning name.
> Proud of their numbers and secure in soul,
> The confident and over-lusty French
> Do the low-rated English play at dice;
> And chide the cripple tardy-gaited night
> Who, like a foul and ugly witch, doth limp
> So tediously away. The poor condemned English,
> Like sacrifices, by their watchful fires
> Sit patiently and inly ruminate
> The morning's danger, and their gesture sad
> Investing lank-lean; cheeks and war-worn coats
> Presenteth them unto the gazing moon

So many horrid ghosts. O now, who will behold
The royal captain of this ruin'd band
Walking from watch to watch, from tent to tent,
Let him cry 'Praise and glory on his head!'
For forth he goes and visits all his host.
Bids them good morrow with a modest smile
And calls them brothers, friends and countrymen.
Upon his royal face there is no note
How dread an army hath enrounded him;
Nor doth he dedicate one jot of color
Unto the weary and all-watched night,
But freshly looks and over-bears attaint
With cheerful semblance and sweet majesty;
That every wretch, pining and pale before,
Beholding him, plucks comfort from his looks:
A largess universal like the sun
His liberal eye doth give to every one,
Thawing cold fear, that mean and gentle all,
Behold, as may unworthiness define,
A little touch of Harry in the night.
And so our scene must to the battle fly;
Where—O for pity!—we shall much disgrace
With four or five most vile and ragged foils,
Right ill-disposed in brawl ridiculous,
The name of Agincourt. Yet sit and see,
Minding true things by what their mockeries be.

Because there are no visuals to go with the play, the Chorus sets the scene, not only by description, but by *sound*. Read this slowly, tasting each word, opening up each vowel and whispering each consonant:

creeping murmur and the poring dark
Fills the wide vessel of the universe.

It sounds creepy, dark, and then open and vast. Now:

That the fixed sentinels almost receive
The secret whispers of each other's watch

All those "s" sounds. Speak that second line really fast; whisper it. Notice the sound of whispering, nervousness, conspiracy, tension in the line? And then—bam!

Steed threatens steed,

You can hear the quick, sharp sound here of the horses:

*Piercing* the night's dull ear

How about this one, later on:

The armourers, accomplishing the knights,
With busy hammers closing rivets up

Shakespeare sets up the armorers—working, hammering away, fixing the shields, sharpening the swords, and polishing the armor. On the second line, he gives you bam-bam-bam regularity of rhythm, which taps off the tongue, quick and sharp.

These are just a few of the major sounds that set the mood in the speech. But go over it again and again, exaggerating what you hear, and tasting each rhythm and word fully. Notice how the vowels and consonants actually give you a visual image and suck your full imagination into the scene. Use them.

## Mediterranean Fire vs. Northern Cool

This is a very general note, but when Shakespeare sets a play in a particular location, he usually gives you thought-patterns and rhythms of that location. For example, *Julius Caesar*, set in Rome, has a lot of logic, oratory, rhetoric—but also a lot of fire. *Hamlet*, set in Denmark, has a lot of darkness, speaking-without-speaking, miscommunication, and *attempts* at balance and will; more airy stuff than the earthy fire of the Mediterranean. *Romeo and Juliet*, set in Italy, has a lot of revenge, fury, and passion. *Measure for Measure* set in Vienna, has a lot of hypocrisy, tidiness-and-filth, tight-laced thinking trying to control more "liberal" attitudes. Just pay careful attention to your thought-patterns and locations, and notice what kind of character and situation notes this gives you. Generally, you will find fiery, heated language in hotter climates, and more introspective struggles in cooler climates.

## Unbuckling Thoughts

This is a tremendously important note, but a bit hard to put down on paper.

Try to "find" thoughts, words, expressions and ideas in your speeches and scenes. It's boring when you come onstage with every word perfectly rehearsed, and perfectly delivered with no struggle to think (in character) of the next word, to discover a new thought, or to find another line. In life, we rarely know exactly what we're going to say, when we're going to say it, and how we're going to say it. We live moment to moment, unless we have a highly specific thing to say to someone that we've carefully practiced before speaking. Why would Shakespeare be any different? The theatre is just a condensation and heightening of life, and although thoughts come more quickly and are sorted into precise situations, you still have to *live* them by *finding* them.

Here's Isabella from *Measure for Measure*, Act II, Scene 4. She's almost always played earnest and desperately serious (which she is). But you can make her funny—funny for the audience *through* that earnest, pious, puritanical persnickety-ness. Her brother, Claudio, has been condemned to death because he knocked up some chick. So Isabella goes to Angelo, a seemingly religious, righteous, straight-laced guy, who temporarily runs the town. He offers Isabella a choice: if she sleeps with him, he'll let her brother live. If she doesn't, her brother will die. Isabella (being a young, virginal nun-in-training), of course, freaks out:

> To whom should I complain? Did I tell this,
> Who would believe me? O perilous mouths,
> That bear in them one and the self-same tongue,
> Either of condemnation or approof;
> Bidding the law make curtsy to their will:
> Hooking both right and wrong to the appetite,
> To follow as it draws! I'll to my brother:
> Though he hath fallen by prompture of the blood,

Yet hath he in him such a mind of honor.
That, had he twenty heads to tender down
On twenty bloody blocks, he'd yield them up,
Before his sister should her body stoop
To such abhorr'd pollution.
Then, Isabel, live chaste, and, brother, die:
More than our brother is our chastity.
I'll tell him yet of Angelo's request,
And fit his mind to death, for his soul's rest.

Now, this monologue *seems* very serious. And it is...for *her*. But the audience shouldn't like Isabella all that much, contrary to how most directors stage the play. All the rotten-toothed life-lovers in the crowd can't figure out why she just doesn't sleep with the guy. After all, she'll save her brother's life, his lover's life, and his kid's future. Isabella drives us nuts with her overblown self-righteousness. I know it's more complicated than that—sin and everything—but the audience *does* get very frustrated with her.

So while you *play* the earnest seriousness, you have to *find* thoughts, expressions, and ideas, which will make your playing real, alive...and funny.

For example, she says:

I'll to my brother:
Though he hath fallen by prompture of the blood,

First, she either makes a strong decision with "I'll to my brother," or she discloses that thought to the audience.

Next, take a look at that funny expression "prompture of the blood." She's far too innocent, coy, young, or modest to say "having sex," or "slipping the bone," or any other expression someone a bit older or more "worldly" might use. She has to *find* these four words.

She must know *something* about sex, but maybe she can't quite come to terms with it, or bring herself to imagine it. She uses, instead, a safer, more acceptable term. "Prompture of the blood...*that's* what the nuns call it," she might think. Or maybe she makes up the expression right there, on the spot. Regardless, she *finds the thought*.

Try this:

> Though he hath fallen by (beat. Hmm...what do I call it? Sex? No, that's too crass.
> How about) *prompture of the blood*

Use those four words with real squeamishness, or red-faced confession. Maybe throw in a little "Ack!" gag or "Tee-hee" giggle afterwards. Maybe smile coyly at the thought, or find the four words distasteful. Regardless, *find the thought* in the moment.

Later on, she says:

> had he twenty heads to tender down
> On twenty bloody blocks, he'd yield them up

which is a very youthful, exaggerated sentiment. You know how we spoke when we were thirteen or fourteen: "Ohmygod! He had, like, *a hundred zits!* Like, *a thousand zits* all over his face!" Same sentiment with *"twenty heads* to tender down/On *twenty bloody blocks."* So you have to *find* that phrase, fresh and spontaneous, in the moment.

And again, with:

> Before his sister should her body stoop
> To such abhorr'd pollution.

Find those two words, "abhorr'd pollution." She's worked herself up through the monologue, and she doesn't know quite what to call the act anymore. It becomes so distasteful to her that she can't even bear the thought. Or, she considers her *brother's* sexual indiscretion "prompture of the blood," while the thought of *her* doing the same thing becomes "abhorr'd pollution." However you find those two words is up to you, but discover them, taste them, use these two words afresh. She doesn't come onstage with everything in order—rather, she lives moment-to-moment, thought-by-thought. *Find* as many expressions, thoughts, and ideas as you can.

## Sad and Funny and Sunny and Fad

Always try to find at least one moment of humor in a very dramatic text, and one moment of sorrow in a funny text. It will depend on your director, and the tone of the production, what you find, when you find it, and how you find it—but always, always try to *lift out an opposite*. These opposites are the nature of life, and the nature of the theatre itself (represented, of course, by those comedy and tragedy masks). They are not separate from each other; merely two ways of looking at the same event.

In life, there is always something sad underneath moments of great joy and laughter—perhaps a fleeting feeling of the too-temporary nature of bliss, or maybe a recognition that ecstasy can only last a short time and that soon our laughter will subside. Or we're laughing hysterically at a very painful situation. And in sorrow, too, there is always a joke, or a joy. No matter how raw or aching we feel at a particular moment, no matter how tragic our lives or situations, there is always something very funny in it. That's part of the truth of being alive, and that's why black comedy and slapstick work so well on an audience's senses. We will always have conflicting emotions, and we can always flip in an instant.

Try to turn around at least one phrase in a text that *seems* uniformly dramatic or comic. Shakespeare almost *always* writes one in—you just have to scan for it with your brain, searching for dynamic opposites. Certainly, you won't want to switch sorrow to joy and joy to sorrow, line-by-line through a whole speech—you'll make the audience schizophrenic. But try at least *one* in every scene.

Here's an example of an angry, raging scene where you can flip on a dime, and find the humor. Hamlet says:

> Now I am alone.
> O, what a rogue and peasant slave am I!
> Is it not monstrous that this player here,
> But in a fiction, in a dream of passion,
> Could force his soul so to his own conceit
> That from her working all his visage wann'd,
> Tears in his eyes, distraction in's aspect,
> A broken voice, and his whole function suiting

With forms to his conceit? and all for nothing!
For Hecuba!
What's Hecuba to him, or he to Hecuba,
That he should weep for her? What would he do,
Had he the motive and the cue for passion
That I have? He would drown the stage with tears
And cleave the general ear with horrid speech,
Make mad the guilty and appal the free,
Confound the ignorant, and amaze indeed
The very faculties of eyes and ears. Yet I,
A dull and muddy-mettled rascal, peak,
Like John-a-dreams, unpregnant of my cause,
And can say nothing; no, not for a king,
Upon whose property and most dear life
A damn'd defeat was made. Am I a coward?
Who calls me villain? breaks my pate across?
Plucks off my beard, and blows it in my face?
Tweaks me by the nose? gives me the lie i' the throat,
As deep as to the lungs? who does me this?
Ha!
'Swounds, I should take it: for it cannot be
But I am pigeon-liver'd and lack gall
To make oppression bitter, or ere this
I should have fatted all the region kites
With this slave's offal: bloody, bawdy villain!
Remorseless, treacherous, lecherous, kindless villain!
O, vengeance!
Why, what an ass am I! This is most brave,
That I, the son of a dear father murder'd,
Prompted to my revenge by heaven and hell,
Must, like a whore, unpack my heart with words,
And fall a-cursing, like a very drab,
A scullion!
Fie upon't! foh! About, my brain! I have heard
That guilty creatures sitting at a play
Have by the very cunning of the scene
Been struck so to the soul that presently

They have proclaim'd their malefactions;
For murder, though it have no tongue, will speak
With most miraculous organ. I'll have these players
Play something like the murder of my father
Before mine uncle: I'll observe his looks;
I'll tent him to the quick: if he but blench,
I know my course. The spirit that I have seen
May be the devil: and the devil hath power
To assume a pleasing shape; yea, and perhaps
Out of my weakness and my melancholy,
As he is very potent with such spirits,
Abuses me to damn me: I'll have grounds
More relative than this: the play's the thing
Wherein I'll catch the conscience of the king.

Did you find one moment? The first thirty-five lines of the text build with apoplectic, ferocious intensity, peaking on:

O, vengeance!

Then, right away Hamlet catches himself, saying:

Why, what an ass am I!

*Catch yourself with this line.* Stop, change direction, and out of nowhere tell the audience:

"Man, I am such a jackass."

Make it funny.
Hamlet then mocks what he's been doing for the past thirty-five lines:

This is most brave,
That I, the son of a dear father murder'd,
Prompted to my revenge by heaven and hell,
Must, like a whore, unpack my heart with words,
And fall a-cursing, like a very drab,
A scullion!

He dismisses his rage with:

Fie upon't! foh!

Which is basically Shakespearean for, "Ah, to hell with it all!"
And then, finally, he starts using his reason on the line:

About, my brain!

Just as you can flip with these high-powered, serious scenes,
you can find moments of sorrow in a funny scene. Here's Falstaff
with a good example:

Peace, good pint-pot; peace, good tickle-brain.
Harry, I do not only marvel where thou spendest thy
time, but also how thou art accompanied: for though
the camomile, the more it is trodden on the faster
it grows, yet youth, the more it is wasted the
sooner it wears. That thou art my son, I have
partly thy mother's word, partly my own opinion,
but chiefly a villanous trick of thine eye and a
foolish-hanging of thy nether lip, that doth warrant
me. If then thou be son to me, here lies the point;
why, being son to me, art thou so pointed at? Shall
the blessed sun of heaven prove a micher and eat
blackberries? A question not to be asked. Shall
the sun of England prove a thief and take purses? A
question to be asked. There is a thing, Harry,
which thou hast often heard of and it is known to
many in our land by the name of pitch: this pitch,
as ancient writers do report, doth defile; so doth
the company thou keepest: for, Harry, now I do not
speak to thee in drink but in tears, not in
pleasure but in passion, not in words only, but in
woes also: and yet there is a virtuous man whom I
have often noted in thy company, but I know not his name.

Yes, there are serious notes from Falstaff, even as he pretends to be the King, mocking and laughing with Harry, offering his advice. But notice the last five lines:

> for, Harry, now I do not
> speak to thee in drink but in tears, not in
> pleasure but in passion, not in words only, but in
> woes also: and yet there is a virtuous man whom I
> have often noted in thy company, but I know not his name.

He is dead serious with the first three lines. Then, try to switch and *laugh off* "woes also." Laughing off sorrow is something we do in life, when we find ourselves uncomfortable with moments of true sadness, or try to dismiss the situation. *Chuckle through this line.* And then, change the subject and refresh the conversation with "and yet." *Lighten* the last two lines, after you've recognized your momentary seriousness.

Practice switching sad and funny, and funny and sad with this speech from Jacques *As You Like It*. In the serious moments, lighten the thoughts. In the funny moments, darken them. Flip things around in this monologue as much as you can:

> All the world's a stage,
> And all the men and women merely players:
> They have their exits and their entrances;
> And one man in his time plays many parts,
> His acts being seven ages. At first the infant,
> Mewling and puking in the nurse's arms.
> And then the whining school-boy, with his satchel
> And shining morning face, creeping like snail
> Unwillingly to school. And then the lover,
> Sighing like furnace, with a woeful ballad
> Made to his mistress' eyebrow. Then a soldier,
> Full of strange oaths and bearded like the pard,
> Jealous in honor, sudden and quick in quarrel,
> Seeking the bubble reputation
> Even in the cannon's mouth. And then the justice,
> In fair round belly with good capon lined,

With eyes severe and beard of formal cut,
Full of wise saws and modern instances;
And so he plays his part. The sixth age shifts
Into the lean and slipper'd pantaloon,
With spectacles on nose and pouch on side,
His youthful hose, well saved, a world too wide
For his shrunk shank; and his big manly voice,
Turning again toward childish treble, pipes
And whistles in his sound. Last scene of all,
That ends this strange eventful history,
Is second childishness and mere oblivion,
Sans teeth, sans eyes, sans taste, sans everything.

## Rhyming Couplets

You'll find a lot of rhyming couplets in Shakespeare's early plays, and very few of them in his late plays. What are they? Well, they're that little sing-song at the end of a monologue that ends the speech. Like:

Shine out, fair sun, till I have bought a glass,
That I may see my shadow as I pass.

where the last syllable in the second last line rhymes with the last syllable in the final line.

## What Do I Do with Them?

First, notice them—but play a rhyming couplet *only subtly*. In a monologue, it's a note of *finality or conclusion*. It's also an *exit* line. It means you should get the hell off the stage by that last word. You should be moving offstage during the last two lines, and be gone as you let the last word linger over the audience.

In dialogue, rhyming couplets are often notes of finality as well. But often, they're just back-and-forth wit-play devices. Clever, snappy stuff. Like:

Dumaine:    As upright as the cedar.
Berowne:                    Stoop, I say—
            Her shoulder is with child.

| | |
|---|---|
| Dumaine: | As fair as day. |
| Berowne: | Ay, as some days, but then no sun must shine. |
| Dumaine: | O that I had my wish! |
| Longaville: | And I had mine! |

It's a note from Shakespeare telling you to keep the banter up, swift, and light.

## Bombast and Doggerel...Boggerel!

Bombast is the beefy-gut twelve or fourteen beats-per-line that we sometimes find in verse. Doggerel is usually a frisky eight beat cadence. Neither is an entirely accurate description, as bombast can sometimes be ten beats-per-line and doggerel can appear as six, seven, or eight. I lump them both together when talking about the obviously different verse you occasionally find in Shakespeare.

Listen to this example of doggerel from *A Midsummer Night's Dream*, Act V, Scene 1:

If we shadows have offended,
Think but this, and all is mended,
That you have but slumber'd here
While these visions did appear.
And this weak and idle theme,
No more yielding but a dream,
Gentles, do not reprehend:
if you pardon, we will mend:
And, as I am an honest Puck,
If we have unearned luck
Now to 'scape the serpent's tongue,
We will make amends ere long;
Else the Puck a liar call;
So, good night unto you all.
Give me your hands, if we be friends,
And Robin shall restore amends.

It's a cutesy-pie jing-jang rhythm—more like a little ditty or song than a piece of verse. It's light, and is usually a *concluding* or *changing* note to a play, scene, or situation. I usually ask my actors to downplay the rhythm because it sticks out so much (which *is* the point). But personally, this stuff tugs on my ear too much—I like to hear *realistic* verse; but I do want you to try and notice these little rhythms. They're light, and bring a note of fantasy or romance to a play.

The *real* bombastic stuff you find in Shakespeare is usually seen when he mocks other playwrights and pokes fun at the overblown verse that came before him. Like this mouthy, big-bellied verse from the Player King in *Hamlet*, Act III, Scene 2. Notice the rhyming couplets on every line:

> I do believe you think what now you speak;
> But what we do determine oft we break.
> Purpose is but the slave to memory,
> Of violent birth, but poor validity;
> Which now, like fruit unripe, sticks on the tree;
> But fall, unshaken, when they mellow be.
> Most necessary 'tis that we forget
> To pay ourselves what to ourselves is debt:
> What to ourselves in passion we propose,
> The passion ending, doth the purpose lose.

When you find this many rhyming couplets in verse, it's meant to be *overdone*, highly *stylized*, *pompous*, or highly *formal*.

## "Concept" Shakespeare

Ahhhh.

For all our work so far, you might think that I'm some kind of a purist. Guess again.

I think the idea of cracking open Shakespeare's text and fiddling around with things is a good one. Most of his text is so strong that no matter what you do, you'll never be able to break him. I try to break his back all the time, searching for what else might be wriggling around in there; sometimes I fail, and sometimes I succeed in finding something new. And finding something makes all the head-pounding worthwhile.

I used to be a "purist" like so many other people. But one day I realized that unless I was playing Shakespeare at the Globe Theatre in the sixteenth century, dressed in pantaloons with a bad haircut, it wasn't "pure." The moment we take Shakespeare out of the Globe, by definition we mess with it. And that's beautiful. He often responds with fresh insight and a renewed boldness to a modern concept. The most killing thing you can do with Shakespeare is to keep him under a dusty glass case and lift him up to the world like a museum-piece. Be inventive, be bold—go wild with his work, because he *will* support you.

Of course, Shakespeare will support you only if your concept makes sense. You can't be an idiot and put *Romeo and Juliet* on roller skates, set in thirty-fourth century Jupiter. Then again, I suppose you can, but there must be a *reason* for it. Look deeply at the text, and find out what the major theme is. Is it about betrayal? Freedom? Lost love? Renewed hope? What is it *about*?

Then, build your concept from that point outwards. Choose what *reflects* the major themes, and what resonates with them. Try to eviscerate his text; try to find some new-jeweled insights that you can hold out to people. Let audiences look at themselves in that old gem now shining with your fresh ideas.

It doesn't matter where you set it or how you costume it, as long as everything in your concept reflects and exalts the *core of the play*. Everything must *support* the true theme, line-by-line, moment-by-moment. Personally, I prefer stripping down, down, down, instead of ballooning outwards.

If you're careful, and if you use your brain, Shakespeare will hold you on his back. Sometimes, he is even made more crystal-clear by modern concepts.

Let me give you an example.

In the Summer of 2001, I had a strong instinct: I wanted to do *The Tempest*. Was there a social or political reason? I don't think so. But I had a strong personal feeling that there was a reason for *me* to do it, and that, for some reason, an audience would respond to the timing. Just a gut-feeling.

So we looked at the space. We found a very ordinary theatre—plain, but for a few strange things. The space was slightly crooked, dark, and dilapidated. There were five or six sets of doors on the walls of the stage (I later found out the theatre used to be an old library). Fire extinguishers, pipes, awkward lips and jutting-out things all over the place gave off a very disconcerting feel.

So I asked what our set budget was. Zero, of course. What was our costume budget? Zero. Just what we could steal or find on the street. Lighting budget? Zero. Could we mask the theatre? No. Who was in our cast? Only men.

Sigh.

Then I began to look at the space more carefully, and to use my imagination. It looked like a lunatic asylum to me. I looked again at *The Tempest* and found that the real core of the play was *freedom*. Every character in the play *needs to be free*. They all have different reasons, and different expressions of that need, but the same theme echoed in every scene: freedom, freedom, freedom.

Freedom. A lunatic asylum. An all-male cast. It began to make sense. We would set the play in an all-male insane asylum. We would make Ferdinand a new inmate sent to the asylum because of his "indiscretion," and play the relationship between he and Miranda (a young man) as a homoerotic one. We would make Miranda a lost, innocent patient who latched himself onto Prospero. We would make Ariel the memory of Prospero's younger self, struggling to free himself from Prospero's clutching reminiscence. We would make Prospero a former doctor, now an inmate. His circle from Naples: fellow doctors, now adrift in the asylum, looking for him. We would make Stephano a violent, Windex-drinking inmate who tortures Trinculo (a frail, pattern-walking wisp). We would have visceral, disturbing scenes of eye-ball-slicing torture and rape. We would make Caliban the only sane person on the ward: the janitor. We would make the ship a bathtub, wrenched out of the bathroom and rowed by mops. We would make the storm and shipwreck a real personal and collective descent into madness. We would make Prospero's magic cloak a shower-curtain, ripped from the stall. We would make the Wedding Scene a pill-time orgy, a sexual free-for-all. And we would make all the characters in Prospero's life: memories, delusions, or fantasies. In the end, we would reveal Prospero, lonely, gabbling away at a few doctors' coats as his madness lifted, and his fantasy faded. The only *actual* people on the ward, we would discover, were Caliban the janitor, Francisco the soiled-underwear bridge between fantasy and reality, Stephano and Trinculo (completely destroyed), and Prospero the ragged, broken lunatic. And for Prospero's epilogue:

> Now my charms are all o'erthrown,
> And what strength I have's mine own,
> Which is most faint: now, 'tis true,
> I must be here confined by you,
> Or sent to Naples. Let me not,
> Since I have my dukedom got
> And pardon'd the deceiver, dwell
> In this bare island by your spell;
> But release me from my bands
> With the help of your good hands:
> Gentle breath of yours my sails
> Must fill, or else my project fails,
> Which was to please. Now I want
> Spirits to enforce, art to enchant,
> And my ending is despair,
> Unless I be relieved by prayer,
> Which pierces so that it assaults
> Mercy itself and frees all faults.
> As you from crimes would pardon'd be,
> Let your indulgence set me free.

He would deliver this to the audience naked; he would carefully plop himself into his bathtub, slice his wrists with Caliban's gum-scraper, and bleed to death. Francisco would applaud with Downs' Syndrome glee, and Caliban—watching the whole time—would throw Prospero's shower curtain over the bathtub, creating his lonely coffin.

Would it work?

It did.

Oh my, it did. No set, no budget, no money—and a mini-miracle.

The audience, of course, was completely polarized. They either loved it or hated it. I never heard such praise in my life, or such venom. Critics uniformly supported it, although some despised its "impurity." I was either trashed as an imbecile, or compared to Peter Brook. Rival theatre directors lined up to wag soggy fingers and dangle complaints in front of my nose

But I say, "Forget it!" Let the purists try to find purity in some monastery somewhere, and let curators protect their museum exhibits. *That's* what the theatre is all about: galvanizing people into deeper depths of living. We need boldness, originality, imagination, invention. The *last* thing we need in the theatre is to maintain the status quo and to pay homage to murky memories of boredom! What I *do* insist on, however, is a very clear text, and very solid acting.

Which is not to say that the production was perfect. Far from it. Through some oversights, I left a few loose threads in the play which were picked apart by the audience—and justly so. I didn't justify a few moments clearly enough, which teetered the production momentarily the wrong way. This lack of justification and detail in a few, short moments was a flaw—but the bulk and freshness of the production completely overshadowed the smaller flaws.

But that's what I mean about "concept" Shakespeare. Go for it. Justify it, and create something *important, immediate,* and *imaginative* for the audience. If you do your work, you'll have both the power of Shakespeare, and the power of new illumination through your concept. And don't worry about poor Willy Shakespeare—his text is stronger than your "mistakes" will ever be.

# IN CONCLUSION

So.

Now you've got your resources. It's time to really start practicing your new skills.

So work.

And keep on working. Read all the plays. Work all the monologues in this book. Get together with other actors and play as many scenes as you can. And when you get as comfortable with Shakespeare's text as you are with everything else—when this becomes second nature to you—throw everything I've taught you away and *live* it.

I strongly encourage you to live as boldly and as deeply as you possibly can. Laugh a lot. Love fiercely. Learn things. Stay up all night making love, and see each new day as a joy. Shake up your life with new discoveries. Surprise yourself, and disturb what you think you know. Delve into other peoples' lives. Change things. Get in touch with your passions and embrace them.

Live.

Because "Shakespeare" isn't about the theatre. It isn't about good acting, or about text, words, or ideas.

It's about *life*.

# APPENDIX

# MONOLOGUES AND SCENES

# TEN GOOD MONOLOGUES FOR WOMEN

Here are ten strong, active monologues for woman; they're perfect for auditions. Each has a range, variation, and complexity to it that will show off your talents, if you really dig into it deeply and apply everything you've learned from this book. Yes, directors have heard them before, but you can bring new insights and fresh perspectives to them, if you do your work. Which should you pick? Why not learn them all?

1. Hermione, from *A Winter's Tale*, Act III, Scene 2:

> Since what I am to say must be but that
> Which contradicts my accusation and
> The testimony on my part no other
> But what comes from myself, it shall scarce boot me
> To say 'not guilty:' mine integrity
> Being counted falsehood, shall, as I express it,
> Be so received. But thus: if powers divine
> Behold our human actions, as they do,
> I doubt not then but innocence shall make
> False accusation blush and tyranny
> Tremble at patience. You, my lord, best know,
> Who least will seem to do so, my past life
> Hath been as continent, as chaste, as true,
> As I am now unhappy; which is more
> Than history can pattern, though devised
> And play'd to take spectators. For behold me
> A fellow of the royal bed, which owe
> A moiety of the throne, a great king's daughter,
> The mother to a hopeful prince, here standing

To prate and talk for life and honor 'fore
Who please to come and hear. For life, I prize it
As I weigh grief, which I would spare: for honor,
'Tis a derivative from me to mine,
And only that I stand for. I appeal
To your own conscience, sir, before Polixenes
Came to your court, how I was in your grace,
How merited to be so; since he came,
With what encounter so uncurrent I
Have strain'd to appear thus: if one jot beyond
The bound of honor, or in act or will
That way inclining, harden'd be the hearts
Of all that hear me, and my near'st of kin
Cry fie upon my grave!

## 2. Hermione, from *A Winter's Tale*, Act III, Scene 2:

Sir, spare your threats:
The bug which you would fright me with I seek.
To me can life be no commodity:
The crown and comfort of my life, your favor,
I do give lost; for I do feel it gone,
But know not how it went. My second joy
And first-fruits of my body, from his presence
I am barr'd, like one infectious. My third comfort
Starr'd most unluckily, is from my breast,
The innocent milk in its most innocent mouth,
Haled out to murder: myself on every post
Proclaimed a strumpet: with immodest hatred
The child-bed privilege denied, which 'longs
To women of all fashion; lastly, hurried
Here to this place, i' the open air, before
I have got strength of limit. Now, my liege,
Tell me what blessings I have here alive,
That I should fear to die? Therefore proceed.
But yet hear this: mistake me not; no life,
I prize it not a straw, but for mine honor,

Which I would free, if I shall be condemn'd
Upon surmises, all proofs sleeping else
But what your jealousies awake, I tell you
'Tis rigor and not law. Your honors all,
I do refer me to the oracle:
Apollo be my judge!

### 3. Lady Anne, from *Richard III*, Act I Scene 2:

Set down, set down your honorable load,
If honor may be shrouded in a hearse,
Whilst I awhile obsequiously lament
The untimely fall of virtuous Lancaster.
Poor key-cold figure of a holy king!
Pale ashes of the house of Lancaster!
Thou bloodless remnant of that royal blood!
Be it lawful that I invocate thy ghost,
To hear the lamentations of Poor Anne,
Wife to thy Edward, to thy slaughter'd son,
Stabb'd by the selfsame hand that made these wounds!
Lo, in these windows that let forth thy life,
I pour the helpless balm of my poor eyes.
Cursed be the hand that made these fatal holes!
Cursed be the heart that had the heart to do it!
Cursed the blood that let this blood from hence!
More direful hap betide that hated wretch,
That makes us wretched by the death of thee,
Than I can wish to adders, spiders, toads,
Or any creeping venom'd thing that lives!
If ever he have child, abortive be it,
Prodigious, and untimely brought to light,
Whose ugly and unnatural aspect
May fright the hopeful mother at the view;
And that be heir to his unhappiness!
If ever he have wife, let her he made
More miserable by the death of him
Than I am made by my poor lord and thee!

Come, now towards Chertsey with your holy load,
Taken from Paul's to be interred there;
And still, as you are weary of the weight,
Rest you, whiles I lament King Henry's corse.

## 4. Juliet, from *Romeo and Juliet*, Act IV, Scene 3:

Farewell! God knows when we shall meet again.
I have a faint cold fear thrills through my veins,
That almost freezes up the heat of life:
I'll call them back again to comfort me:
Nurse! What should she do here?
My dismal scene I needs must act alone.
Come, vial.
What if this mixture do not work at all?
Shall I be married then tomorrow morning?
No, no: this shall forbid it: lie thou there.
*Laying down her dagger*
What if it be a poison, which the friar
Subtly hath minister'd to have me dead,
Lest in this marriage he should be dishonor'd,
Because he married me before to Romeo?
I fear it is: and yet, methinks, it should not,
For he hath still been tried a holy man.
How if, when I am laid into the tomb,
I wake before the time that Romeo
Come to redeem me? there's a fearful point!
Shall I not, then, be stifled in the vault,
To whose foul mouth no healthsome air breathes in,
And there die strangled ere my Romeo comes?
Or, if I live, is it not very like,
The horrible conceit of death and night,
Together with the terror of the place,
As in a vault, an ancient receptacle,
Where, for these many hundred years, the bones
Of all my buried ancestors are packed:
Where bloody Tybalt, yet but green in earth,

Lies festering in his shroud; where, as they say,
At some hours in the night spirits resort;—
Alack, alack, is it not like that I,
So early waking, what with loathsome smells,
And shrieks like mandrakes' torn out of the earth,
That living mortals, hearing them, run mad:
O, if I wake, shall I not be distraught,
Environed with all these hideous fears?
And madly play with my forefather's joints?
And pluck the mangled Tybalt from his shroud?
And, in this rage, with some great kinsman's bone,
As with a club, dash out my desperate brains?
O, look! methinks I see my cousin's ghost
Seeking out Romeo, that did spit his body
Upon a rapier's point: stay, Tybalt, stay!
Romeo, I come! This do I drink to thee.
*She falls upon her bed, within the curtains*

## 5. Katherine, from *The Taming of the Shrew*, Act V, Scene 2:

Fie, fie! unknit that threatening unkind brow,
And dart not scornful glances from those eyes,
To wound thy lord, thy king, thy governor:
It blots thy beauty as frosts do bite the meads,
Confounds thy fame as whirlwinds shake fair buds,
And in no sense is meet or amiable.
A woman moved is like a fountain troubled,
Muddy, ill-seeming, thick, bereft of beauty;
And while it is so, none so dry or thirsty
Will deign to sip or touch one drop of it.
Thy husband is thy lord, thy life, thy keeper,
Thy head, thy sovereign; one that cares for thee,
And for thy maintenance commits his body
To painful labor both by sea and land,
To watch the night in storms, the day in cold,
Whilst thou liest warm at home, secure and safe;
And craves no other tribute at thy hands

But love, fair looks and true obedience;
Too little payment for so great a debt.
Such duty as the subject owes the prince
Even such a woman oweth to her husband;
And when she is froward, peevish, sullen, sour,
And not obedient to his honest will,
What is she but a foul contending rebel
And graceless traitor to her loving lord?
I am ashamed that women are so simple
To offer war where they should kneel for peace;
Or seek for rule, supremacy and sway,
When they are bound to serve, love and obey.
Why are our bodies soft and weak and smooth,
Unapt to toil and trouble in the world,
But that our soft conditions and our hearts
Should well agree with our external parts?
Come, come, you froward and unable worms!
My mind hath been as big as one of yours,
My heart as great, my reason haply more,
To bandy word for word and frown for frown;
But now I see our lances are but straws,
Our strength as weak, our weakness past compare,
That seeming to be most which we indeed least are.
Then vail your stomachs, for it is no boot,
And place your hands below your husband's foot:
In token of which duty, if he please,
My hand is ready; may it do him ease.

## 6. Rosalind, from *As You Like It*, Act III, Scene 5:

And why, I pray you? Who might be your mother,
That you insult, exult, and all at once,
Over the wretched? What though you have no beauty,
As, by my faith, I see no more in you
Than without candle may go dark to bed
Must you be therefore proud and pitiless?
Why, what means this? Why do you look on me?

I see no more in you than in the ordinary
Of nature's sale-work. Od's my little life,
I think she means to tangle my eyes too!
No, faith, proud mistress, hope not after it:
'Tis not your inky brows, your black silk hair,
Your bugle eyeballs, nor your cheek of cream,
That can entame my spirits to your worship.
You foolish shepherd, wherefore do you follow her,
Like foggy south puffing with wind and rain?
You are a thousand times a properer man
Than she a woman: 'tis such fools as you
That makes the world full of ill-favor'd children:
'Tis not her glass, but you, that flatters her;
And out of you she sees herself more proper
Than any of her lineaments can show her.
But, mistress, know yourself: down on your knees,
And thank heaven, fasting, for a good man's love:
For I must tell you friendly in your ear,
Sell when you can: you are not for all markets:
Cry the man mercy; love him; take his offer:
Foul is most foul, being foul to be a scoffer.
So take her to thee, shepherd: fare you well.

## 7. Tamora, from *Titus Andronicus*, Act 2 Scene 3:

Have I not reason, think you, to look pale?
These two have 'ticed me hither to this place:
A barren detested vale, you see it is;
The trees, though summer, yet forlorn and lean,
O'ercome with moss and baleful mistletoe:
Here never shines the sun; here nothing breeds,
Unless the nightly owl or fatal raven:
And when they show'd me this abhorred pit,
They told me, here, at dead time of the night,
A thousand fiends, a thousand hissing snakes,
Ten thousand swelling toads, as many urchins,
Would make such fearful and confused cries

As any mortal body hearing it
Should straight fall mad, or else die suddenly.
No sooner had they told this hellish tale,
But straight they told me they would bind me here
Unto the body of a dismal yew,
And leave me to this miserable death:
And then they call'd me foul adulteress,
Lascivious Goth, and all the bitterest terms
That ever ear did hear to such effect:
And, had you not by wondrous fortune come,
This vengeance on me had they executed.
Revenge it, as you love your mother's life,
Or be ye not henceforth call'd my children.

## 8. Duchess, from *Henry the Sixth, Part* Two, Act II, Scene 4:

Ah, Gloucester, teach me to forget myself!
For whilst I think I am thy married wife
And thou a prince, protector of this land,
Methinks I should not thus be led along,
Mail'd up in shame, with papers on my back,
And followed with a rabble that rejoice
To see my tears and hear my deep-set groans.
The ruthless flint doth cut my tender feet,
And when I start, the envious people laugh
And bid me be advised how I tread.
Ah, Humphrey, can I bear this shameful yoke?
Trow'st thou that e'er I'll look upon the world,
Or count them happy that enjoy the sun?
No; dark shall be my light and night my day;
To think upon my pomp shall be my hell.
Sometime I'll say, I am Duke Humphrey's wife,
And he a prince and ruler of the land:
Yet so he ruled and such a prince he was
As he stood by whilst I, his forlorn duchess,
Was made a wonder and a pointing-stock
To every idle rascal follower.

But be thou mild and blush not at my shame,
Nor stir at nothing till the axe of death
Hang over thee, as, sure, it shortly will;
For Suffolk, he that can do all in all
With her that hateth thee and hates us all,
And York and impious Beaufort, that false priest,
Have all limed bushes to betray thy wings,
And, fly thou how thou canst, they'll tangle thee:
But fear not thou, until thy foot be snared,
Nor never seek prevention of thy foes.

## 9. Hostess, from *Henry V*, Act II, Scene 3:

Nay, sure, he's not in hell: he's in Arthur's bosom, if ever man went
to Arthur's bosom. A' made a finer end and went away an it had
been any christom child; a' parted even just between twelve and
one, even at the turning o' the tide: for after I saw him fumble with
the sheets and play with flowers and smile upon his fingers' ends, I
knew there was but one way; for his nose was as sharp as a pen, and
a' babbled of green fields. 'How now, sir John!' quoth I 'what, man!
be o' good cheer.' So a' cried out 'God, God, God!' three or four
times. Now I, to comfort him, bid him a' should not think of God; I
hoped there was no need to trouble himself with any such
thoughts yet. So a' bade me lay more clothes on his feet: I put my
hand into the bed and felt them, and they were as cold as any
stone; then I felt to his knees, and they were as cold as any stone,
and so upward and upward, and all was as cold as any stone.

## 10. Lady Macbeth, from *Macbeth*, Act I, Scene 5:

Lady Macbeth: *(reading a letter)*

'They met me in the day of success: and I have
learned by the perfectest report, they have more in
them than mortal knowledge. When I burned in desire
to question them further, they made themselves air,
into which they vanished. Whiles I stood rapt in
the wonder of it, came missives from the king, who
all-hailed me 'Thane of Cawdor'; by which title,

before, these weird sisters saluted me, and referred
me to the coming on of time, with 'Hail, king that
shalt be!' This have I thought good to deliver
thee, my dearest partner of greatness, that thou
mightst not lose the dues of rejoicing, by being
ignorant of what greatness is promised thee. Lay it
to thy heart, and farewell.'
Glamis thou art, and Cawdor; and shalt be
What thou art promised: yet do I fear thy nature;
It is too full o' the milk of human kindness
To catch the nearest way: thou wouldst be great;
Art not without ambition, but without
The illness should attend it: what thou wouldst highly,
That wouldst thou holily; wouldst not play false,
And yet wouldst wrongly win: thou'ldst have, great Glamis,
That which cries 'Thus thou must do, if thou have it;
And that which rather thou dost fear to do
Than wishest should be undone.' Hie thee hither,
That I may pour my spirits in thine ear;
And chastise with the valor of my tongue
All that impedes thee from the golden round,
Which fate and metaphysical aid doth seem
To have thee crown'd withal.
*Enter a Messenger*
What is your tidings?

Messenger:      The king comes here tonight.

Lady Macbeth:  Thou'rt mad to say it:
Is not thy master with him? who, were't so,
Would have inform'd for preparation.

Messenger:      So please you, it is true: our thane is coming:
One of my fellows had the speed of him,
Who, almost dead for breath, had scarcely more
Than would make up his message.

Lady Macbeth:  Give him tending;
He brings great news.
*Exit Messenger*
The raven himself is hoarse
That croaks the fatal entrance of Duncan
Under my battlements. Come, you spirits
That tend on mortal thoughts, unsex me here,

And fill me from the crown to the toe top-full
Of direst cruelty! make thick my blood;
Stop up the access and passage to remorse,
That no compunctious visitings of nature
Shake my fell purpose, nor keep peace between
The effect and it! Come to my woman's breasts,
And take my milk for gall, you murdering ministers,
Wherever in your sightless substances
You wait on nature's mischief! Come, thick night,
And pall thee in the dunnest smoke of hell,
That my keen knife see not the wound it makes,
Nor heaven peep through the blanket of the dark,
To cry 'Hold, hold!'

# TEN GOOD MONOLOGUES FOR MEN

1. Iachimo, from *Cymbeline*, Act II, Scene 2:

*Iachimo comes from the trunk*
The crickets sing, and man's o'er-labor'd sense
Repairs itself by rest. Our Tarquin thus
Did softly press the rushes, ere he waken'd
The chastity he wounded. Cytherea,
How bravely thou becomest thy bed, fresh lily,
And whiter than the sheets! That I might touch!
But kiss; one kiss! Rubies unparagon'd,
How dearly they do't! 'Tis her breathing that
Perfumes the chamber thus: the flame o' the taper
Bows toward her, and would under-peep her lids,
To see the enclosed lights, now canopied
Under these windows, white and azure laced
With blue of heaven's own tinct. But my design,
To note the chamber: I will write all down:
Such and such pictures; there the window; such
The adornment of her bed; the arras; figures,
Why, such and such; and the contents o' the story.
Ah, but some natural notes about her body,
Above ten thousand meaner moveables
Would testify, to enrich mine inventory.
O sleep, thou ape of death, lie dull upon her!
And be her sense but as a monument,
Thus in a chapel lying! Come off, come off:
*Taking off her bracelet*
As slippery as the Gordian knot was hard!
'Tis mine; and this will witness outwardly,

As strongly as the conscience does within,
To the madding of her lord. On her left breast
A mole cinque-spotted, like the crimson drops
I' the bottom of a cowslip: here's a voucher,
Stronger than ever law could make: this secret
Will force him think I have pick'd the lock and ta'en
The treasure of her honor. No more. To what end?
Why should I write this down, that's riveted,
Screw'd to my memory? She hath been reading late
The tale of Tereus; here the leaf's turn'd down
Where Philomel gave up. I have enough:
To the trunk again, and shut the spring of it.
Swift, swift, you dragons of the night, that dawning
May bare the raven's eye! I lodge in fear;
Though this a heavenly angel, hell is here.
*Clock strikes*
One, two, three: time, time!
*Goes into the trunk.*

## 2. King Richard, from *Richard II*, Act III, Scene 3:

We are amazed; and thus long have we stood
To watch the fearful bending of thy knee,
Because we thought ourself thy lawful king:
And if we be, how dare thy joints forget
To pay their awful duty to our presence?
If we be not, show us the hand of God
That hath dismissed us from our stewardship;
For well we know, no hand of blood and bone
Can gripe the sacred handle of our sceptre,
Unless he do profane, steal, or usurp.
And though you think that all, as you have done,
Have torn their souls by turning them from us,
And we are barren and bereft of friends;
Yet know, my master, God omnipotent,
Is mustering in his clouds on our behalf
Armies of pestilence; and they shall strike

Your children yet unborn and unbegot,
That lift your vassal hands against my head
And threat the glory of my precious crown.
Tell Bolingbroke—for yond methinks he stands—
That every stride he makes upon my land
Is dangerous treason: he is come to ope
The purple testament of bleeding war;
But ere the crown he looks for live in peace,
Ten thousand bloody crowns of mothers' sons
Shall ill become the flower of England's face,
Change the complexion of her maid-pale peace
To scarlet indignation and bedew
Her pastures' grass with faithful English blood.

### 3. Richard, from *Richard III*, Act I, Scene 2:

Was ever woman in this humor woo'd?
Was ever woman in this humor won?
I'll have her; but I will not keep her long.
What! I, that kill'd her husband and his father,
To take her in her heart's extremest hate,
With curses in her mouth, tears in her eyes,
The bleeding witness of her hatred by;
Having God, her conscience, and these bars against me,
And I nothing to back my suit at all,
But the plain devil and dissembling looks,
And yet to win her, all the world to nothing!
Ha!
Hath she forgot already that brave prince,
Edward, her lord, whom I, some three months since,
Stabb'd in my angry mood at Tewksbury?
A sweeter and a lovelier gentleman,
Framed in the prodigality of nature,
Young, valiant, wise, and, no doubt, right royal,
The spacious world cannot again afford
And will she yet debase her eyes on me,
That cropp'd the golden prime of this sweet prince,

And made her widow to a woful bed?
On me, whose all not equals Edward's moiety?
On me, that halt and am unshapen thus?
My dukedom to a beggarly denier,
I do mistake my person all this while:
Upon my life, she finds, although I cannot,
Myself to be a marvellous proper man.
I'll be at charges for a looking-glass,
And entertain some score or two of tailors,
To study fashions to adorn my body:
Since I am crept in favor with myself,
Will maintain it with some little cost.
But first I'll turn yon fellow in his grave;
And then return lamenting to my love.
Shine out, fair sun, till I have bought a glass,
That I may see my shadow as I pass.

## 4. Lewis, from *King John*, Act V, Scene 2:

Your grace shall pardon me, I will not back:
I am too high-born to be propertied,
To be a secondary at control,
Or useful serving-man and instrument,
To any sovereign state throughout the world.
Your breath first kindled the dead coal of wars
Between this chastised kingdom and myself,
And brought in matter that should feed this fire;
And now 'tis far too huge to be blown out
With that same weak wind which enkindled it.
You taught me how to know the face of right,
Acquainted me with interest to this land,
Yea, thrust this enterprise into my heart;
And come ye now to tell me John hath made
His peace with Rome? What is that peace to me?
I, by the honor of my marriage-bed,
After young Arthur, claim this land for mine;
And, now it is half-conquer'd, must I back

Because that John hath made his peace with Rome?
Am I Rome's slave? What penny hath Rome borne,
What men provided, what munition sent,
To underprop this action? Is't not I
That undergo this charge? who else but I,
And such as to my claim are liable,
Sweat in this business and maintain this war?
Have I not heard these islanders shout out
'Vive le roi!' as I have bank'd their towns?
Have I not here the best cards for the game,
To win this easy match play'd for a crown?
And shall I now give o'er the yielded set?
No, no, on my soul, it never shall be said.

## 5. Bastard, from *King John*, Act II, Scene 1:

Mad world! mad kings! mad composition!
John, to stop Arthur's title in the whole,
Hath willingly departed with a part,
And France, whose armor conscience buckled on,
Whom zeal and charity brought to the field
As God's own soldier, rounded in the ear
With that same purpose-changer, that sly devil,
That broker, that still breaks the pate of faith,
That daily break-vow, he that wins of all,
Of kings, of beggars, old men, young men, maids,
Who, having no external thing to lose
But the word 'maid,' cheats the poor maid of that,
That smooth-faced gentleman, tickling Commodity,
Commodity, the bias of the world,
The world, who of itself is peized well,
Made to run even upon even ground,
Till this advantage, this vile-drawing bias,
This sway of motion, this Commodity,
Makes it take head from all indifferency,
From all direction, purpose, course, intent:
And this same bias, this Commodity,
This bawd, this broker, this all-changing word,

Clapp'd on the outward eye of fickle France,
Hath drawn him from his own determined aid,
From a resolved and honorable war,
To a most base and vile-concluded peace.
And why rail I on this Commodity?
But for because he hath not woo'd me yet:
Not that I have the power to clutch my hand,
When his fair angels would salute my palm;
But for my hand, as unattempted yet,
Like a poor beggar, raileth on the rich.
Well, whiles I am a beggar, I will rail
And say there is no sin but to be rich;
And being rich, my virtue then shall be
To say there is no vice but beggary.
Since kings break faith upon Commodity,
Gain, be my lord, for I will worship thee.

## 6. King Henry, from *Henry V*, Act IV, Scene 1:

Upon the king! let us our lives, our souls,
Our debts, our careful wives,
Our children and our sins lay on the king!
We must bear all. O hard condition,
Twin-born with greatness, subject to the breath
Of every fool, whose sense no more can feel
But his own wringing! What infinite heart's-ease
Must kings neglect, that private men enjoy!
And what have kings, that privates have not too,
Save ceremony, save general ceremony?
And what art thou, thou idle ceremony?
What kind of god art thou, that suffer'st more
Of mortal griefs than do thy worshippers?
What are thy rents? what are thy comings in?
O ceremony, show me but thy worth!
What is thy soul of adoration?
Art thou aught else but place, degree and form,
Creating awe and fear in other men?
Wherein thou art less happy being fear'd

Than they in fearing.
What drink'st thou oft, instead of homage sweet,
But poison'd flattery? O, be sick, great greatness,
And bid thy ceremony give thee cure!
Think'st thou the fiery fever will go out
With titles blown from adulation?
Will it give place to flexure and low bending?
Canst thou, when thou command'st the beggar's knee,
Command the health of it? No, thou proud dream,
That play'st so subtly with a king's repose;
I am a king that find thee, and I know
'Tis not the balm, the scepter and the ball,
The sword, the mace, the crown imperial,
The intertissued robe of gold and pearl,
The farced title running 'fore the king,
The throne he sits on, nor the tide of pomp
That beats upon the high shore of this world,
No, not all these, thrice-gorgeous ceremony,
Not all these, laid in bed majestical,
Can sleep so soundly as the wretched slave,
Who with a body fill'd and vacant mind
Gets him to rest, cramm'd with distressful bread;
Never sees horrid night, the child of hell,
But, like a lackey, from the rise to set
Sweats in the eye of Phoebus and all night
Sleeps in Elysium; next day after dawn,
Doth rise and help Hyperion to his horse,
And follows so the ever-running year,
With profitable labor, to his grave:
And, but for ceremony, such a wretch,
Winding up days with toil and nights with sleep,
Had the fore-hand and vantage of a king.
The slave, a member of the country's peace,
Enjoys it; but in gross brain little wots
What watch the king keeps to maintain the peace,
Whose hours the peasant best advantages.

## 7. Angelo, from *Measure for Measure*, Act II, Scene 4:

Who will believe thee, Isabel?
My unsoil'd name, the austereness of my life,
My vouch against you, and my place i' the state,
Will so your accusation overweigh,
That you shall stifle in your own report
And smell of calumny. I have begun,
And now I give my sensual race the rein:
Fit thy consent to my sharp appetite;
Lay by all nicety and prolixious blushes,
That banish what they sue for; redeem thy brother
By yielding up thy body to my will;
Or else he must not only die the death,
But thy unkindness shall his death draw out
To lingering sufferance. Answer me to-morrow,
Or, by the affection that now guides me most,
I'll prove a tyrant to him. As for you,
Say what you can, my false o'erweighs your true.

## 8. Iago, from *Othello*, Act I, Scene 3:

Thus do I ever make my fool my purse:
For I mine own gain'd knowledge should profane,
If I would time expend with such a snipe.
But for my sport and profit. I hate the Moor:
And it is thought abroad, that 'twixt my sheets
He has done my office: I know not if't be true;
But I, for mere suspicion in that kind,
Will do as if for surety. He holds me well;
The better shall my purpose work on him.
Cassio's a proper man: let me see now:
To get his place and to plume up my will
In double knavery—How, how? Let's see:
After some time, to abuse Othello's ear
That he is too familiar with his wife.
He hath a person and a smooth dispose

To be suspected, framed to make women false.
The Moor is of a free and open nature,
That thinks men honest that but seem to be so,
And will as tenderly be led by the nose
As asses are.
I have't. It is engender'd. Hell and night
Must bring this monstrous birth to the world's light.

## 9. Malvolio, from *Twelfth Night*, Act II, Scene 5:

M, O, A, I; this simulation is not as the former: and
yet, to crush this a little, it would bow to me, for
every one of these letters are in my name. Soft!
here follows prose.
*Reads*
'If this fall into thy hand, revolve. In my stars I
am above thee; but be not afraid of greatness: some
are born great, some achieve greatness, and some
have greatness thrust upon 'em. Thy Fates open
their hands; let thy blood and spirit embrace them;
and, to inure thyself to what thou art like to be,
cast thy humble slough and appear fresh. Be
opposite with a kinsman, surly with servants; let
thy tongue tang arguments of state; put thyself into
the trick of singularity: she thus advises thee
that sighs for thee. Remember who commended thy
yellow stockings, and wished to see thee ever
cross-gartered: I say, remember. Go to, thou art
made, if thou desirest to be so; if not, let me see
thee a steward still, the fellow of servants, and
not worthy to touch Fortune's fingers. Farewell.
She that would alter services with thee,
THE FORTUNATE-UNHAPPY.'
Daylight and champagne discovers not more: this is
open. I will be proud, I will read politic authors,
I will baffle Sir Toby, I will wash off gross
acquaintance, I will be point-devise the very man.

I do not now fool myself, to let imagination jade
me; for every reason excites to this, that my lady
loves me. She did commend my yellow stockings of
late, she did praise my leg being cross-gartered;
and in this she manifests herself to my love, and
with a kind of injunction drives me to these habits
of her liking. I thank my stars I am happy. I will
be strange, stout, in yellow stockings, and
cross-gartered, even with the swiftness of putting
on. Jove and my stars be praised! Here is yet a
postscript.
*Reads*
'Thou canst not choose but know who I am. If thou
entertainest my love, let it appear in thy smiling;
thy smiles become thee well; therefore in my
presence still smile, dear my sweet, I prithee.'
Jove, I thank thee: I will smile; I will do
everything that thou wilt have me.

## 10. Mercutio, from *Romeo and Juliet*, Act I, Scene 4:

Mercutio:    O, then, I see Queen Mab hath been with you.
             She is the fairies' midwife, and she comes
             In shape no bigger than an agate-stone
             On the fore-finger of an alderman,
             Drawn with a team of little atomies
             Athwart men's noses as they lie asleep;
             Her wagon-spokes made of long spiders' legs,
             The cover of the wings of grasshoppers,
             The traces of the smallest spider's web,
             The collars of the moonshine's watery beams,
             Her whip of cricket's bone, the lash of film,
             Her wagoner a small grey-coated gnat,
             Not so big as a round little worm
             Prick'd from the lazy finger of a maid;
             Her chariot is an empty hazel-nut
             Made by the joiner squirrel or old grub,
             Time out o' mind the fairies' coachmakers.

        And in this state she gallops night by night
        Through lovers' brains, and then they dream of love;
        O'er courtiers' knees, that dream on court'sies straight,
        O'er lawyers' fingers, who straight dream on fees,
        O'er ladies ' lips, who straight on kisses dream,
        Which oft the angry Mab with blisters plagues,
        Because their breaths with sweetmeats tainted are:
        Sometime she gallops o'er a courtier's nose,
        And then dreams he of smelling out a suit;
        And sometime comes she with a tithe-pig's tail
        Tickling a parson's nose as a' lies asleep,
        Then dreams, he of another benefice:
        Sometime she driveth o'er a soldier's neck,
        And then dreams he of cutting foreign throats,
        Of breaches, ambuscadoes, Spanish blades,
        Of healths five-fathom deep; and then anon
        Drums in his ear, at which he starts and wakes,
        And being thus frighted swears a prayer or two
        And sleeps again. This is that very Mab
        That plats the manes of horses in the night,
        And bakes the elflocks in foul sluttish hairs,
        Which once untangled, much misfortune bodes:
        This is the hag, when maids lie on their backs,
        That presses them and learns them first to bear,
        Making them women of good carriage:
        This is she—
Romeo:    Peace, peace, Mercutio, peace!
        Thou talk'st of nothing.
Mercutio:  True, I talk of dreams,
        Which are the children of an idle brain,
        Begot of nothing but vain fantasy,
        Which is as thin of substance as the air
        And more inconstant than the wind, who wooes
        Even now the frozen bosom of the north,
        And, being anger'd, puffs away from thence,
        Turning his face to the dew-dropping south.

# TEN ALTERNATIVE MONOLOGUES FOR WOMEN

A director won't get tired of hearing the same old monologue again and again, if it is done *extremely* well. But it always piques curiosity, and shows a strong imagination and insight if you choose one that he or she has never heard before. Here, I give you ten for women and ten for men, because there's no need to keep rehashing the same stuff over and over again. There are scores of excellent monologues in Shakespeare's work that people rarely sniff out. Enjoy these, and *use* them.

1. Queen Katharine, from *Henry VIII*, Act II, Scene 4:

Sir, I desire you do me right and justice;
And to bestow your pity on me: for
I am a most poor woman, and a stranger,
Born out of your dominions; having here
No judge indifferent, nor no more assurance
Of equal friendship and proceeding. Alas, sir,
In what have I offended you? What cause
Hath my behavior given to your displeasure,
That thus you should proceed to put me off,
And take your good grace from me? Heaven witness,
I have been to you a true and humble wife,
At all times to your will conformable;
Ever in fear to kindle your dislike,
Yea, subject to your countenance, glad or sorry
As I saw it inclined: when was the hour
I ever contradicted your desire,
Or made it not mine too? Or which of your friends

Have I not strove to love, although I knew
He were mine enemy? What friend of mine
That had to him derived your anger, did I
Continue in my liking? Nay, gave notice
He was from thence discharged. Sir, call to mind
That I have been your wife, in this obedience,
Upward of twenty years, and have been blest
With many children by you: if, in the course
And process of this time, you can report,
And prove it too, against mine honor aught,
My bond to wedlock, or my love and duty,
Against your sacred person, in God's name,
Turn me away; and let the foul'st contempt
Shut door upon me, and so give me up
To the sharp'st kind of justice. Please you sir,
The king, your father, was reputed for
A prince most prudent, of an excellent
And unmatch'd wit and judgment: Ferdinand,
My father, king of Spain, was reckon'd one
The wisest prince that there had reign'd by many
A year before: it is not to be question'd
That they had gather'd a wise council to them
Of every realm, that did debate this business,
Who deem'd our marriage lawful: wherefore I humbly
Beseech you, sir, to spare me, till I may
Be by my friends in Spain advised; whose counsel
I will implore: if not, i' the name of God,
Your pleasure be fulfill'd!

## 2. Constance, from *King John*, Act III, Scene 1:

You have beguiled me with a counterfeit
Resembling majesty, which, being touch'd and tried,
Proves valueless: you are forsworn, forsworn;
You came in arms to spill mine enemies' blood,
But now in arms you strengthen it with yours:
The grappling vigor and rough frown of war

Is cold in amity and painted peace,
And our oppression hath made up this league.
Arm, arm, you heavens, against these perjured kings!
A widow cries; be husband to me, heavens!
Let not the hours of this ungodly day
Wear out the day in peace; but, ere sunset,
Set armed discord 'twixt these perjured kings!
Hear me, O, hear me!
War! War! No peace! Peace is to me a war
O Lymoges! O Austria! thou dost shame
That bloody spoil: thou slave, thou wretch, thou coward!
Thou little valiant, great in villany!
Thou ever strong upon the stronger side!
Thou Fortune's champion that dost never fight
But when her humorous ladyship is by
To teach thee safety! Thou art perjured too,
And soothest up greatness. What a fool art thou,
A ramping fool, to brag and stamp and swear
Upon my party! Thou cold-blooded slave,
Hast thou not spoke like thunder on my side,
Been sworn my soldier, bidding me depend
Upon thy stars, thy fortune and thy strength,
And dost thou now fall over to my foes?
Thou wear a lion's hide! doff it for shame,
And hang a calf's-skin on those recreant limbs.

## 3. Paulina, from *The Winter's Tale*, Act III, Scene 2:

What studied torments, tyrant, hast for me?
What wheels? racks? fires? what flaying? boiling?
In leads or oils? what old or newer torture
Must I receive, whose every word deserves
To taste of thy most worst? Thy tyranny
Together working with thy jealousies,
Fancies too weak for boys, too green and idle
For girls of nine, O, think what they have done
And then run mad indeed, stark mad! for all

Thy bygone fooleries were but spices of it.
That thou betray'dst Polixenes,'twas nothing;
That did but show thee, of a fool, inconstant
And damnable ingrateful: nor was't much,
Thou wouldst have poison'd good Camillo's honor,
To have him kill a king: poor trespasses,
More monstrous standing by: whereof I reckon
The casting forth to crows thy baby-daughter
To be or none or little; though a devil
Would have shed water out of fire ere done't:
Nor is't directly laid to thee, the death
Of the young prince, whose honorable thoughts,
Thoughts high for one so tender, cleft the heart
That could conceive a gross and foolish sire
Blemish'd his gracious dam: this is not, no,
Laid to thy answer: but the last, O lords,
When I have said, cry 'woe!' the queen, the queen,
The sweet'st, dear'st creature's dead, and vengeance for't
Not dropp'd down yet.

## 4. Helena, from *All's Well That Ends Well*, Act I, Scene 3:

Then, I confess,
Here on my knee, before high heaven and you,
That before you, and next unto high heaven,
I love your son.
My friends were poor, but honest; so's my love:
Be not offended; for it hurts not him
That he is loved of me: I follow him not
By any token of presumptuous suit;
Nor would I have him till I do deserve him;
Yet never know how that desert should be.
I know I love in vain, strive against hope;
Yet in this captious and intenible sieve
I still pour in the waters of my love
And lack not to lose still: thus, Indian-like,
Religious in mine error, I adore

The sun, that looks upon his worshipper,
But knows of him no more. My dearest madam,
Let not your hate encounter with my love
For loving where you do: but if yourself,
Whose aged honor cites a virtuous youth,
Did ever in so true a flame of liking
Wish chastely and love dearly, that your Dian
Was both herself and love: O, then, give pity
To her, whose state is such that cannot choose
But lend and give where she is sure to lose;
That seeks not to find that her search implies,
But riddle-like lives sweetly where she dies!

## 5. Constance, from *King John*, Act III, Scene 1:

Gone to be married! gone to swear a peace!
False blood to false blood join'd! gone to be friends!
Shall Lewis have Blanch, and Blanch those provinces?
It is not so; thou hast misspoke, misheard:
Be well advised, tell o'er thy tale again:
It cannot be; thou dost but say 'tis so:
I trust I may not trust thee; for thy word
Is but the vain breath of a common man:
Believe me, I do not believe thee, man;
I have a king's oath to the contrary.
Thou shalt be punish'd for thus frighting me,
For I am sick and capable of fears,
Oppress'd with wrongs and therefore full of fears,
A widow, husbandless, subject to fears,
A woman, naturally born to fears;
And though thou now confess thou didst but jest,
With my vex'd spirits I cannot take a truce,
But they will quake and tremble all this day.
What dost thou mean by shaking of thy head?
Why dost thou look so sadly on my son?
What means that hand upon that breast of thine?
Why holds thine eye that lamentable rheum,

Like a proud river peering o'er his bounds?
Be these sad signs confirmers of thy words?
Then speak again; not all thy former tale,
But this one word, whether thy tale be true.

## 6. Imogen, from *Cymbeline*, Act III, Scene 6:

I see a man's life is a tedious one:
I have tired myself, and for two nights together
Have made the ground my bed. I should be sick,
But that my resolution helps me. Milford,
When from the mountain-top Pisanio show'd thee,
Thou wast within a ken: O Jove! I think
Foundations fly the wretched; such, I mean,
Where they should be relieved. Two beggars told me
I could not miss my way: will poor folks lie,
That have afflictions on them, knowing 'tis
A punishment or trial? Yes; no wonder,
When rich ones scarce tell true. To lapse in fulness
Is sorer than to lie for need, and falsehood
Is worse in kings than beggars. My dear lord!
Thou art one o' the false ones. Now I think on thee,
My hunger's gone; but even before, I was
At point to sink for food. But what is this?
Here is a path to't: 'tis some savage hold:
I were best not to call; I dare not call: yet famine,
Ere clean it o'erthrow nature, makes it valiant,
Plenty and peace breeds cowards: hardness ever
Of hardiness is mother. Ho! who's here?
If any thing that's civil, speak; if savage,
Take or lend. Ho! No answer? Then I'll enter.
Best draw my sword: and if mine enemy
But fear the sword like me, he'll scarcely look on't.
Such a foe, good heavens!

## 7. Adriana, from *The Comedy of Errors*, Act II, Scene 1:

His company must do his minions grace,
Whilst I at home starve for a merry look.
Hath homely age the alluring beauty took
From my poor cheek? then he hath wasted it:
Are my discourses dull? barren my wit?
If voluble and sharp discourse be marr'd,
Unkindness blunts it more than marble hard:
Do their gay vestments his affections bait?
That's not my fault: he's master of my state:
What ruins are in me that can be found,
By him not ruin'd? then is he the ground
Of my defeatures. My decayed fair
A sunny look of his would soon repair
But, too unruly deer, he breaks the pale
And feeds from home; poor I am but his stale.
Unfeeling fools can with such wrongs dispense.
I know his eye doth homage otherwhere,
Or else what lets it but he would be here?
Sister, you know he promised me a chain;
Would that alone, alone he would detain,
So he would keep fair quarter with his bed!
I see the jewel best enamelled
Will lose his beauty; yet the gold bides still,
That others touch, and often touching will
Wear gold: and no man that hath a name,
By falsehood and corruption doth it shame.
Since that my beauty cannot please his eye,
I'll weep what's left away, and weeping die.

## 8. Countess, from *All's Well That Ends Well*, Act I, Scene 3:

Yes, Helen, you might be my daughter-in-law:
God shield you mean it not! daughter and mother
So strive upon your pulse. What, pale again?
My fear hath catch'd your fondness: now I see
The mystery of your loneliness, and find
Your salt tears' head: now to all sense 'tis gross
You love my son; invention is ashamed,
Against the proclamation of thy passion,
To say thou dost not: therefore tell me true;
But tell me then, 'tis so; for, look thy cheeks
Confess it, th' one to th' other; and thine eyes
See it so grossly shown in thy behaviors
That in their kind they speak it: only sin
And hellish obstinacy tie thy tongue,
That truth should be suspected. Speak, is't so?
If it be so, you have wound a goodly clew;
If it be not, forswear't: howe'er, I charge thee,
As heaven shall work in me for thine avail,
Tell me truly.

## 9. Queen, from *Cymbeline*, Act III, Scene 1:

    That opportunity,
Which then they had to take from 's, to resume
We have again. Remember, sir, my liege,
The kings your ancestors, together with
The natural bravery of your isle, which stands
As Neptune's park, ribbed and paled in
With rocks unscalable and roaring waters,
With sands that will not bear your enemies' boats,
But suck them up to the topmast. A kind of conquest
Caesar made here; but made not here his brag
Of 'came' and 'saw' and 'overcame: 'with shame—
That first that ever touch'd him—he was carried
From off our coast, twice beaten; and his shipping—

Poor ignorant baubles! Upon our terrible seas,
Like egg-shells moved upon their surges, crack'd
As easily 'gainst our rocks: for joy whereof
The famed Cassibelan, who was once at point—
O giglot fortune!—To master Caesar's sword,
Made Lud's town with rejoicing fires bright
And Britons strut with courage.

## 10. Constance, from *King John,* Act III, Scene 1:

If thou, that bid'st me be content, wert grim,
Ugly and slanderous to thy mother's womb,
Full of unpleasing blots and sightless stains,
Lame, foolish, crooked, swart, prodigious,
Patch'd with foul moles and eye-offending marks,
I would not care, I then would be content,
For then I should not love thee, no, nor thou
Become thy great birth nor deserve a crown.
But thou art fair, and at thy birth, dear boy,
Nature and Fortune join'd to make thee great:
Of Nature's gifts thou mayst with lilies boast,
And with the half-blown rose. But Fortune, O,
She is corrupted, changed and won from thee;
She adulterates hourly with thine uncle John,
And with her golden hand hath pluck'd on France
To tread down fair respect of sovereignty,
And made his majesty the bawd to theirs.
France is a bawd to Fortune and King John,
That strumpet Fortune, that usurping John!
Tell me, thou fellow, is not France forsworn?
Envenom him with words, or get thee gone
And leave those woes alone which I alone
Am bound to under-bear.

# TEN ALTERNATIVE MONOLOGUES FOR MEN

1. Timon, from *Timon of Athens*, Act IV, Scene 3:

Not by his breath that is more miserable.
Thou art a slave, whom Fortune's tender arm
With favor never clasp'd; but bred a dog.
Hadst thou, like us from our first swath, proceeded
The sweet degrees that this brief world affords
To such as may the passive drugs of it
Freely command, thou wouldst have plunged thyself
In general riot; melted down thy youth
In different beds of lust; and never learn'd
The icy precepts of respect, but follow'd
The sugar'd game before thee. But myself,
Who had the world as my confectionary,
The mouths, the tongues, the eyes and hearts of men
At duty, more than I could frame employment,
That numberless upon me stuck as leaves
Do on the oak, hive with one winter's brush
Fell from their boughs and left me open, bare
For every storm that blows: I, to bear this,
That never knew but better, is some burden:
Thy nature did commence in sufferance, time
Hath made thee hard in't. Why shouldst thou hate men?
They never flatter'd thee: what hast thou given?
If thou wilt curse, thy father, that poor rag,
Must be thy subject, who in spite put stuff
To some she beggar and compounded thee
Poor rogue hereditary. Hence, be gone!
If thou hadst not been born the worst of men,
Thou hadst been a knave and flatterer.

## 2. Timon, from *Timon of Athens*, Act IV, Scene 3:

Nor on the beasts themselves, the birds, and fishes;
You must eat men. Yet thanks I must you con
That you are thieves profess'd, that you work not
In holier shapes: for there is boundless theft
In limited professions. Rascal thieves,
Here's gold. Go, suck the subtle blood o' the grape,
Till the high fever seethe your blood to froth,
And so 'scape hanging: trust not the physician;
His antidotes are poison, and he slays
Moe than you rob: take wealth and lives together;
Do villany, do, since you protest to do't,
Like workmen. I'll example you with thievery.
The sun's a thief, and with his great attraction
Robs the vast sea: the moon's an arrant thief,
And her pale fire she snatches from the sun:
The sea's a thief, whose liquid surge resolves
The moon into salt tears: the earth's a thief,
That feeds and breeds by a composture stolen
From general excrement: each thing's a thief:
The laws, your curb and whip, in their rough power
Have uncheque'd theft. Love not yourselves: away,
Rob one another. There's more gold. Cut throats:
All that you meet are thieves: to Athens go,
Break open shops; nothing can you steal,
But thieves do lose it: steal no less for this
I give you; and gold confound you howsoe'er! Amen.

## 3. Bastard, from *King John*, Act I, Scene 1:

Brother, adieu: good fortune come to thee!
For thou wast got i' the way of honesty.
*Exeunt all but Bastard*
A foot of honor better than I was;
But many a many foot of land the worse.
Well, now can I make any Joan a lady.
'Good den, sir Richard!'—'God-a-mercy, fellow!'—

And if his name be George, I'll call him Peter;
For new-made honor doth forget men's names;
'Tis too respective and too sociable
For your conversion. Now your traveller,
He and his toothpick at my worship's mess,
And when my knightly stomach is sufficed,
Why then I suck my teeth and catechise
My picked man of countries: 'My dear sir,'
Thus, leaning on mine elbow, I begin,
'I shall beseech you'—that is question now;
And then comes answer like an Absey book:
'O sir,' says answer, 'at your best command;
At your employment; at your service, sir;'
'No, sir,' says question, 'I, sweet sir, at yours:'
And so, ere answer knows what question would,
Saving in dialogue of compliment,
And talking of the Alps and Apennines,
The Pyrenean and the river Po,
It draws toward supper in conclusion so.
But this is worshipful society
And fits the mounting spirit like myself,
For he is but a bastard to the time
That doth not smack of observation;
And so am I, whether I smack or no;
And not alone in habit and device,
Exterior form, outward accoutrement,
But from the inward motion to deliver
Sweet, sweet, sweet poison for the age's tooth:
Which, though I will not practice to deceive,
Yet, to avoid deceit, I mean to learn;
For it shall strew the footsteps of my rising.
But who comes in such haste in riding-robes?
What woman-post is this? hath she no husband
That will take pains to blow a horn before her?
*Enter Lady Faulconbridge and Gurney*
O me! it is my mother. How now, good lady!
What brings you here to court so hastily?

## 4. King John, from *King John*, Act II, Scene 1:

For our advantage; therefore hear us first.
These flags of France, that are advanced here
Before the eye and prospect of your town,
Have hither march'd to your endamagement:
The cannons have their bowels full of wrath,
And ready mounted are they to spit forth
Their iron indignation 'gainst your walls:
All preparation for a bloody siege
All merciless proceeding by these French
Confronts your city's eyes, your winking gates;
And but for our approach those sleeping stones,
That as a waist doth girdle you about,
By the compulsion of their ordinance
By this time from their fixed beds of lime
Had been dishabited, and wide havoc made
For bloody power to rush upon your peace.
But on the sight of us your lawful king,
Who painfully with much expedient march
Have brought a countercheque before your gates,
To save unscratch'd your city's threatened cheeks,
Behold, the French amazed vouchsafe a parle;
And now, instead of bullets wrapp'd in fire,
To make a shaking fever in your walls,
They shoot but calm words folded up in smoke,
To make a faithless error in your ears:
Which trust accordingly, kind citizens,
And let us in, your king, whose labor'd spirits,
Forwearied in this action of swift speed,
Crave harbourage within your city walls.

## 5. Ford, from *The Merry Wives of Windsor*, Act II, Scene 2:

What a damned Epicurean rascal is this! My heart is
ready to crack with impatience. Who says this is
improvident jealousy? my wife hath sent to him; the
hour is fixed; the match is made. Would any man

have thought this? See the hell of having a false
woman! My bed shall be abused, my coffers
ransacked, my reputation gnawn at; and I shall not
only receive this villanous wrong, but stand under
the adoption of abominable terms, and by him that
does me this wrong. Terms! Names! Amaimon sounds
well; Lucifer, well; Barbason, well; yet they are
devils' additions, the names of fiends: but Cuckold!
Wittol!—Cuckold! the devil himself hath not such a name.
Page is an ass, a secure ass: he will trust his wife; he will
not be jealous. I will rather trust a Fleming with my butter,
Parson Hugh the Welshman with my cheese, an Irishman
with my aqua-vitae bottle, or a thief to walk my ambling
gelding, than my wife with herself; then she plots,
then she ruminates, then she devises; and what they
think in their hearts they may effect, they will
break their hearts but they will effect. God be
praised for my jealousy! Eleven o'clock the hour.
I will prevent this, detect my wife, be revenged on
Falstaff, and laugh at Page. I will about it;
better three hours too soon than a minute too late.
Fie, fie, fie! cuckold! cuckold! cuckold!

## 6. Melun, from *King John*, Act V, Scene 4:

Have I not hideous death within my view,
Retaining but a quantity of life,
Which bleeds away, even as a form of wax
Resolveth from his figure 'gainst the fire?
What in the world should make me now deceive,
Since I must lose the use of all deceit?
Why should I then be false, since it is true
That I must die here and live hence by truth?
I say again, if Lewis do win the day,
He is forsworn, if e'er those eyes of yours
Behold another day break in the east:
But even this night, whose black contagious breath
Already smokes about the burning crest

Of the old, feeble and day-wearied sun,
Even this ill night, your breathing shall expire,
Paying the fine of rated treachery
Even with a treacherous fine of all your lives,
If Lewis by your assistance win the day.
Commend me to one Hubert with your king:
The love of him, and this respect besides,
For that my grandsire was an Englishman,
Awakes my conscience to confess all this.
In lieu whereof, I pray you, bear me hence
From forth the noise and rumor of the field,
Where I may think the remnant of my thoughts
In peace, and part this body and my soul
With contemplation and devout desires.

## 7. Salisbury, from *King John*, Act V, Scene 2:

Upon our sides it never shall be broken.
And, noble Dauphin, albeit we swear
A voluntary zeal and an unurged faith
To your proceedings; yet believe me, prince,
I am not glad that such a sore of time
Should seek a plaster by contemn'd revolt,
And heal the inveterate canker of one wound
By making many. O, it grieves my soul,
That I must draw this metal from my side
To be a widow-maker! O, and there
Where honorable rescue and defense
Cries out upon the name of Salisbury!
But such is the infection of the time,
That, for the health and physic of our right,
We cannot deal but with the very hand
Of stern injustice and confused wrong.
And is't not pity, O my grieved friends,
That we, the sons and children of this isle,
Were born to see so sad an hour as this;
Wherein we step after a stranger march
Upon her gentle bosom, and fill up

Her enemies' ranks—I must withdraw and weep
Upon the spot of this enforced cause—
To grace the gentry of a land remote,
And follow unacquainted colors here?
What, here? O nation, that thou couldst remove!
That Neptune's arms, who clippeth thee about,
Would bear thee from the knowledge of thyself,
And grapple thee unto a pagan shore;
Where these two Christian armies might combine
The blood of malice in a vein of league,
And not to spend it so unneighborly!

### 8. Coriolanus, from *Coriolanus*, Act III, Scene 1:

'Shall'!
O good but most unwise patricians! Why,
You grave but reckless senators, have you thus
Given Hydra here to choose an officer,
That with his peremptory 'shall,' being but
The horn and noise o' the monster's, wants not spirit
To say he'll turn your current in a ditch,
And make your channel his? If he have power
Then veil your ignorance; if none, awake
Your dangerous lenity. If you are learn'd,
Be not as common fools; if you are not,
Let them have cushions by you. You are plebeians,
If they be senators: and they are no less,
When, both your voices blended, the great'st taste
Most palates theirs. They choose their magistrate,
And such a one as he, who puts his 'shall,'
His popular 'shall' against a graver bench
Than ever frown in Greece. By Jove himself!
It makes the consuls base: and my soul aches
To know, when two authorities are up,
Neither supreme, how soon confusion
May enter 'twixt the gap of both and take
The one by the other.

## 9. Bastard, from *King John*, Act V, Scene 2:

By all the blood that ever fury breathed,
The youth says well. Now hear our English king;
For thus his royalty doth speak in me.
He is prepared, and reason too he should:
This apish and unmannerly approach,
This harness'd masque and unadvised revel,
This unhair'd sauciness and boyish troops,
The king doth smile at; and is well prepared
To whip this dwarfish war, these pigmy arms,
From out the circle of his territories.
That hand which had the strength, even at your door,
To cudgel you and make you take the hatch,
To dive like buckets in concealed wells,
To crouch in litter of your stable planks,
To lie like pawns lock'd up in chests and trunks,
To hug with swine, to seek sweet safety out
In vaults and prisons, and to thrill and shake
Even at the crying of your nation's crow,
Thinking his voice an armed Englishman;
Shall that victorious hand be feebled here,
That in your chambers gave you chastisement?
No: know the gallant monarch is in arms
And like an eagle o'er his aery towers,
To souse annoyance that comes near his nest.
And you degenerate, you ingrate revolts,
You bloody Neroes, ripping up the womb
Of your dear mother England, blush for shame;
For your own ladies and pale-visaged maids
Like Amazons come tripping after drums,
Their thimbles into armed gauntlets change,
Their needles to lances, and their gentle hearts
To fierce and bloody inclination.

## 10. Pericles, from *Pericles*, Act I, Scene 1:

How courtesy would seem to cover sin,
When what is done is like an hypocrite,
The which is good in nothing but in sight!
If it be true that I interpret false,
Then were it certain you were not so bad
As with foul incest to abuse your soul;
Where now you're both a father and a son,
By your untimely claspings with your child,
Which pleasure fits an husband, not a father;
And she an eater of her mother's flesh,
By the defiling of her parent's bed;
And both like serpents are, who though they feed
On sweetest flowers, yet they poison breed.
Antioch, farewell! for wisdom sees, those men
Blush not in actions blacker than the night,
Will shun no course to keep them from the light.
One sin, I know, another doth provoke;
Murder's as near to lust as flame to smoke:
Poison and treason are the hands of sin,
Ay, and the targets, to put off the shame:
Then, lest my lie be cropp'd to keep you clear,
By flight I'll shun the danger which I fear.

# TWO GOOD SCENES

Here are two of my favorite scenes from Shakespeare. Both are excellent for your practice. Apply everything you've learned to these scenes, and work them carefully, and slowly. For the *Much Ado About Nothing* scene, you'll need to get in touch with the moments in your life when you've been completely open, honest, and unblocked when confessing your love to someone. For the *Richard III* scene, you'll need to find your manipulation, your locked-target focus, and your charm; your Anne will need to find her rage, exhaustion, confusion, and dark vulnerability.

1. From *Much Ado About Nothing*, Act IV, Scene 1:

| | |
|---|---|
| Benedick | Lady Beatrice, have you wept all this while? |
| Beatrice | Yea, and I will weep a while longer. |
| Benedick | I will not desire that. |
| Beatrice | You have no reason; I do it freely. |
| Benedick | Surely I do believe your fair cousin is wronged. |
| Beatrice | Ah, how much might the man deserve of me that would right her! |
| Benedick | Is there any way to show such friendship? |
| Beatrice | A very even way, but no such friend. |
| Benedick | May a man do it? |
| Beatrice | It is a man's office, but not yours. |
| Benedick | I do love nothing in the world so well as you: is not that strange? |
| Beatrice | As strange as the thing I know not. It were as possible for me to say I loved nothing so well as you: but believe me not; and yet I lie not; I confess nothing, nor I deny nothing. I am sorry for my cousin. |
| Benedick | By my sword, Beatrice, thou lovest me. |

| | |
|---|---|
| Beatrice | Do not swear, and eat it. |
| Benedick | I will swear by it that you love me; and I will make him eat it that says I love not you. |
| Beatrice | Will you not eat your word? |
| Benedick | With no sauce that can be devised to it. I protest I love thee. |
| Beatrice | Why, then, God forgive me! |
| Benedick | What offence, sweet Beatrice? |
| Beatrice | You have stayed me in a happy hour: I was about to protest I loved you. |
| Benedick | And do it with all thy heart. |
| Beatrice | I love you with so much of my heart that none is left to protest. |
| Benedick | Come, bid me do any thing for thee. |
| Beatrice | Kill Claudio. |
| Benedick | Ha! not for the wide world. |
| Beatrice | You kill me to deny it. Farewell. |
| Benedick | Tarry, sweet Beatrice. |
| Beatrice | I am gone, though I am here: there is no love in you: nay, I pray you, let me go. |
| Benedick | Beatrice— |
| Beatrice | In faith, I will go. |
| Benedick | We'll be friends first. |
| Beatrice | You dare easier be friends with me than fight with mine enemy. |
| Benedick | Is Claudio thine enemy? |
| Beatrice | Is he not approved in the height a villain, that hath slandered, scorned, dishonored my kinswoman? O that I were a man! What, bear her in hand until they come to take hands; and then, with public accusation, uncovered slander, unmitigated rancor, —O God, that I were a man! I would eat his heart in the market-place. |
| Benedick | Hear me, Beatrice— |
| Beatrice | Talk with a man out at a window! A proper saying! |
| Benedick | Nay, but, Beatrice— |
| Beatrice | Sweet Hero! She is wronged, she is slandered, she is undone. |
| Benedick | Beat— |

| Beatrice | Princes and counties! Surely, a princely testimony, a goodly count, Count Comfect; a sweet gallant, surely! O that I were a man for his sake! or that I had any friend would be a man for my sake! But manhood is melted into courtesies, valor into compliment, and men are only turned into tongue, and trim ones too: he is now as valiant as Hercules that only tells a lie and swears it. I cannot be a man with wishing, therefore I will die a woman with grieving. |
|---|---|
| Benedick | Tarry, good Beatrice. By this hand, I love thee. |
| Beatrice | Use it for my love some other way than swearing by it. |
| Benedick | Think you in your soul the Count Claudio hath wronged Hero? |
| Beatrice | Yea, as sure as I have a thought or a soul. |
| Benedick | Enough! I am engaged; I will challenge him. I will kiss your hand, and so I leave you. By this hand, Claudio shall render me a dear account. As you hear of me, so think of me. Go, comfort your cousin: I must say she is dead: and so, farewell. |
| | *Exeunt* |

## 2. From *Richard III*, Act I, Scene 2:

| Gloucester | Sweet saint, for charity, be not so curst. |
|---|---|
| Lady Anne | Foul devil, for God's sake, hence, and trouble us not; |
| | For thou hast made the happy earth thy hell, |
| | Fill'd it with cursing cries and deep exclaims. |
| | If thou delight to view thy heinous deeds, |
| | Behold this pattern of thy butcheries. |
| | O, gentlemen; see, see! dead Henry's wounds |
| | Open their congeal'd mouths and bleed afresh! |
| | Blush, blush, thou lump of foul deformity; |
| | For 'tis thy presence that exhales this blood |
| | From cold and empty veins, where no blood dwells; |
| | Thy deed, inhuman and unnatural, |
| | Provokes this deluge most unnatural. |
| | O God, which this blood madest, revenge his death! |
| | O earth, which this blood drink'st revenge his death! |
| | Either heaven with lightning strike the murderer dead, |
| | Or earth, gape open wide and eat him quick, |

As thou dost swallow up this good king's blood
Which his hell-govern'd arm hath butchered!

**Gloucester**  Lady, you know no rules of charity,
Which renders good for bad, blessings for curses.

**Lady Anne**  Villain, thou know'st no law of God nor man:
No beast so fierce but knows some touch of pity.

**Gloucester**  But I know none, and therefore am no beast.

**Lady Anne**  O wonderful, when devils tell the truth!

**Gloucester**  More wonderful, when angels are so angry.
Vouchsafe, divine perfection of a woman,
Of these supposed evils, to give me leave,
By circumstance, but to acquit myself.

**Lady Anne**  Vouchsafe, diffused infection of a man,
For these known evils, but to give me leave,
By circumstance, to curse thy cursed self.

**Gloucester**  Fairer than tongue can name thee, let me have
Some patient leisure to excuse myself.

**Lady Anne**  Fouler than heart can think thee, thou canst make
No excuse current, but to hang thyself.

**Gloucester**  By such despair, I should accuse myself.

**Lady Anne**  And, by despairing, shouldst thou stand excused;
For doing worthy vengeance on thyself,
Which didst unworthy slaughter upon others.

**Gloucester**  Say that I slew them not.

**Lady Anne**                                    Why, then they are not dead:
But dead they are, and devilish slave, by thee.

**Gloucester**  I did not kill your husband.

**Lady Anne**                                    Why, then he is alive.

**Gloucester**  Nay, he is dead; and slain by Edward's hand.

**Lady Anne**  In thy foul throat thou liest: Queen Margaret saw
Thy murderous falchion smoking in his blood;
The which thou once didst bend against her breast,
But that thy brothers beat aside the point.

**Gloucester**  I was provoked by her sland'rous tongue,
Which laid their guilt upon my guiltless shoulders.

**Lady Anne**  Thou wast provoked by thy bloody mind.
Which never dreamt on aught but butcheries:
Didst thou not kill this king?

**Gloucester**                                    I grant ye.

| | |
|---|---|
| Lady Anne | Dost grant me, hedgehog? Then, God grant me too |
| | Thou mayst be damned for that wicked deed! |
| | O, he was gentle, mild, and virtuous! |
| Gloucester | The fitter for the King of heaven, that hath him. |
| Lady Anne | He is in heaven, where thou shalt never come. |
| Gloucester | Let him thank me, that holp to send him thither; |
| | For he was fitter for that place than earth. |
| Lady Anne | And thou unfit for any place but hell. |
| Gloucester | Yes, one place else, if you will hear me name it. |
| Lady Anne | Some dungeon. |
| Gloucester | Your bedchamber. |
| Lady Anne | Ill rest betide the chamber where thou liest! |
| Gloucester | So will it, madam till I lie with you. |
| Lady Anne | I hope so. |
| Gloucester | I know so. But, gentle Lady Anne, |
| | To leave this keen encounter of our wits, |
| | And fall somewhat into a slower method, |
| | Is not the causer of the timeless deaths |
| | Of these Plantagenets, Henry and Edward, |
| | As blameful as the executioner? |
| Lady Anne | Thou art the cause, and most accursed effect. |
| Gloucester | Your beauty was the cause of that effect; |
| | Your beauty, that did haunt me in my sleep |
| | To undertake the death of all the world, |
| | So I might live one hour in your sweet bosom. |
| Lady Anne | If I thought that, I tell thee, homicide, |
| | These nails should rend that beauty from my cheeks. |
| Gloucester | These eyes could never endure sweet beauty's wreck; |
| | You should not blemish it, if I stood by: |
| | As all the world is cheered by the sun, |
| | So I by that; it is my day, my life. |
| Lady Anne | Black night o'ershade thy day, and death thy life! |
| Gloucester | Curse not thyself, fair creature thou art both. |
| Lady Anne | I would I were, to be revenged on thee. |
| Gloucester | It is a quarrel most unnatural, |
| | To be revenged on him that loveth thee. |
| Lady Anne | It is a quarrel just and reasonable, |
| | To be revenged on him that slew my husband. |
| Gloucester | He that bereft thee, lady, of thy husband, |
| | Did it to help thee to a better husband. |

Lady Anne His better doth not breathe upon the earth.
Gloucester He lives that loves thee better than he could.
Lady Anne Name him.
Gloucester        Plantagenet.
Lady Anne            Why, that was he.
Gloucester The selfsame name, but one of better nature.
Lady Anne Where is he?
Gloucester      Here.
*She spitteth at him*
            Why dost thou spit at me?
Lady Anne Would it were mortal poison, for thy sake!
Gloucester Never came poison from so sweet a place.
Lady Anne Never hung poison on a fouler toad.
          Out of my sight! thou dost infect my eyes.
Gloucester Thine eyes, sweet lady, have infected mine.
Lady Anne Would they were basilisks, to strike thee dead!
Gloucester I would they were, that I might die at once;
          For now they kill me with a living death.
          Those eyes of thine from mine have drawn salt tears,
          Shamed their aspect with store of childish drops:
          These eyes that never shed remorseful tear,
          No, when my father York and Edward wept,
          To hear the piteous moan that Rutland made
          When black-faced Clifford shook his sword at him;
          Nor when thy warlike father, like a child,
          Told the sad story of my father's death,
          And twenty times made pause to sob and weep,
          That all the standers-by had wet their cheeks
          Like trees bedash'd with rain: in that sad time
          My manly eyes did scorn an humble tear;
          And what these sorrows could not thence exhale,
          Thy beauty hath, and made them blind with weeping.
          I never sued to friend nor enemy;
          My tongue could never learn sweet smoothing word;
          But now thy beauty is proposed my fee,
          My proud heart sues, and prompts my tongue to speak.
*She looks scornfully at him*
          Teach not thy lip such scorn, for it was made
          For kissing, lady, not for such contempt.

If thy revengeful heart cannot forgive,
Lo, here I lend thee this sharp-pointed sword;
Which if thou please to hide in this true bosom.
And let the soul forth that adoreth thee,
I lay it naked to the deadly stroke,
And humbly beg the death upon my knee.
*He lays his breast open: she offers at it with his sword*
Nay, do not pause; for I did kill King Henry,
But 'twas thy beauty that provoked me.
Nay, now dispatch; 'twas I that stabb'd young Edward,
But 'twas thy heavenly face that set me on.
*She lets fall the sword*
Take up the sword again, or take up me.

|  |  |
|---|---|
| Lady Anne | Arise, dissembler: though I wish thy death, I will not be thy executioner. |
| Gloucester | Then bid me kill myself, and I will do it. |
| Lady Anne | I have already. |
| Gloucester | That was in thy rage: Speak it again, and, even with the word, That hand, which, for thy love, did kill thy love, Shall, for thy love, kill a far truer love; To both their deaths thou shalt be accessary. |
| Lady Anne | I would I knew thy heart. |
| Gloucester | 'Tis figured in my tongue. |
| Lady Anne | I fear me both are false. |
| Gloucester | Then never man was true. |
| Lady Anne | Well, well, put up your sword. |
| Gloucester | Say, then, my peace is made. |
| Lady Anne | That shall you know hereafter. |
| Gloucester | But shall I live in hope? |
| Lady Anne | All men, I hope, live so. |
| Gloucester | Vouchsafe to wear this ring. |
| Lady Anne | To take is not to give. |
| Gloucester | Look, how this ring encompasseth finger. Even so thy breast encloseth my poor heart; Wear both of them, for both of them are thine. And if thy poor devoted servant may But beg one favor at thy gracious hand, Thou dost confirm his happiness for ever. |

| | |
|---|---|
| Lady Anne | What is it? |
| Gloucester | That it would please thee leave these sad designs |
| | To him that hath more cause to be a mourner, |
| | And presently repair to Crosby Place; |
| | Where, after I have solemnly interr'd |
| | At Chertsey monastery this noble king, |
| | And wet his grave with my repentant tears, |
| | I will with all expedient duty see you: |
| | For divers unknown reasons. I beseech you, |
| | Grant me this boon. |
| Lady Anne | With all my heart; and much it joys me too, |
| | To see you are become so penitent. |
| | Tressel and Berkeley, go along with me. |
| Gloucester | Bid me farewell. |
| Lady Anne |                   'Tis more than you deserve; |
| | But since you teach me how to flatter you, |
| | Imagine I have said farewell already. |

# ABOUT THE AUTHOR

Theatre wunderkind Madd Harold is an actor, director, producer, teacher, and writer. Born March 9, 1973, his numerous stage productions have alternately earned him the title "genius" and "rapscallion." As an actor, he has appeared in many film and television parts, and on both contemporary and classical stages. He has performed in and directed many Shakespeare productions, and his recent awards include "Best Director" (Montreal English Critics' Circle Award) for his work on an adaptation of *Henry V*. His radically imaginative and novel work has been seen in New York, London, Edinburgh, Montreal, and Toronto.

# FOR THE ACTOR

### HOW TO AGENT YOUR AGENT
*by Nancy Rainford*

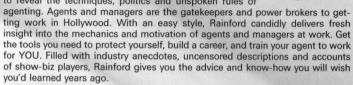

NEW RELEASE!

Nancy Rainford takes the reader behind the scenes to reveal the techniques, politics and unspoken rules of agenting. Agents and managers are the gatekeepers and power brokers to getting work in Hollywood. With an easy style, Rainford candidly delivers fresh insight into the mechanics and motivation of agents and managers at work. Get the tools you need to protect yourself, build a career, and train your agent to work for YOU. Filled with industry anecdotes, uncensored descriptions and accounts of show-biz players, Rainford gives you the advice and know-how you will wish you'd learned years ago.
**$17.95, ISBN 1580650422**

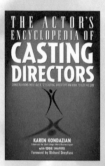

### THE ACTOR'S ENCYCLOPEDIA OF CASTING DIRECTORS
**Interviews with Over 100 Casting Directors on How to Get the Job**
*by Karen Kondazian with Eddie Shapiro, foreword by Richard Dreyfuss*

Kondazian has compiled insider information and intimate profiles from talking to premier casting directors in film, television, theatre and commercials from Los Angeles to New York. Casting directors speak on the record to reflect and convey expert advice about how to get in the door and how to prepare effectively for readings. Find out from casting directors what's hot and what's not.
**$19.95, ISBN 1580650139**

### HOW TO GET THE PART... WITHOUT FALLING APART!
**Featuring the Haber Phrase Technique® for Actors**
*by Margie Haber with Barbara Babchick, foreword by Heather Locklear*

Acting coach to the stars Margie Haber has created a revolutionary phrase technique to get actors through readings without stumbling over the script. The book helps actors break through the psychological roadblocks to auditioning with a 10-step method for breaking down the scene. Actors learn to prepare thoroughly, whether they have twenty minutes or two weeks. Includes celebrity photos and audition stories.
**$17.95, ISBN 1580650147**

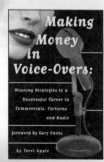

### MAKING MONEY IN VOICE-OVERS
**Winning Strategies to a Successful Career in TV, Commercials, Radio and Animation**
*by Terri Apple, foreword by Gary Owens*

This book helps the actor, radio DJ, vocal impressionist or amateur cartoon voice succeed in voice-overs, no matter where you live. From assessing one's competitive advantages to creating a demo tape to handling initial sessions, Apple provides a clear guide full of insider tips and strategies helpful to both beginners and experienced professionals.
**$16.95, ISBN 1580650112**

# FOR THE SCREENWRITER

## POWER SCREENWRITING
### The 12 Stages of Story Development
*by Michael Chase Walker*

Michael Chase Walker offers a clear and straightforward framework upon which to build story plots. Standing on the broad shoulders of Joseph Campbell, Christopher Vogler, and others who have demonstrated how mythology is used, Walker brings passion, insight and clarity to a whole new range of story traditions never before examined. Walker offers a wide variety of alternative principles and techniques that are more flexible, adaptable and relevant for the modern story-teller. This book gives insight into the art of storytelling as a way to give depth and texture to any screenplay.

**$19.95, ISBN 1580650414**

## HOW NOT TO WRITE A SCREENPLAY
### 101 Common Mistakes Most Screenwriters Make
*by Denny Martin Flinn*

Having read tons of screenplays as an executive, Denny Martin Flinn has come to understand that while all good screenplays are unique, all bad screenplays are the same. Flinn's book will teach the reader how to avoid the pitfalls of bad screen-writing, and arrive at one's own destination intact. Every example used is gleaned from a legitimate screenplay. Flinn's advice is a no-nonsense analysis of the latest techniques for crafting first-rate screenplays that sell.

**$16.95, ISBN 1580650155**

## ELEMENTS OF STYLE FOR SCREENWRITERS
### The Essential Manual for Writers of Screenplays
*by Paul Argentini*

Paul Argentini presents an essential reference masterpiece in the art of clear and concise principles of screenplay formatting, structure and style for screenwriters. Argentini explains how to design and format manuscripts to impress any film school professor, story editor, agent, producer or studio executive. A to Z listing of format terms and examples. Includes a special section on stage play format-ting.

**$11.95, ISBN 1580650031**

## THE COMPLETE WRITER'S GUIDE TO HEROES & HEROINES
### Sixteen Master Archetypes
*by Tami D. Cowden,*
*Caro LaFever, Sue Viders*

By following the guidelines of the archetypes presented in this comprehensive reference work, writers can create extraordinarily memorable characters and ele-vate their writing to a higher level. The authors give examples of well-known heroes and heroines from television and film so the reader can picture the arche-type in his or her mind. The core archetype tells the writer how heroes or hero-ines think and feel, what drives them and how they reach their goals.

**$17.95, ISBN 1580650244**

# HOLLYWOOD CREATIVE DIRECTORY

*Hollywood Creative Directory* publishes the most complete and up-to-date directories featuring film and television professionals. Our directories are meticulously researched and compiled using strict listing qualifications. Each company listing contains staff names, titles, addresses, phone and fax numbers, email addresses, and Web sites. All books feature comprehensive indices for easy reference.

## PRODUCERS, 47th Edition

- Over 9,900 film and TV producers, studio and network executives
- Over 1,750 production companies, studios and networks
- Includes addresses, phone and fax numbers, staff names and titles
- Selected credits and studio deals
- Special TV Show section
- Cross-referenced indices by name, type and deal
- Web sites and email addresses
- Published every April, August and December

| | |
|---|---|
| Single issue | $59.95 |
| 1-year print subscription | $149.95 |
| 2-year print subscription | $249.95 |
| 1-year online subscription | $199.95 |

## AGENTS & MANAGERS, 24th Edition

- Over 5,500 names of agents and managers
- Over 1,500 talent and literary agencies and management companies coast to coast
- Includes addresses, phone and fax numbers, staff names and titles
- Cross-referenced indices by name and type
- Bonus: Film and TV Casting Directors and Publicity Companies
- Published every March and September

| | |
|---|---|
| Single issue | $59.95 |
| 1-year print subscription | $99.95 |
| 2-year print subscription | $189.95 |
| 1-year online subscription | $149.95 |

## DISTRIBUTORS, 14th Edition

- Over 4,500 domestic film and TV distribution executives, sales agents, marketing and merchandising executives, producer and distributor reps and financing company executives
- Over 500 international film and TV buyers and distributors worldwide
- Includes publicity companies

| | |
|---|---|
| Single issue | $59.95 |
| 1-year online subscription | $149.95 |